Asian Perspectives on Animal Ethics

To date, philosophical discussions of animal ethics and Critical Animal Studies have been dominated by Western perspectives and Western thinkers. This book makes a novel contribution to animal ethics in showing the range and richness of ideas offered to these fields by diverse Asian traditions.

Asian Perspectives on Animal Ethics is the first of its kind to include the intersection of Asian and European traditions with respect to human and nonhuman relations. Presenting a series of studies focusing on specific Asian traditions, as well as studies that put those traditions in dialogue with Western thinkers, this book looks at Asian philosophical doctrines concerning compassion and nonviolence as these apply to nonhuman animals, as well as the moral rights and status of nonhuman animals in Asian traditions. Using Asian perspectives to explore ontological, ethical, and political questions, contributors analyze humanism and post-humanism in Asian and comparative traditions and offer insight into the special ethical relations between humans and other particular species of animals.

This book will be of interest to students and scholars of Asian religion and philosophy, as well as to those interested in animal ethics and Critical Animal Studies.

Neil Dalal is Assistant Professor of South Asian Philosophy and Religious Thought in the Philosophy Department and Religious Studies Program at the University of Alberta, Canada. He holds a PhD from the Department of Asian Studies at the University of Texas at Austin.

Chloë Taylor is Assistant Professor of Philosophy and Women's and Gender Studies at the University of Alberta, Canada. She has a PhD in Philosophy from the University of Toronto and was a Social Sciences and Humanities Research Council of Canada and Tomlinson postdoctoral fellow in Philosophy at McGill University.

Routledge studies in Asian religion and philosophy

1 **Deconstruction and the Ethical in Asian Thought**
Edited by Youru Wang

2 **An Introduction to Daoist Thought**
Action, language, and ethics in Zhuangzi
Eske Møllgaard

3 **Religious Commodifications in Asia**
Marketing gods
Edited by Pattana Kitiarsa

4 **Christianity and the State in Asia**
Complicity and conflict
Edited by Julius Bautista and Francis Khek Gee Lim

5 **Christianity in Contemporary China**
Socio-cultural perspectives
Edited by Francis Khek Gee Lim

6 **The Buddha and Religious Diversity**
J. Abraham Velez de Cea

7 **Japanese Religions and Globalization**
Ugo Dessi

8 **Religion and the Subtle Body in Asia and the West**
Between mind and body
Geoffrey Samuel and Jay Johnston

9 **'Yogini' in South Asia**
Interdisciplinary approaches
Edited by Istvan Keul

10 The Confucian Philosophy of Harmony
Chenyang Li

11 Postcolonial Resistance and Asian Theology
Simon Shui-Man Kwa

12 Asian Perspectives on Animal Ethics
Rethinking the nonhuman
Edited by Neil Dalal and Chloë Taylor

Asian Perspectives on Animal Ethics

Rethinking the nonhuman

Edited by Neil Dalal and Chloë Taylor

Routledge
Taylor & Francis Group
LONDON AND NEW YORK

First published 2014
by Routledge
2 Park Square, Milton Park, Abingdon, Oxon OX14 4RN

and by Routledge
711 Third Avenue, New York, NY 10017

Routledge is an imprint of the Taylor & Francis Group, an informa business

British Library Cataloguing in Publication Data
A catalogue record for this book is available from the British Library

Library of Congress Cataloging in Publication Data
Asian perspectives on animal ethics : rethinking the nonhuman / [edited by] Neil Dalal and Chloe Taylor.
pages cm. – (Routledge studies in Asian religion and philosophy ; 12)
Includes bibliographical references and index.
1. Human-animal relationships–Asia. 2. Animals–Symbolic aspects–Asia. 3. Animal welfare–Moral and ethical aspects–Cross-cultural studies. 4. Human-animal relationships–Cross-cultural studies 5. Animals–Religious aspects. 6. Nonviolence–Religious aspects. I. Dalal, Neil, editor of compilation.
QL85.D35 2014
179'.3–dc23 2013038671

ISBN: 978-0-415-72986-4 (hbk)
ISBN: 978-1-315-79624-6 (ebk)

Typeset in Times New Roman
by Wearset Ltd, Boldon, Tyne and Wear

Printed and bound in the United States of America by Publishers Graphics, LLC on sustainably sourced paper.

For Jillian
For Mishka (1997–2012)

Contents

Illustrations

Figures

Table

Contributors

Amy L. Allocco is Assistant Professor of Religious Studies at Elon University. In 2013 she was appointed the Distinguished Emerging Scholar in Religious Studies and in 2012 she received the Elon College of Arts and Science's Excellence in Teaching Award. Allocco earned her PhD in Emory University's Program in West and South Asian Religions in the Graduate Division of Religion and also holds degrees from Harvard Divinity School and Colgate University. Trained both as an ethnographer of South Asian religions and in approaches to Hindu textual traditions, Allocco has developed specializations in performance and ritual studies as well as gender and religion. Allocco's current book project analyses contemporary snake goddess traditions in South India and the repertoire of ritual therapies performed to mitigate *nāga dōṣam* (snake blemish), a malignant horoscopic condition understood to cause delayed marriage and infertility.

Bao-Er is a lawyer practicing primarily in the area of child protection law, in Sydney, New South Wales, Australia. His undergraduate studies at Macquarie University were in philosophy, Chinese, and law. He undertook research in Chinese law and society at the University of Sydney Law School and was awarded a Master of Laws (Hon I) in 1998 and Doctor of Philosophy in 2005. He has had a long-standing interest in Chinese culture and society, first visiting China as a student in 1983, he taught at a tertiary college in Anhui Province during 1999/2000, and presented papers on child protection law at conferences in Beijing and Shanghai in 2005. In recent years his research interests have included "nonhuman animals" and his law firm, The Blue Mountains Legal Research Centre, undertakes research on issues concerning the role law plays in the lives of children and animals in both China and Australia.

Christopher Key Chapple is Doshi Professor of Indic and Comparative Theology and Director of the Master of Arts in Yoga Studies at Loyola Marymount University in Los Angeles. He has published more than a dozen books, including *Nonviolence to Animals, Earth, and Self in Asian Traditions* and *Yoga and the Luminous: Patanjali's Spiritual Path to Freedom*. He serves on the advisory boards for the Green Yoga Association (Oakland), the Ahimsa

Center (Pomona), and the Forum on Religion and Ecology (Yale). He edits the journal *Worldviews: Global Religions, Culture, and Ecology* (Brill).

Neil Dalal is Assistant Professor of South Asian Philosophy and Religious Thought at the University of Alberta. He holds a PhD in Asian Cultures and Languages from the University of Texas at Austin where he studied Indian philosophy, the history of Indian religions, and Sanskrit. He is the co-director of *Gurukulam*, a feature length ethnographic film on a contemporary Advaita Vedānta tradition in South India, and his articles have appeared in *Method and Theory in the Study of Religion* and the *International Journal of Hindu Studies*. He is currently working on a book manuscript analyzing the intersection of texts and contemplative practices in early Advaita Vedānta.

Christopher Framarin is an Associate Professor in the Philosophy and Religious Studies Departments at the University of Calgary in Alberta, Canada. He is the author of *Desire and Motivation in Indian Philosophy* (2009) and *Hinduism and Environmental Ethics: Law, Literature, and Philosophy* (2014), both with Routledge.

Pankaj Jain is the author of *Dharma and Ecology of Hindu Communities: Sustenance and Sustainability* (May 2011), which won the 2012 DANAM Book Award and the 2011 Uberoi Book Award. He is an Assistant Professor in the department of Anthropology and the department of Philosophy and Religion Studies at the University of North Texas where he teaches courses on religions, cultures, ecologies, and films of India and Asia. He has published articles in journals such as *Religious Studies Review*, *Worldviews*, *Religion Compass*, *Journal of Vaishnava Studies*, *Union Seminary Quarterly Review* and the *Journal of Visual Anthropology*. He has received the Fulbright-Nehru Environmental Leadership Fellowship in 2012 to study the cultures and sustainability initiatives in the Himalayas. He is also the director of the Eco-Dharma and Bhumi-Seva Project and is working with the Hindu and Jain temples in North America for their "greening" efforts.

Katharine Loevy is Assistant Professor of Philosophy at Pacific University. Her graduate work was completed at Vanderbilt University, where she received a PhD in philosophy, an MA in Art History, and an MA in the History and Critical Theory of Religion. She has published essays on Hegel and Levinas, and is currently pursuing the animal question in relation to certain key figures in Continental philosophy.

James McRae holds a PhD in comparative philosophy from the University of Hawaii at Manoa and serves as an Associate Professor of Asian Philosophy and Religion and the Coordinator for Asian Studies at Westminster College in Fulton, Missouri. His publications include the books *The Philosophy of Ang Lee* (with Robert Arp and Adam Barkman, University Press of Kentucky, 2013) and *Environmental Philosophy in Asian Traditions of Thought* (with J. Baird Callicott, State University of New York Press, 2014).

Chloë Taylor is Assistant Professor in the Departments of Philosophy and Women's and Gender Studies at the University of Alberta. She has a PhD from the University of Toronto and was a postdoctoral fellow in the Philosophy Department at McGill University. She is the author of *The Culture of Confession from Augustine to Foucault* (Routledge 2008, 2010) as well as a number of articles in journals such as *Hypatia*, *Philosophy Today*, *Ancient Philosophy* and *Postmodern Culture*. She is currently working on two book manuscripts, entitled *Bucolic Pleasures? Foucault, Feminism, and Sex Crime* and *Abnormal Appetites: Foucault and the Politics of Food.*

Anne Vallely's work falls within the field of the Anthropology of South Asian Religion, with a focus on Jainism. Her research interests include human/non-human boundaries, religion and animals, death rituals and mourning, spirit possession, and asceticism. She is author of *Guardians of the Transcendent: An Ethnography of a Jain Ascetic Community* and co-editor of *Animals and the Human Imagination.*

Mario Wenning is Assistant Professor at the University of Macau as well as Humboldt Research Fellow at the University of Frankfurt. He has published a number of articles in the areas of Critical Theory, German Idealism, and philosophical Daoism. His work emphasizes productive engagements between these traditions. Currently he is completing a book on the role of utopia in the Critical Theory tradition and edits a collection of essays on novel interpretations of the concept of resistance. He has also translated recent German philosophers such as Sloterdijk, Schmitt, and Jaspers into English.

Acknowledgments

We would like to thank the Social Sciences and Humanities Research Council of Canada for funding the workshop for which many of the papers for this volume were originally written. We would also like to thank our research assistants, Ela Przybylo, Emma Kennedy, and Roxana Akhbari.

Introduction

Neil Dalal

In recent years scholars have produced a number of studies on Asian approaches to nature, ecology, and environmental ethics.[1] Though these touch on nonhuman animals,[2] few works specifically deal with the range and richness of Asian perspectives on nonhuman animals.[3] Asian religious and philosophical traditions have also remained on the margins of the burgeoning field of Critical Animal Studies, which has been dominated by Western thinkers and perspectives despite a common view that Asian traditions are examples of more compassionate attitudes towards the nonhuman animal world. This volume is the first of its kind to include the intersection of Asian and continental traditions with respect to human and nonhuman animal relations. The chapters contained in this volume use Asian perspectives to explore crucial ontological, ethical, and political questions concerning the nonhuman animal world and our ethical engagements with other animals.

Asian traditions are incredibly diverse and stretch over a vast geographical region and period of time. They do not always lend themselves to an identifiable systematic moral philosophy, and their complexity and historical evolution make drawing simple or straightforward conclusions from them a difficult endeavor. But over the centuries they have clearly held a deep concern for nonhuman animals and our moral obligations towards them. In some cases this concern was prudent rather than altruistic or compassionate, such as the fear that harmed nonhuman animals will retaliate in the next world. Nevertheless, Asian traditions have grappled with understanding how to relate to nonhuman animals, where they fit in the world, and how to avoid harming them though specific practices. They provide a variety of conceptual resources and different possible worldviews, which include philosophical positions as well as mythologies, rituals, cosmologies, legal codes, hagiographies and other religious manifestations. And contrary to dominant nonhuman animal views inherited from the history of Western thought, many Asian traditions depict other animals as having families and community, possessing forms of communication and consciousness, and as subjects who experience joy, suffering, and other forms of mental life. Understanding the depth and breadth of these views is a vital contribution to the study of Asian religions and philosophies and to Critical Animal Studies. They have the potential to expand the moral horizon of our perspectives on nonhuman animal ethics.

Asian perspectives on nonhuman animals provide a valuable viewpoint to better understand Western ones. It is all too easy for our vision to be corralled by the walls of ingrained ideologies and unconscious assumptions. Engaging an understanding and dialogue with Asian traditions provides new perspectives, spaces for reflection and reevaluation of ossified views and blind spots. For this reason, it is worthwhile to look elsewhere to understand how we can conceptualize and understand nonhuman animals differently. This encounter moves in both directions to facilitate gradual modification, mutual accommodation, and alternative accounts. At times it is a stark confrontation that questions entrenched ideas like the dichotomy of human and animal, or notions of purity and pollution, or the assumption of ethical anthropocentrism and human superiority.

It may be naïve and uncritically romantic, however, to assume that Asian traditions are the panacea for our moral quagmires and troubled relationships with nonhuman animals. Such idealized views ignore certain aspects of them that are decidedly not nonhuman animal friendly. And some contemporary concerns may not fit neatly into philosophies and religious ideologies that evolved in earlier time periods. In addition, despite Asian doctrines that appear to logically ensure the safety, respect for, and rights of nonhuman animals, there is generally only a selective application of such concepts in actual practice. In reality, nonhuman animals continue to suffer from exploitation, instrumental use, habitat destruction, and a variety of other problems throughout the Asian world. There is a gap between religious or philosophical ideologies and the lived realities of nonhuman animals. However, the chapters in this volume implicitly challenge the idea of an irreconcilable dichotomy between religious imaginaries and lived reality. Rather than focusing on the contemporary treatment of and practices concerning animals in Asian countries, they explore the religious and philosophical presuppositions that constitute a foundational source from which we can better understand the lived realities of nonhuman animals and our ethical relationships to them.

Asian philosophies and religions do not always entail ethical action towards nonhuman animals, but they can provide alternative ontologies and relationships with other animals that lead to different moral implications. They possess symbolic resources to help ground a nonhuman animal ethic, particularly for people within those traditions or living in Asian cultures. Mythology and ritual for example provide windows to understand psychology and archetypal relationships with nonhuman animals. They describe human/nonhuman animal interrelationships found in popular religious consciousness, and act normatively to maintain those views or raise the possibility of intimacy, connection, and participation with nonhuman animals. Sacred narratives and ritual theories often function as means to transform nonhuman animals from profane to sacred entities, emphasizing their divine nature or connection to the heavenly or ancestral worlds.

From the time of ancient trade networks to colonialism and globalization, Asian traditions have not lived in complete isolation amongst themselves or from Western traditions. Today, transnational diaspora populations and North

American and European converts continue to increase. International political and environmental concerns have deeply impacted Asian traditions and their relationship to nonhuman animals, and have helped inspire efforts to protect nonhuman animals. Many adherents of Asian religions now strive to close the gap between traditional views that champion other animals and practices that exploit them. By retrieving nonhuman animal friendly doctrines found in their traditions and selectively incorporating new principles and practices, they engage in constructive cross-cultural efforts that respect orthodox authorities and embrace contemporary nonhuman animal concerns.

Grounding nonhuman animal ethics in Asian philosophies and religions is a complicated undertaking. Critical Animal Studies, in the ways contemporary academics construe it, is a Western discourse. Using Western frameworks and philosophical terms to understand or map Asian traditions may be a helpful endeavor. They can help articulate the material in more useful and precise ways, incorporate the insights of Western moral philosophy, and serve as bridges for comparisons. However, we need not approach Asian traditions solely from a Western framework. To insist on Western approaches leads to certain pitfalls because they are framed with assumptions that do not always fit Asian material. Scholars must be wary of supplanting ideas of one culture for another or engaging in forms of intellectual hegemony. In addition, it is all too easy to cherry pick doctrines, practices, or textual passages that are amenable to an agenda foreign to a particular Asian tradition, and then anachronistically project that agenda back on to the tradition. Such projects of selective reading may fail to clearly understand the greater context and history of the tradition and inadvertently distort it. One must first carefully analyze Asian traditions to understand nonhuman animal doctrines in their own terms and to situate them in broader worldviews. Only then can we responsibly move across cultural and spatial boundaries to construct a fruitful comparative dialogue.

The essays in this volume exemplify a responsible approach to the material by being deeply aware of underlying metaphysical and epistemological structures, as well as historical concerns and doctrinal differences within the diversity of each tradition. They initiate new areas of exploration and dialogue and contribute significant steps towards constructing a new discourse on nonhuman animals. The main themes of the volume, with two to three chapters dedicated to each theme, are: Asian philosophical doctrines concerning compassion and nonviolence as these apply to nonhuman animals; humanism and posthumanism in Asian traditions; the moral rights and status of nonhuman animals in Asian traditions; and, finally, special ethical relations between humans and particular species of nonhuman animals.

The following sections provide brief descriptions of major themes, doctrines, and practices that influence human and nonhuman animal relationships in some of the major Asian traditions, as well as summaries of the corresponding chapters found in this volume. The introductory sections include overviews of South Asian and East Asian philosophical and religious approaches to nonhuman animals, as well as overviews specific to Buddhism, Hinduism, Jainism,

Confucianism, and Daoism. For the sake of brevity, these descriptions cannot do justice to historical, religious, cultural, and linguistic differences, and leave a number of other Asian traditions and geographical regions untouched; however, they provide a stepping stone towards further research and a general background to help readers appreciate the particularities, deeper structures, and subtle insights in each chapter.[4]

South Asian approaches to nonhuman animals

The philosophical and religious traditions that arose in South Asia are vast and varied, originating in various regions and time periods, and often engaging in dialogue and influencing each other. In this milieu, Hindu, Buddhist, and Jain traditions developed unique worldviews that offer insights and approaches for understanding and respecting nonhuman animals. By the middle of the first millennium BCE, the Brahmanical tradition, one of the primary roots of Hinduism, composed the Upanishads, a genre of texts found within the Vedas that explore the nature of reality and the hidden meanings of Vedic rituals. During the same period Buddhism and Jainism developed in northeast India.[5] It is difficult to understand the mutual influences these traditions had on each other due to the sparse textual and archaeological record from the time period; however, we find a number of common themes and structures that contributed to their views on nonhuman animals.

These traditions, particularly Buddhism and Jainism, developed as renouncer traditions. Individuals renounced family, wealth, and society to become renunciates, ascetics, and monks in order to pursue liberation to the exclusion of all else. In the ancient Indian cultural context, liberation presupposes the doctrines of *karma* and rebirth. The Vedic belief that actions, particularly ritual actions, elicit future unseen consequences eventually developed into an ethicized notion of action, resulting in merit and demerit. *Karma*, the fruits of actions in the forms of merit and demerit, pushes the individual to reincarnate in other worlds and forms after death. He or she then experiences karmic consequences, which lead to more action and karmic fruits to be experienced. This forms a continuous cycle of birth and death (*saṃsāra*), where one must experience new human births, other worldly bodies in heavens and hells, as well as nonhuman births. The renouncer seeks to escape this cycle, which is fraught with repeated pain and suffering. Each tradition developed important differences in their understanding of *saṃsāra*, *karma*, the moral order they presuppose, and the ways to find freedom. But within this common cultural container we find parallel views on nonhuman animals.

Buddhism, Jainism, Brahmanism, and later forms of Hinduism, stress the importance of nonviolence or non-injury (*ahiṃsā*). The general agreement among these traditions is that abstaining from violence allows the agent of action to avoid negative *karma* and difficult rebirths. In addition, violence cultivates polluted mental states, which lead to personal suffering and obstruct meditation and other contemplative practices indispensible for gaining liberation. One cannot engage violence and simultaneously pursue the renunciate path due to their mutual opposition. Nonviolence extends beyond the human world to include nonhuman animals. Intentional, and in some cases even unintentional harm or killing of other animals, conflicts with the moral order and results in negative *karma*. For this reason, these traditions favor a vegetarian diet and avoid direct killing of nonhuman animals for instrumental dietary use. One may argue that refraining from violence to avoid negative *karma* is merely prudent egoistic action on behalf of the agent; however this criticism ignores the presupposition of an underlying moral order. Individuals have an intrinsic duty to avoid conflict with the moral order and to maintain moral harmony. South Asian traditions often focus on avoidance of harm rather than prescriptive actions, but compassion to nonhuman animals, being empathetic to their suffering, and altruistic action towards them also hold great importance. The importance of nonviolence throughout these traditions demonstrates the intrinsic value of nonhuman animal life and a recognition that they suffer from harm.

The South Asian doctrine of rebirth radically informs one's relationship to nonhuman animals.[6] Every human has taken a number of nonhuman animal births in the past, and may be born as another animal in the future. And nonhuman animals in this lifetime may have been human in a previous life or will become one in the future. Thus the evolution is not a linear progression from nonhuman animal to human. Some traditions believe that in rare cases one can even remember one's former incarnations as nonhuman animals or may recognize other animals as past relatives. Despite the significant differences among the traditions regarding the nature of the self or soul and what exactly transmigrates, rebirth affirms a continuity of life irrespective of embodied form, and views life as a web of interconnected beings. And it must be noted that both humans and nonhuman animals are subject to the laws and conditions of *karma*. In this way rebirth minimizes human and nonhuman animal dichotomies and hierarchies.

One could argue that the belief in rebirth leads to a position of equality and justice between humans and nonhumans. Not knowing our future birth or future special interests is akin to John Rawl's veil of ignorance and ought to lead to fairness, mutual respect, and freedom without subordinating the interests of nonhuman animals to those of humans. The distinct possibility that I, or my parents, may be an abused factory fed cow or a hunted whale in the next life behooves me to treat other animals fairly now. However, rebirth and *karma* ironically provide hierarchy, for nonhuman animal births are generally considered lower ones resulting from negative *karma*. Nonhuman animals are perceived to live in greater suffering, are unlikely or unable to gain liberation due to a lack of wisdom, are unaware of morality, do not have an aptitude for ritual, and may not be able to produce positive *karma*.[7] The Indian traditions tend not to explore this ambivalent tension in rebirth and its implications for either equality or the instrumental use of other animals. Viewing nonhuman animal births as the result of negative *karma* potentially wedges open a distinction of nonhuman animals as other, leading to their lower intrinsic value in relation to humans.

Buddhism

In many ways, nonhuman animals hold a high profile in Buddhist traditions. In some texts nonhuman animal births are glorified. The *Jātaka* stories, for example, describe the previous births of the Buddha, Siddhārtha Gautama. In many of these tales he incarnates in the forms of nonhuman animals, such as a rabbit, swan, fish, quail, ape, elephant, and deer.[8] The tales often characterize these nonhuman animals as having meritorious qualities that people should emulate. They demonstrate compassion and supererogatory altruism, even sacrificing their own lives for the sake of others, whether as humans sacrificing life for nonhuman animals, or as nonhuman animals sacrificing life for others. Some examples include a rabbit that jumps in a fire to save a starving brahmin, and humans who sacrifice their own flesh for the sake of a starving tigress and her cubs or to satisfy a hawk prevented from eating his natural prey. Such tales emphasize the importance of alleviating nonhuman suffering and the value of their lives.

The first and most important precept for Buddhist monks, nuns, and laity is abstaining from taking life. This precept is directed towards human life, but extends to include nonhuman animals as well. The basic Buddhist eight-fold path also reflects this awareness of the value of nonhuman animal life. Right livelihood, the fifth factor, is based on the importance of not harming any beings. For example, it proscribes professions such as butchering or dealing in weapons or poisons. Right speech and right action also apply to nonhuman animals.[9] This value for other animal life and avoiding any nonhuman animal suffering led early Buddhists to strongly critique Vedic sacrifices as unethical.

Buddhist morality is not limited to action itself. It includes intention and mental states as well. Mental states resulting from wrong views, sense desires, and anger may result in harmful and murderous intentions, intentions that produce negative *karma* even if they do not culminate in harmful action. Thus the Buddhist ideally avoids such intentions and works to eradicate their roots in desire, greed, and ignorance. This practice minimizes harm to nonhumans, and results in psychological purity for one's self as well. According to Buddhists, understanding one's self, or rather the lack of any ultimate, essential, or enduring self, helps one to empathize with the fear and pain that all beings struggle with. A wise person understands the fact that all beings hold their selves extremely dear.[10] A being's love for his or her self entails the intrinsic value of individual life, whether human or nonhuman animal. From this perspective the Buddhist principle of *ahiṃsā* is a tradition of abstention as well as the valuation of life.[11]

Another reason to avoid harming nonhuman animals is the retaliatory measures they may take in the future. One could be reborn as a nonhuman animal or in a hell world where the very beings one abused has the opportunity to harm and torment him or her.[12] Buddhists generally view nonhuman animal births negatively. The nonhuman animal world itself is one of six distinct realms that comprise a hierarchical taxonomy consisting of gods, hell beings, humans, nonhuman animals, and hungry ghosts. Moving from a human to a nonhuman animal birth results from negative *karma*. For example, some texts claim that a robber or a hunter, who deals with stealing or killing, is likely to be reborn as a snake or a scorpion, and lazy students may be born as parrots and swans.[13] On the other hand, achieving a human birth is considered a moral achievement for only humans are eligible to enter the Buddhist monastic order. In fact the initiation ceremony includes the question, "Are you a human being?"[14]

Prudent reasons such as self-protection and self-purity are not the only rationalizations for nonviolence and compassion. The primary motivation and justification is the happiness and harmony of living beings.[15] This Buddhist ethic was not limited to the monastic order. At times it was encouraged throughout the subcontinent with royal patronage. Buddhist teachings inspired Aśoka, the third century BCE emperor of the Mauryan Empire, to prescribe compassion, nonviolence, and harmony on rock and pillar edicts. In Mahāyāna Buddhism, this motivation culminates in the *bodhisattva* vows of cultivating compassion for all beings and working for their liberation from suffering. Nonhuman animals clearly have an important place in Buddhist morality despite competing claims of anthropocentrism and human superiority.

Ceremonies of releasing nonhuman animals back into the wild, prevalent in East Asian Buddhist traditions, are another manifestation of *ahiṃsā* and compassion. The boundary between the human and nonhuman animal world is permeable, for nonhumans may literally have been one's relatives in other lives. Ceremonies to liberate living beings are grounded in the *Brahmajāla Sūtra*'s recognition of other animals as parents and family, and its stories of the Buddha saving and liberating nonhuman animals. For example in one story he saves 10,000 fish by having elephants bring water to their pond which is almost dried up.[16] These ceremonies emphasize altruism to nonhuman animals and recognize their suffering. Though we must note that despite good intentions there are numerous difficulties with these rituals. Many are intertwined with economic influences and issues of political power. Nonhuman animals need to be captured first to be re-released, and many die in the process.[17] This underlying antimony between ethics and practice alludes to a contradiction—Buddhist traditions recognize captivity as harm but often allow it in order to promote human interests.[18]

According to Buddhist monastic law codes, the consequences for killing nonhuman animals are less than that of killing humans.[19] This reflects a human/nonhuman animal value hierarchy and discontinuity. Killing a human person results in permanent expulsion from the monastic order, while killing nonhuman animals can be rectified with expiatory rights. Interestingly, this offense does not distinguish the value of different nonhuman animals or their levels of intelligence. The penalty for killing an elephant is no different from killing an earthworm.[20]

The universal Buddhist value of nonviolence naturally influences dietary restrictions within the monastic community. Surprisingly though, most Buddhists in South Asia did not have a strictly vegetarian diet. As mendicants,

Buddhist monks and nuns receive alms from the laity. Early Indian Buddhism did not forbid eating nonhuman animals, other than elephants, horses, dogs, snakes, lions, tigers, leopards, bears, and hyenas.[21] And the Buddha is said to have made vegetarianism optional.[22] This apparent contradiction between nonviolence and meat eating is due to competing factors. One factor is the Buddhist emphasis on intention. Most monastic codes explicitly prohibit the intentional destruction of any being's life.[23] However, most codes allow a monk to be passively complicit in meat consumption. There are two conditions to this. The first is factual. The donor should not have butchered the nonhuman animal for that monk in particular. And the second, a psychological condition, holds that the monk must never knowingly eat the flesh of a nonhuman animal butchered for his or her consumption.[24] One may criticize this practice as being passively complicit to killing nonhuman animals; however, the monk is not intentionally contributing to that killing. In addition, the religious context of receiving alms obligates a monk to selflessly accept meat. Monks are fields of merit for the laity. To refuse meat would interfere with the karmic fruit the layperson gains from feeding a monk. In the monk's perspective, the merit the layperson accrues from providing alms outweighs any demerit the monk might gain from eating meat or being passively complicit to the pain and slaughtering of the nonhuman animal.

The Mahāyāna tradition developed a greater emphasis on vegetarianism, at times refuting the complicit passive eating of flesh. This became especially prevalent in Chinese Buddhist traditions that adhered to the *Brahmajāla Sūtra*, a fifth century monastic code. In fact, vegetarianism became identified with Buddhism in China. One potential factor influencing Chinese Buddhist vegetarianism was the *tathāgatagarbha* doctrine, which taught that all incarnate sentient beings are interrelated and have the capacity to attain buddhahood. Thus it would not be correct to eat a being embodying this spiritual principle.[25] This was not the case with all Mahāyāna traditions. Tibetan Buddhists ate meat partly out of necessity when living in rugged mountainous areas not suitable for year-round agriculture. However, most Tibetan Buddhists in exile continue to eat meat in areas where vegetables and grains are plentiful. This is not simply due to a meat addiction or blindness to nonhuman animal suffering, but because they abide by the *Mūlasarvāstivāda Vinaya*, a monastic law code which allows non-intentional meat eating.[26] Making changes to ancient *Vinaya* rules is a complicated and arduous process even when there is a clear case.

Buddhist metaphysics also provide unique avenues to reconsider the nature of nonhuman animals. The Buddhist doctrines of dependent origination and no-self (*anātman*) show that individuals possess no essential unchanging self or soul. They are rather composed of constantly changing aggregates (*skandha*s). By extension, one cannot find any essential distinction between humans and nonhuman animals. Later Mahāyāna philosophies, such as Mādhyamika and Yogācāra, which spread into East Asia and Tibet, developed different interpretations of emptiness (*śūnyatā*). They point out the absence of any unchanging essence for any entity, or the absence of any difference between entities and the individual mind apprehending them. Such ideas affirm the non-distinction of humans and nonhuman animals from the absolute perspective. The Huayan (Flower Garland) School in China posits the interconnection of all phenomena in the world, where each phenomenon reflects every other and interpenetrates all existence. Such metaphysical doctrines reject dichotomies. They invite a radical consideration of self-identity in regard to nonhuman animals or alienation between self and other.

Chapter summaries

James McRae's "Cutting the cat in one: Zen Master Dōgen on the moral status of nonhuman animals," brings out the nuances of Buddhist nonhuman animal ethics within Japan's Sōtō Zen tradition through Dōgen's interpretation of "Nansen's cat" *koan*. Dōgen, the thirteenth century founder of the Sōtō school of Zen, discusses this *koan* in his *Shōbōgenzō Zuimonki*. In the well-known *koan*, Zen master Nansen cuts a cat in half in a rather surprising effort to impart wisdom to his students. The story, if read literally, is rather shocking and contradicts popular notions of Buddhism that take for granted a fixed Buddhist position of nonviolence and compassion for all nonhuman animals. How could a Buddhist monk, wedded to his monastic precept of nonviolence, kill an innocent cat? McRae uses the *koan* as a launching point to discuss Zen ethics in general, and more specifically the Buddhist theory of causality and how it leads to an understanding of interconnection and compassion to all beings. He then proceeds to probe Dōgen's understanding of human obligation to nonhuman animals, a position of weak rights based on the potential to achieve enlightenment. The last section of the chapter returns to the apparent contradiction of non-injury and Nansen's cat. McRea challenges the assumption that Zen holds absolute moral values. He affirms the important position of nonviolence in Dōgen's thought, but teases out the ways in which Zen allows exceptions to human obligations to the nonhuman animal world, particularly through the application of skillful means. The doctrine of skillful means, which can be interpreted to legitimize certain actions on utilitarian grounds, provides a potential gray area where one may transgress prohibited actions to move individuals towards enlightenment. This gray area is a controversial one though, a space that McRae believes Dōgen may have been uneasy with.

In "Animal compassion: what the *Jātakas* teach Lévinas about giving 'the bread from one's own mouth,'" Katharine Loevy puts the ethical phenomenology of French philosopher and Talmudic scholar Emmanuel Levinas in conversation with the Buddhist literary genre of the *Jātaka* tales. Although Levinas was famously dismissive of the intellectual and philosophical contributions that have emerged out of Asia, Loevy demonstrates that the *Jātaka* tales in fact reveal and address a blindspot in Levinas's own ethical theory. Loevy points out that while "giving the bread from one's own mouth" is Levinas's "preferred narrative for describing the transformation of the subject of enjoyment into ethical subjectivity," he fails to address the fact that this "bread" or "gift" that we give to another may itself be an Other, or may be the kind of being to which we owe an ethical response; that is, very often the food that humans enjoy, with which we nourish ourselves and others, consists of the flesh of other animals. Loevy argues that the *Jātaka* stories show acts of hyperbolic compassion with regard to the issue of hunger in a way that resonates deeply with Lévinas's trope of "taking the bread from one's own mouth," but that the *Jātaka* tales show these acts of compassion as taking place across the boundary that separates humans from non-human animals. Through stories of extreme sacrifice in which humans and other animals offer their own flesh to be eaten to stave off the hunger of another animal or human, the *Jātaka* tales resonate with the resources that Levinas provides us for thematizing this kind of an ethical summons and the ethical attunements that are required as a result, however they simultaneously offer a corrective to Levinas' oft-criticized humanism.

Hinduism

"Hinduism" denotes an astounding diversity of traditions both contemporary and ancient, including but not limited to Vedicism, post-Vedic Brahminism, Vaiṣṇavism, Śaivism, Tantra, Vedānta, Yoga, and a number of popular movements and vernacular traditions. It is difficult to identify a common essential core of these traditions. Though they share a family resemblance, they possess important differences regarding metaphysics, theism, authoritative texts, religious practices, as well as perspectives on nonhuman animals. Despite its diversity, Hinduism is commonly identified with vegetarianism, nonviolence, and reverence to cows and other sacred nonhuman animals. Such stereotypical characterizations are to some degree problematic essentialisms that invite either a romanticization or in some cases naïve derision of Hindu and nonhuman animal relationships. However, cows are indeed objects of devotion and worship among some Hindu communities, particularly those devoted to the deity Viṣṇu or his form as Kṛṣṇa. There is also a broad movement among Hindus in India to protect cows and give them sanctuary in old age and sickness. Many contemporary Hindus consider the cow a sacred symbol representing divinity, the universe, and even nationhood. And traditional sources view the five products of the cow (*pañcagavya*), consisting of milk, curd, clarified butter, urine, and dung as pure substances suitable for ritual, medical, or consumptive use.[27]

Ancient India did not always view nonviolence towards nonhuman animals as necessarily following from their sacred status. The oral texts of the Vedic culture, perhaps the earliest root of Hinduism, endorse the sacrifice and normative consumption of nonhuman animals within the confines of specific rituals. Vedic sacrifice was limited to a select few domestic animals such as cows, bulls, horses, sheep, and goats. And though most modern Hindus may be averse to such practices, the underlying theory of sacrifice need not be reduced simply to instrumental use and unethical slaughter. Though religiously sanctioned sacrifice may, prima facie, appear morally unjustifiable due to the consequential imbalance between ritual merit gained and loss of life, such a view misses its higher dimensions that point to the great value nonhuman animals possess in the Vedic worldview.[28] The intricate mythologies, ritual theories, and taxonomies implicit to sacrificial practices provide a window into ancient Indian conceptions of nonhuman animals. These perspectives often emphasize their intrinsic sacrality and even divinity, which makes them ritually efficacious, pleasing to the gods, and helpful in maintaining cosmic harmony. For example both the cow and the horse are homologized as microcosms for the universe and symbols of creation. The *Atharva Veda* identifies the cow as the "all-containing universe."[29] The opening verse of the *Bṛhadāraṇyaka Upaniṣad* homologizes the body of the sacrificial horse with the universe. Its head is the dawn, its sight is the sun, its back is the sky, and its underbelly the earth, just to name a handful of its associations.

Zoological taxonomies in Vedic and later legal literature also provide a window into conceived human/nonhuman animal relationships. Nonhuman animals are classified according to various criteria. Pedal structure forms one type of anatomical taxonomy. This includes whether a being possesses whole hooves (horses, donkeys), cloven hooves (cattle, goats, and sheep), or claws/nails (humans, apes, cats, etc.), as well as their number of feet, whether two feet or four feet. Dental structure forms another criterion. Beings are divided on the basis of having incisors in only the lower jaw, or both the upper and lower jaws. Modes of procreation comprise another taxonomical division depending on whether one is born from an egg, embryo, moisture, or sprouts. We also find a fundamental differentiation of domesticated nonhuman animals in the village from wild ones living in the forest. These taxonomies overlap, mutually enforce each other, and dictate which nonhuman animals are suitable in the ritual arena.[30] They are also grounded in animal cosmogonies.

Cosmogonies provide another window to Hindu conceptions of nonhuman animals. For example, *Bṛhadāraṇyaka Upaniṣad* 1.4.1–4 discusses the primal first person (*puruṣa*), who divides into man and woman and through their union gives birth to humans. They then proceed to give birth to various nonhuman animals by changing into each nonhuman animal male and female pair. This process includes cattle, horses, donkeys, goats, sheep, and all other beings down to ants. In another creation myth, the creator deity Prajāpati emits humans and nonhuman animals. From his mind he emits humans; from his eye, the horse; from his breath the cow; from his ear, the ram; and from his voice, the goat.[31]

Such cosmogonies and taxonomies place humans in an exceptional status, a hierarchy that pervades most forms of Hinduism. They are the first-born, the sacrificers, and the eaters, as opposed to the eaten. This type of superiority is based on a nutritional chain moving from supernatural entities, to humans, to nonhuman animals, to plants, and finally water.[32] The eaters are superior to their food just as the strong are superior to the weak. However, an important point to notice is that humans are not in a totally separate category or considered wholly other. They overlap with nonhuman animals based on taxonomy and cosmogony. The above cosmogonies, for example, understand humans as ontologically ultimately identified with nonhuman animals. This is also reflected in the fact that humans are included as one of the animals to be sacrificed (though human sacrifice was unlikely put into actual practice) and in later periods excluded from sacrifices along with other animals.[33] With the eventual rise of *ahiṃsā*, sacrificing and eating nonhuman animals became increasingly taboo because they were seen as non-other than human. To sacrifice and eat them becomes a form of cannibalism.[34] From this perspective, we find an opportunity to grant nonhuman animals the intrinsic value assumed for humans.

There is some debate whether the move towards embracing *ahiṃsā* and the subsequent rejection of nonhuman animal sacrifice and meat eating developed from within Vedic ritual theory and practice or from external influences. It is possible that *ahiṃsā* was a broader pan-Indian movement that swept through most Indian religious traditions, or that the influence of Jainism, Buddhism, and other renouncer traditions brought *ahiṃsā* into the Vedic worldview.[35] In any case, nonhuman sacrifice and consumption was frowned upon by the beginning of the Common Era, at least for brahmins who made up the priestly class. Exceptions were made for such acts, perhaps due to an unwillingness to challenge the authority of earlier Vedic texts, but textual sources such as the *Dharma Śāstra* and *Mahābhārata* demonstrate ambivalence and disconcertment regarding these practices.[36] Instead they increasingly prescribe vegetarianism and the use of animal effigies made of butter, flour, or other non-meat substances as substitutions for living animals.[37] Hindu ascetics who renounced rituals were more closely bound by *ahiṃsā*, and in their initiation vows must assure all beings that they will not cause them harm.[38]

Substitution effigies and other vegetable offerings are supposed to maintain the same ritual efficacy as animal sacrifice, but avoid the potential demerit of killing. By the early centuries CE, Hindus increasingly perceived nonhuman animals as conscious subjects that can experience suffering and deserve compassion. Therefore they should not become objects only fit for instrumental use. This is in part due to the importance of the *ahiṃsā* doctrine and the view that killing or cruelty towards living beings transgresses *dharma*, the universal moral order, and conflicts with moral virtues. Another factor is the broad acceptance of reincarnation. Nonhuman animals possess subtle bodies (*sūkṣmaśarīra*s) that are only temporarily encapsulated in animal forms. The subtle body, or soul, which transmigrates from birth to birth, is ultimately more real than its embodied form, whether human or nonhuman. Similar to Buddhism, reincarnation and the belief in the afterworld also encourage the fear that partaking in such violence will lead one to be reborn in a more difficult birth or a hell realm where those very slaughtered nonhuman animals will seek retaliation. In fact, Manu's *Dharma Śāstra* provides the following etymology for the term "*māṃsa*" (meat). " 'Me he (*māṃ sa*) will eat in the next world, whose meat (*māṃsa*) I eat in this world'—this, the wise declare, is what gave the name to and discloses the true nature of 'meat' (*māṃsa*)."[39] Despite such classical legal and theological proscriptions on meat eating, we should not assume that all Hindus are or were vegetarian. Different Hindu traditions, cultural groups, and class and caste identities, maintained varying positions on meat restrictions. And today, cosmopolitanism, globalization, and diasporic acculturation exert normative pressures to transgress vegetarianism.

Many other sources in classical Hinduism emphasize the veneration of nonhuman animals and their continuity with the human realm. Sacred narratives associate nonhuman animals with deities, often as their mounts (*vāhana*s). For example, Śiva is associated with the bull, Brahmā and Saraswatī with the swan, Skanda with the peacock, Gaṇeśa with the mouse, Lakṣmī with the elephant, and Dūrgā with the lion or tiger.[40] These nonhuman animals are emblematic of their particular deity, and thus gain an exalted and sacred status. It is common for such nonhuman animals to become dear to devotees who provide offerings to them in worship. Offering food or other ritual substances to nonhuman animals, whether in their actual living forms or iconographic or symbolic forms, is widespread in Hindu life. In addition, one of the five great daily and obligatory ritual practices of householders includes feeding nonhumans.[41] And it is common in Hindu death rites (*śrāddha*) to feed one's ancestors by offering rice balls to crows.

Classical Hinduism characterizes personal identity as having permeable boundaries.[42] This understanding is found in Indian mythologies that posit continuities between nonhuman animals, humans, and deities by which one may transform into the other or combine nonhuman animal and human characteristics. For example, there are semi-divine nonhuman animals that possess heightened intelligence and power. In the great epic, the *Rāmāyaṇa*, we meet the wise vulture Jaṭāyu, the divine bear Jāmbavān, and noble Hanumān, one of the *vānaras*, a group of divine monkeys. The *Purāṇas* narrate the lives of celestial snakes, like Vāsuki or Ādiśeṣa, the exploits of Garuda, the eagle mount of Viṣṇu who is sometimes half man/half eagle, or of Nandi, the mount of Śiva, sometimes depicted as half bull/half man. We also encounter Viṣṇu's hybrid forms such as Narasiṃha, who is half man/half lion, and Hayagrīva, who possesses the head of a horse. And one of the most popular and ubiquitous gods in Hinduism is Gaṇeśa, with his human body and elephant head. In many cases we find humans or gods transforming into other animals, a kind of theriomorphic shape shifting that mirrors the continuity of life implicit to reincarnation. For example, Viṣṇu incarnates as a fish, tortoise, and boar to rescue the world.

In many mythological contexts, sages, great ascetics, celestial beings, or demons transform into nonhuman animals. And occasionally these individuals are able to gain liberation while in nonhuman animal form. From the perspective of these narratives, one should be wary of disregarding nonhuman animals for they may be divine beings or wise sages even in their present form.[43] In other narratives, certain ascetics live as one among a group of nonhuman animals, even learning to speak their language.[44] And such narratives may not be far removed from actual ascetic practices in ancient India. Wild nonhuman animals provided models and archetypes for asceticism. Just as they live in a world removed from the domestic village and prohibited from the ritual space, so too did ascetics. Many ascetics eschewed society and domesticity, and intentionally retreated to the forest to step outside social, familial, and ritual duties. They lived more like nonhuman animals, perhaps not showering and shaving, sleeping in caves or at the base of a tree, and not using fire to cook or stay warm. Some even took such practices a step further by literally imitating nonhuman animals. These individuals vowed to act as a particular nonhuman animal. Some walked on all fours as though a dog. Others acted like a deer or a cow, wandering freely in the forest and using their mouths to eat food from the ground without any utensils.[45] Such austerities radically question human and nonhuman animal hierarchies, and perceive nonhuman animal lifestyles and qualities as efficacious for self-purification, contemplation, and absolute freedom. These ascetics challenge the idea that the lives of wild nonhuman animals or domesticated ones such as dogs are ritually impure and to be avoided.

Despite such resources that challenge hierarchies and affirm the value and importance of nonhuman animals, much of classical and contemporary Hinduism maintains anthropocentrism and hierarchy by assigning greater value to humans. This has its roots in the Vedic worldview and ironically in reincarnation. Hindus broadly conceive nonhuman animal births as lower births resulting from negative actions.[46] And, in many narratives, a grave ethical transgression forces a sage or a scoundrel to transform into a nonhuman animal unwillingly. Mirroring this hierarchy is a conception of religious purity and pollution. Humans lie on a spectrum of religious purity and pollution based on class, ritual action, diet, intention, and other forms of innate and extrinsic contact. Nonhuman animals are similarly conceived. Even though captive elephants may provide blessings in a temple, or venerated cows may possess a great deal of purity that parallels the purity of a brahmin, nonhuman animals in general are considered unclean and less ritually pure than humans. A dog, for example, mirrors the impurity of an outcaste and may be regarded as untouchable.[47] Such forms of hierarchy are a slippery slope, easily leading to a lack of intrinsic value and compassion, and the exploitation or neglect of nonhuman animals. On the other hand, the notion that nonhuman animals are impure encourages Hindus to avoid consuming flesh, which pollutes body and mind.

More recently there have been attempts to ground or construct views of nonhuman animals and environmental ethics in Hindu metaphysical doctrines. Though such attempts may not translate easily into lived religious practice, they still constitute a rich resource. Like Buddhist and Daoist metaphysics, a variety of Hindu philosophies challenge accepted notions of self-identity. Sāṅkhya and Pātañjali Yoga argue that the essential identity of each living being is pure consciousness distinct from material nature. Other philosophical traditions like Advaita Vedānta, Viśiṣṭādvaita Vedānta, and Tantra posit realities of continuity, oneness, and shared identity. Advaita Vedānta, for example, claims an ultimate reality of nonduality. In this perspective, the sustaining reality of all individuals is a single self, which is pure non-intentional consciousness unlimited by individual distinctions or forms. Furthermore, the experienced empirical world of multiplicity and distinction is considered a divine manifestation, the material body of *Īśvara* (God), facilitating the idea that all living beings are sacred. The endeavor to ascribe moral value to nonhuman animals by taking such positions and leaping the chasm between transcendent and empirical realities is fraught with philosophical difficulties.[48] But, if possible, these traditions implicitly affirm nonhuman animals as possessing consciousness and intrinsic value, and deserving compassion and some degree of equality.

Chapter summaries

In "The Argument for *Ahiṃsā* in the *Anuśāsanaparvan* of the *Mahābhārata*," Christopher Framarin analyzes a dialogue between Yudhiṣṭhira and Bhīṣma in the *Mahābhārata* regarding moral obligations humans have towards nonhuman animals. Framarin argues that the passage asserts human obligations to nonhuman animals based on their sentience and ability to experience pleasure and pain. Framarin challenges a trend among some Indian philosophers who claim the ethical treatment of animals and/or ecosystems in texts such as the *Mahābhārata* or the *Dharma Śāstra* are based solely on prudential concerns where one avoids injuring others in order to simply avoid negative karmic repercussions. Framarin argues that prudential concerns are based on a pre-existing moral order, and that nonhuman animals have direct moral standing, meaning they must be considered for their own sake. A key position of Framarin's argument is that the value or disvalue of pleasure and pain are not wholly extrinsic. If the value of pleasure and pain are intrinsic, then any entity that can experience pleasure or pain must possess intrinsic value. He explains that sentiency itself indicates an experiencing subject, with intrinsic value and direct moral standing. Framarin also argues that life itself has intrinsic value, while death has intrinsic disvalue. Therefore humans have an obligation not to infringe on the longevity of other nonhuman animals. He briefly extends similar arguments to physical health, strength, freedom, etc., arguing that they are intrinsically valuable, and therefore extend direct moral standing to nonhuman animals.

Amy Allocco's chapter, "Snakes in the dark age: human action, karmic retribution, and the possibilities for Hindu animal ethics," explores rarely studied vernacular snake worship traditions in Tamil Nadu, India, and theorizes them as a model for human and nonhuman animal interaction. Utilizing ethnographic fieldwork and oral narratives, Allocco contextualizes the place of sacred snakes (*nāga*s), their power, and the forms of their worship. She outlines common manifestations *nāga*s take in worship, as anthropomorphic goddess, an anthill, a divine serpent, and a stone *nāga* image, and describes practices involved in their worship. One of the popular reasons people propitiate *nāga*s is the fear of their curses. *Nāga dōṣam* (snake blemish), a type of curse caused by harming or killing a snake, manifests as an astrological flaw and leads to many potential problems, particularly fertility and marriage problems among women. Specific rituals to *nāga*s help remove this blemish and its manifestations. Interestingly, such *nāga* worship cuts across caste and class distinctions and continues to grow in popularity. In her fieldwork, Allocco has found that *nāga dōṣam* is embedded in Hindu understandings of cosmic time, specifically the current Kali Yuga age, the fourth and final age of the world in which society, religion, and ethics continue to deteriorate. According to her informants and textual sources, in this age we grow further alienated from and destructive of the environment and nonhuman animals, which is why *nāga* worship and avoiding their harm is all the more important. Allocco theorizes that *nāga*s and the Kali Yuga cosmology are models from which an indigenous environmental and nonhuman animal ethic can be retrieved. Rather than a fatalistic or passive disregard for nonhuman animals, belief in the Kali Yuga and the example of human/nonhuman animal relationships within *nāga* worship, engender moral responsibility for nonhuman animals and the environment.

In "Bovine *dharma*: nonhuman animals in the Swadhyaya Parivar," Pankaj Jain examines nonhuman animal perspectives in the Swadhyaya movement, a contemporary Hindu based tradition founded by Pandurang Shastri Athavale in the mid-twentieth century. Jain discusses the ways this religious tradition provides a unique indigenous ethic towards nonhuman animals. Athavale developed a novel approach, grounded in classical texts, of a dharmic way of life that includes deep respect and reverence for nonhuman animals and the environment. Jain explains that the underlying root for this respect is the belief that God resides in all things. This manifests clearly in what Jain calls "bovine *dharma*," in which the qualities and virtues of cows, a manifestation of divine presence, become a model or metaphor for developing human moral virtues. Other types of dharmic moral virtues are located in a variety of other nonhuman animals. Athavale discussed other models based on his interpretations of the *Bhagavad Purāṇa* and the *Bhagavad Gītā*. Jain outlines these nonhuman animals, such as the pigeon, python, elephant, and deer, and explains how they inspire human ethics. This nonhuman animal *dharma*, derived from textual reverence for nature, is a model for spiritual and ethical transformation among Swadhyaya adherents. Jain's discussion shows how religious devotional practices and ideologies can manifest as powerful means for an environmental and nonhuman animal ethic.

Jainism

Jainism is arguably the oldest living renouncer tradition in India. According to Jain history, there were twenty-four Tīrthaṇkaras (literally "Ford-makers"), liberated teachers who perfected their knowledge and paved the way towards enlightenment. The last Tīrthaṇkara and influential propagator of Jainism was Vardhamāna Mahāvīra. He probably lived in the fifth or sixth century BCE, shortly before the Buddha and in the same general region. Of all South Asian traditions, Jainism is most renowned for its commitment to avoid harm to other living beings. Non-injury (*ahiṃsā*) comprises the cornerstone of Jain philosophy and forms its central religious practices and pursuit of liberation. Jain monks, nuns, and laity are well known for their meticulous measures to minimize any kind of violence to nonhuman animals.

Jain cosmology views the world as three tiered, with an upper heavenly realm, middle earthly realm, and lower hell realm, each of which has its own subdivisions. These realms mirror the four destinies that a being can take in rebirth, as heavenly beings, hell beings, animals, or plants.[49] Humans, nonhuman animals, insects, plants, and microorganisms all inhabit the same earthly realm. Jainism categorizes all living beings in a hierarchical taxonomy based on their number of senses. Plants, microorganisms (*nigoda*), and basic element-bodied beings are one-sensed beings, limited to touch alone. Two-sensed ones, such as worms and mollusks possess touch and taste. Ants, beetles, centipedes, and other similar three-sensed beings possess touch, taste, and smell. Insects such as bees, mosquitoes, and scorpions possess touch, taste, smell, and sight. Humans and other animals, including fish and marine life, possess all five senses, touch, taste, smell, sight, and hearing.[50] All living beings share the basic sense of touch. From the possession of touch, Jains reason that beings, even one-sensed ones, are sentient and can experience pain, suffering, and craving.

Jains view every living being as possessing a pure soul with intrinsic functions of consciousness, bliss, and energy.[51] The true nature and splendor of the soul is covered by *karma*. According to Jains, *karma* is a viscous sticky material or dust that clings to an individual based on his or her actions. Each individual has the capacity to eliminate this karmic pollution through religious practices and ultimately perfect liberating knowledge, a potential innate to nonhuman animals as well. Even though it may take them several lifetimes to gain a suitable birth, this potential along with their sentience and capacity to suffer establish their intrinsic worth. These facts underlie the Jain emphasis on *ahiṃsā* towards nonhuman animals. Jains employ a number of practices and restraints to lighten the karmic burdens covering their souls, and to eliminate harm to others. The focus on *ahiṃsā* leads Jains to an orientation of great attentiveness. Cultivating spiritual progress requires an exquisite mindfulness to maintain *ahiṃsā* in all actions and intentions. For laity, the focus is on two to five-sensed beings, but for monks, the progression of this careful awareness includes less developed one-sensed beings. Jain ethics includes intentions, actions, and results. Further, one's ignorance is no excuse for unintentional violence. Thus, for Jains, individuals are responsible for recognizing violence and taking personal responsibility in action. Thus it is necessary to understand what harm is and its causes, when animals are suffering, how they suffer, etc.

Maintaining *ahiṃsā* requires strict vegetarianism. All Jains, without exception, must subsist on one-sensed beings (plants) and milk products.[52] This excludes nonhuman animals unintentionally killed for providing food as alms, or the flesh of animals dead by natural causes.[53] Jain ascetics criticized others, such as Buddhists, for their lax restrictions on vegetarianism, and condemned Brahmanical nonhuman animal sacrifice.[54] Monks often carry whisk brooms to clear insects from the road or seat, and some sects wear mouth shields to avoid killing flying beings. There are additional restrictions on travel, digging, and bathing to avoid causing harm. Lay Jains cannot take up harmful occupations like hunting or fishing, and also avoid cooking and eating after sunrise so no insects are killed in the fire. Nonhuman animals are not to be beaten, branded, mutilated, held in captivity, forced to carry overly heavy burdens, or given insufficient water and food.[55] Jains are also known for setting up nonhuman animal shelters and hospital (*pinjrapole*s).

Ahiṃsā and the respect for life manifest on an intellectual level as a respect for the opinions of others. Jainism is well known for its philosophical position of nonabsolutism (*anekāntavāda*), an inclusive epistemology which claims every judgment is relative. According to this position, particular points of view, which lead to judgments, hold only partial knowledge. The classic example is a group of blind men touching different parts of an elephant and coming to various partially correct conclusions, but not recognizing the elephant itself. According to *anekāntavāda*, we ought to be tolerant and open to multiple points of view. Alternative perspectives are other angles on reality that we may overlook. This mentality of perspectivalism can extend to nonhuman animals, and help open humans to their views and needs. *Anekāntavāda* encourages a disposition to look beyond anthropocentrism, and to acknowledge the plight of nonhuman animals and emphasize with their suffering.[56]

Even though humans and nonhuman animals share the same hierarchical position of five-sensed beings in the sensory taxonomy, Jains consider nonhuman animal births lower than human ones. They entail greater difficulty in spiritual progression because nonhuman animals are more entangled in passions, cravings, and ignorance than humans. Nonhuman animal births may also result from deceit or other unethical actions. For Jains, this hierarchy does not legitimate subjugation or killing of nonhuman animals. And Jainism is unique among Indian traditions for attributing particular abilities to five-sensed nonhuman animals believed to have reason.[57] These nonhuman animals not only possess the innate seeds to propel them towards liberation, but also moral agency and volition to affect their destiny.[58] They may remember prior lives, engage religious practices such as fasting and contemplation, and can give up habits such as predatory lifestyles.[59]

Nonhuman animals with reason can potentially progress through some of the important early spiritual stages on the Jain path to liberation. This includes *samyak-darśana*, a deep but momentary insight into the true nature of one's soul. This flash of insight generates purity, weakens karmic obstructions, and helps develop the desire to take Jain vows.[60] The circular assembly where a Tīrthaṇkara shares his wisdom, called the *samavasaraṇa*, perhaps best illustrates that nonhuman animals long to understand their true nature and are capable of receiving instruction. The Tīrthaṇkara is able to communicate with all the beings in the *samavasaraṇa*, including various five-sensed animals who gather in harmony and form the second ring of the congregation.[61] A number of other stories in Jain narrative literature attest to the aspirations and religious abilities of nonhuman animals to gain insight and take religious vows.[62] Such stories reinforce the Jain commitment not to interfere with nonhuman animal life in any way that might restrict their path to liberation.

Nonhuman animals often play a vital role in the lives of Tīrthaṇkaras, and Jains identify each Tīrthaṇkara with a particular animal. For example, Ariṣṭanemi, the twenty-second Tīrthaṇkara, refused to marry Princess Rājimati after learning caged nonhuman animals would be killed for the wedding. He then saved these animals and retired to an ascetic life. Pārśvanātha, the twenty-third

Tīrthaṇkara saved a pair of snakes being unknowingly burnt in the logs of an ascetic's fire.[63] Mahāvīra received instruction from two Jain monks in a previous life while embodied in the form of a lion. Despite his nonhuman lion form he awoke to his true nature, desisted from his violent lion ways, and took the lesser vows of a lay Jain. Refraining from killing and eating flesh, he died of starvation and was reborn in a heavenly world.[64]

Jains engage in self-sacrificing action or inaction to maximize the interests of others, and to remain detached from the violence of the world. This is sometimes clearly demanding for the individual. However, one may argue that Jainism's altruistic embrace of *ahiṃsā* is in reality egoistic, not purely out of compassion or selflessness. To act out anger and violence creates negative *karma* and fuels negative passions. The primary reason for reducing harm, acting kindly, and alleviating suffering of nonhuman animals is to reduce one's karmic burden. This is true in one sense, for the Jain goal is ultimately individual liberation. But in the case of Jainism there is a convergence of ethical egoism and altruism. From the standpoint of Jain philosophy, the action that maximizes the individual Jain's own self interest is the same action that minimizes harm to other beings. Thus, even though *ahiṃsā* can be boiled down to self-interest, the very soteriological value system of Jainism inverts ethical egoism to account for the moral welfare of other beings.

Chapter summaries

In looking at certain Hindu and Buddhist traditions in South Asia, it is tempting to focus on ideas of nonduality and interconnection that parallel contemporary movements like deep ecology, or which may be interpreted as an affirmation of equality and criticism of human exceptionalism and hierarchy. Anne Vallely's "Being sentiently with others: the shared existential trajectory among humans and nonhumans in Jainism," highlights a different approach in the Jain tradition. Jainism privileges humans as a superior category and demarcates a clear ontological difference between humans and nonhuman animals. The primary reason for this is the greater human potential for attaining final liberation. Jains also seek distance from nonhuman animals. Yet at the same time, an ethic of nonviolence towards the nonhuman world forms the very basis for the Jain tradition. Vallely addresses how Janism's anthropocentric classification does not lead to an exploitive relationship with nonhuman animals. On the contrary, in the Jain worldview humans must avoid any harm to other beings. Jains view the world as animate and intelligent, with different categories of living beings forming a cosmological hierarchy based on the senses. Every organism, however, possesses the sense of touch, indicating the presence of a soul with its defining characteristic of sentience and the capacity to suffer. Furthermore, all beings are moving from birth to birth in different life forms. Vallely's chapter discusses the commonalities of all beings consisting of shared sentiency, suffering, and an "existential trajectory" aimed towards liberation. She argues that with more complex beings there is a shared sense of alienation and thus a compassion for and commiseration with them. Understanding this shared plight of all beings cultivates empathy towards nonhuman animals due to an awareness of "being with other beings" in a world that is fundamentally communicative and relational.

Christopher Key Chapple's chapter, "Nonhuman animals and the question of rights from an Asian perspective," juxtaposes Asian views on nonhuman animal personhood with the approach found in various declarations of rights. Chapple discusses the United Nations Declaration of Rights, the Earth Charter, and the Great Ape Project, and their assertions of human rights, environmental rights, and the rights of nonhuman primates. The Earth Charter and the Great Ape Project, approaches modeled on the UN Declaration of Rights, extend such rights and their presupposition of the importance of individual dignity to nonhuman animals and even ecological systems. Chapple points out that these charters assign an entity's measure of worth based on humans. Nonhuman primates, for example, are given rights due to their similarities to humans. Unfortunately such approaches fail to assign rights to many other kinds of nonhuman animals. Chapple then turns his attention to South Asian perspectives that do not operate from an anthropocentric standpoint. He concisely explains Yoga, Hindu, Jain, and Buddhist perspectives on nonhuman animals as well as the example of the Bishnoi community, who have become renowned in India for their fierce protection of nonhuman animals. Utilizing sacred narratives, philosophical positions, and reincarnation theory, he finds a common thread through these traditions that see all beings as kin and companions, a view that ascribes innate dignity and personhood to all nonhuman animals. This position can develop a deeper level of compassion, humility, and empathy towards other animals.

East Asian approaches to nonhuman animals

Early Chinese cosmology points out a seamless continuum between the human and nonhuman animal worlds. Rather than a sharp boundary or dichotomy, there is a porous demarcation between the two. Common to many Chinese philosophical schools is a complex evolution of multiplicity out of a single simple unity. The world is composed of *qi*. Though difficult to define, *qi* is something akin to an irreducible continuous energy field or animating fluid. *Qi* pervades all things without distinguishing essential and changing aspects.[65] It divides into *yin* and *yang*, heaven and earth, makes up everything including the subtle breath of the body, and is constantly in a process of change and transformation.

This *qi* worldview, with its constant transformation of all things, a type of "processional cosmology," is a pervasive background to Daoism and Confucianism.[66] It dovetails with the unitary nature of the *dao*, which is never frozen or fixed. The *dao*'s constant transformations include the arbitrary forms and fluid potential between human and nonhuman animal forms. On the other hand, even though *qi* does not lend itself to simple divisions, its moral manifestation contributes to human/nonhuman animal distinctions. For Confucians, *qi* (and blood) is the physiological substrate of beings, as well as the function of moral temperament.[67] The Confucian sage, Mencius (Mengzi), for example, believed that one's moral *qi* must be nourished through a process of growth and extension to achieve self-actualization.[68] Confucianism and some other Chinese traditions believe moral characteristics of humans, rather than biological perfections, distinguish humans from nonhuman animals.[69]

Early Chinese philosophers devised a number of ways to classify nonhuman animals within the larger project of understanding the cosmos as a whole. This classification was largely part of textual and ritual orders and based on correlation rather than differentiation.[70] For example, one model of correlative classification in the third century BCE was based on the conceptual scheme of *yinyang* and the five phases (*wuxing*) of wood, fire, earth, metal, and water. In one manifestation of this model, animals are classified into five categories based on correlations of skin and the five phases. Scaly animals are identified with wood, feathered ones with fire, naked ones with earth, hairy ones with metal, and armored ones with water. Each animal category is correlated further with other manifestations of each phase, such as seasons, cardinal directions, and colors.[71] This framework includes humans as naked animals, rather than grouping them as an essentially different species. Humans are just part of the greater whole. From the standpoint of the *yinyang* and *wuxing* models, there is no permanent human/nonhuman animal distinction, and all beings are interrelated, continuous, and interdependent with each other and the totality of cosmic forces. Linear hierarchies based on scales of perfection, that place humans at the pinnacle of all species are absent in such classificatory models.[72]

Nonhuman animals hold a number of important functions in pre-Buddhist Chinese religion. One function was as intermediaries for human communication with the spirit world. Turtles, for example, were associated with divine powers, immortality, and the advent of trigrams and writing. Diviners of the ancient Shang dynasty used the plastron portion of the turtle shell for divination, as well as the scapula bones of domestic oxen. Dogs, with their domestic familiarity, straddled the human and nonhuman animal worlds as well as the realms of the living and the dead.[73] Nonhuman animal sacrifice was central to religious, social, and political life in early China. In these rituals, nonhuman animals served in particular as sacrificial cuisine, a vital part of such practices. There is also some evidence that nonhuman animals, or their spirits, were objects of ritual worship, particularly for agriculture and military affairs. Religious groups from various periods and locations worshipped nonhuman animal spirits such as horses, dragons, chickens, tigers, and snakes. Though unlike South Asia, deities rarely took the shape of nonhuman animals and were generally not symbolized by other animals.[74]

Around the first century CE, elements of Buddhism entered China with Buddhist monks or pious lay people attached to caravans traveling the trade routes. Over the following centuries Buddhism would steadily grow in popularity and interact with other Chinese traditions. Chinese Buddhist traditions such as Ch'an, Tiantai, and Huayan, evolved and developed traditions quite distinct from South Asian Buddhism, but maintained a strong focus on nonviolence and compassion to nonhuman animals. The moral obligation to protect nonhuman animal life, to some degree, influenced Daoist and Confucian worldviews as well. And vegetarianism is still closely associated with Buddhism in China.

Buddhism, Daoism, and neo-Confucianism were major influences on Japan's rich religious history and its views on nonhuman animals. The sixth century CE arrival of Buddhism in Japan brought an emphasis on nonhuman animal suffering and liberation, which led in part to decrees against killing nonhuman animals, especially large domestic ones. Along with its belief in nonhuman animal sentience, Buddhism also brought new forms of hierarchy between human and nonhuman animals with its theories of rebirth. It would quickly become intertwined with indigenous traditions and inspire hybrid traditions.[75] Prior to the influence of continental traditions, the indigenous traditions of pre-Buddhist Japan incorporated aspects of animism and shamanism, often viewing nonhuman animals as numinous beings inhabiting a space between human and divine realms. Japanese folklore and mythology demonstrate a fluid boundary between human, nonhuman animal, and divine worlds, with nonhuman animals functioning as omens, intermediaries, and symbols of cosmic order.[76] Shinto, for example, incorporates nonhuman animal spirits to guard shrines, and has a number of tales about shape-shifting animals and magical creatures. Nonhuman animals were revered and feared in such spiritualized perspectives; revered for their divine connection, but also feared as threatening forces proximate to monsters and demonic spirits. Wolves, for example, were divine messengers at Shinto shrines, but also looked upon as demons that might attack people.[77] Modern Japan continues to face these kinds of ambivalent dichotomies. On the one hand the Japanese religious imagination views nonhuman animals as possessing an otherworldly sacred status and forming part of a harmonious and aesthetically prized relationship with nature and humans. On the other hand, modern Japan's utilitarian perspective often supersedes these views in favor of utilizing nonhuman animals as commodities or eradicating them as pests.

Confucianism

Confucianism holds a variety of views regarding animals, some of which appear to contradict each other at face value. On the one hand we find a Confucian concern with extending kindness to nonhuman animals and reducing their suffering; however, on the other hand, a robust Confucian ethic towards the nonhuman animal world faces the difficulties of human superiority and a lack of intrinsic value for nonhuman animals. These obstacles are grounded in the Confucian view that moral virtues are tied to the human world. Humans have high intrinsic value and nonhuman animals are morally inferior to humans. From another perspective, it is not that humans are necessarily superior, but that humans should associate with other humans, and thus put human beings first. From this standpoint, even if nonhuman animals have innate qualities that are the same or similar to humans, they still would not hold equal rights.[78]

Confucianism, unlike some other East Asian and South Asian traditions that endorse the importance of asceticism and renunciation, focuses on one's obligations to family and society. This is clearly apparent in the five primary Confucian human relationships of king–subject, father–son, husband–wife, elder brother–younger brother, and friend–friend. The Confucian individual is a moral agent who cultivates filial piety, virtues, and inner flourishing through these primary relationships. The human being is thus fundamentally social in nature, and to become fully human is a process to be pursued within society. To step away from this and become a hermit not only shirks harmony, one's virtues, and duties, but also moves one towards nonhuman animals, a movement which Confucius (Kongzi) ardently criticized.[79] To become less than human was to lose one's status as a fully developed moral agent.[80]

The instrumental use of nonhuman animals required by Confucian sacrificial rituals demonstrates the primacy of socio-familial relationships and one's reverence to heaven. Performing ritual is imperative for the individual as well as to restore order and maintain harmony. Ritual practice is grounded in the Confucian fidelity to the ancients and the reverence one has for ancestors, deities, and humans. Furthermore, ritual practice is a primary arena in which the noble person (*junzi*) develops virtues and harmony between internal disposition and external activity.[81] The commitment of fulfilling virtues of love and reverence to gods, spirits, and humans unequivocally includes sacrificial nonhuman animals. Offering their valuable lives is a mark of the seriousness of ritual, and ignoring sacrifice does irreparable damage to the rituals and leads to disorder. This strict ritual observance excludes ritual reform, such as that found in ancient India, where animal sacrifice in Vedic religion mostly died out due to the classical Brahmanical emphasis on nonviolence. Confucians are also generally not vegetarian. One may view meat eating and even hunting as an extension of Confucian ritual sacrifice, where all social interaction is patterned ritually.

Despite maintaining the ancient Chinese *qi* worldview and cosmology of constant change and transformation, Confucianism does not support the equality of all things. Human transformation through cultivating culture and moral virtue elevates the human towards the divine and away from the base nonhuman animal world.[82] In defense of its vertical hierarchical worldview where human wellbeing supersedes nonhuman animal wellbeing, Confucianism critiques equality of love or equality of rights as an empty claim leading to no love or no rights.[83] Despite this, Confucianism prescribes a caring or sympathetic love towards nonhuman animals. Even though this caring is trumped by reverence, devotion, and benevolence towards humans, it still provides a powerful ground for better treatment of nonhuman animals. Nonhuman animals should not be killed without reason. They are to be treated well, free from cruelty and poor living conditions, when raised for ritual use or sustenance.[84] Intimate nonhuman animals, either pets or those used for labor, are not to be killed and may deserve death rituals such as burial. Restrictions are not limited to domestic animals. When hunting other animals one should not use wasteful or unsportsmanlike methods, which take unfair advantage of them and compromise one's moral virtue.[85] Confucians disapproved of using nonhuman animals for sports such as cock fighting, bull fighting, and horse racing. Such pastimes may have been popular through the centuries, but are not oriented towards cultivating noble virtues. They are frivolous and thrive on the corrupt force of greed.[86]

Confucians support consequentialist utilitarian-like guidelines towards nonhuman animals. The noble Confucian is sensitive to nonhuman animals and should avoid harming them or directly taking their life. It is for this reason that Mencius advises the noble person to avoid the kitchen.[87] When we perceive suffering, even of nonhuman animals, it reminds us of our own. Our inability to bear their suffering brings out our own compassion and humane treatment of nonhuman animals.[88] Ideally this circle of compassion and care extends to everything in the world with developed sagehood. In addition, later neo-Confucian doctrines held the idea of the unity of all beings. This notion, of forming one body with all things, further grounds sensitivity to the suffering and distress of other animals.[89]

Chapter summary

Bao-Er's "China's Confucian horses: the place of nonhuman animals in a Confucian world order," investigates the possibilities and difficulties of nonhuman animal ethics in Confucianism. He focuses on the related themes of humanity, hierarchy, and harmony. Relational hierarchies form the structural basis of Confucian social and moral order and self-identity. Knowing one's role and place in the intricate social web of relationships and acting appropriately results in harmony and stability. Humaneness is cultivated within harmonious interrelational participation. Bao-Er explains the intrinsic human value required by this scheme to the exclusion of nonhuman animals that were ritually sacrificed as the means to connect with the divine. However, developing humanity faces a tension; compassion must be cultivated to develop moral virtue, including a sensitivity to nonhuman animal suffering, yet upholding social harmony, even at the expense of nonhuman animals, is of utmost importance. Bao-Er questions how to retrieve a nonhuman animal ethic from Confucianism, particularly as China expands the creation of Confucian institutes as part of its promotion of Chinese culture and desire to unite ethnic Chinese. The challenge for a Confucian nonhuman animal ethic is to view nonhuman animals as intrinsically valuable, and to find a path that extends humane love to other animals without subordinating them to human kinship love.

Daoism

The term "Daoism" is somewhat vague. Daoism, similar to Hinduism, has no single founder with disciples who share a single identity. A number of different Daoist traditions with varying doctrines and practices arose over the centuries, some of which were independent and not necessarily aware of each other. As their doctrines, rituals, and practices evolved they created a large corpus of Daoist literary work, not limited to the two well-known fourth century BCE mystical/philosophical texts, the *Daodejing* ascribed to Laozi (Lao Tzu), and

Zhuangzi's *Zhuangzi*. Daoist views on nonhuman animals vary, mirroring its obscure historical origins, lack of a single unified school, and the particularities of its complex evolution.

Given the diversity of Daoisms, it is not surprising to find a sense of ambivalence and tension towards nonhuman animals. On the one hand, few moral prohibitions against their appropriation are stated or put into practice. Some Daoists considered killing nonhuman animals for the sake of human consumption in terms of food, clothing, and medication, as natural and appropriate, just as some animals and insects eat others or prey on humans. Though traditional Chinese communities engaged in animal sacrifice, and some contemporary traditions continue to tolerate sacrifice,[90] there is little evidence of such rituals in early Daoism. During the late Han period, Daoist movements supported ritual reform through a ban of blood sacrifice.[91]

Daoism provides a number of original nonhuman animal friendly doctrines, cosmologies, and mythologies. Daoists seek to live in accordance with the *dao*, or way. The *dao*, which is the true nature, order, and unitary structure underlying the world, is too subtle to be grasped by words. All entities of the universe differentiate out of this fundamental unity. The *Daodejing*, for example, states,

> [*Dao* produced] the One. The One produced the two. The two produced the three. And the three produced the ten thousand things. The ten thousand things carry the *yin* and embrace the *yang*, and through the blending of the material force they achieve harmony.[92]

This important overarching cosmological reality overshadows distinctions, for from its standpoint one cannot draw a boundary between human and nature or separate the human and nonhuman.[93] There is a constant continuum without distinction that cannot be divided into linear hierarchical orders, gradations, or scales of perfection that exclude nonhuman animals.[94]

According to the Daoist view, all things in the world are in a process of constant change and transformation. The human form is arbitrary and just one of many possibilities. With time the human form will die and change into something else.[95] While this should not be conflated with South Asian theories of reincarnation, it can lead to similar results regarding nonhuman animals. Here again we find a continuum between human and nonhuman animals, where identities are unstable and porous. No permanent line can be drawn because humans can potentially change to nonhuman animals and vice versa. The fluidity of *qi* and the inevitable cosmological flow is a worldview that inhibits freezing the whole into parts that involve fixed ontological demarcations. This opens up the possibility of compassion and empathy based on the equality of a shared existential reality.

For Daoists, nonhuman animals are metaphors for teaching and sources of emulation and learning. Observing other animals and incorporating their movement inspires forms of Daoist martial arts and health practices. However, Daoist doctrines move beyond such animal emulation to seeing them as sources for human conduct and more aptly following the proper way. Similar to other traditions that lean towards forest dwelling and reject social institutions, Daoism looks to nonhuman animals as possessing the ideal attributes of detachment, simplicity, and great perspective. Nonhuman animals live freely, spontaneously, and simply in nature. Humans should return to nature and live similarly to them.[96] Zhuangzi even recommends the radical move of becoming or thinking the nonhuman animal, such as the horse, the yak, or the butterfly, to move beyond the confines of human speech and thought.[97] Opening one's perspective to the nonhuman animal, and in some sense becoming the nonhuman animal, allows one to move beyond the limitations of language and essentialized human identity. Stepping into other animal perspectives resists human exceptionalism and breaks the anthropocentric and anthropomorphic limitations that bind us.[98]

Following the path of the *dao* includes cultivating one's self to live in harmony with nature. From an abstract sense, this blending or yielding with nature may manifest as less domination, intervention, and control of both ecosystems and nonhuman animals.

Approaching wild nonhuman animals as ideal beings who are free, naturally follow the *dao*, and who possess their own *dao*, leads to a position of respect and non-intervention.[99] This ties into the Daoist doctrine of *wu wei*, a position of responsible non-action where one's egotistical concerns and passions do not dictate action. Instead, one remains gentle and strives to abstain from forceful interference that causes disruption and disorder. If *wu wei* is extended to nonhuman animals, then it is best to avoid forcing them to act contrary to their nature. It is better to allow them to live freely and pursue their own future instead of competing with them or making them instrumental sources of our material needs. Daoists recognize that nonhuman animals value their own lives and self-preservation, enjoy freedom, and thrive in their natural environment. The *Zhuangzi*, for example, repeatedly states that we should not make nonhuman animals act contrary to their nature. For example, wild marsh pheasants do not ask to be put in a cage,[100] wild horses are happier than captive ones,[101] and a turtle would rather drag its tail through the mud than be honored with its remains preserved in an ancestral shrine.[102] One could argue that this implies nonhuman animals possess intrinsic value and direct moral standing. When taken to its logical conclusion, Daoist ideology should lead to a transformative symbiotic relationship with nonhuman animals, without competition and with mutual benefit and interdependence. Respecting nonhumans will help humans flourish.[103]

Even though the non-interventionist strategy of *wu wei* lends itself to a conservation ethic, it may not satisfy an animal activist agenda. Daoist traditions generally do not focus on ethical obligations for adherents or assign rights to nonhuman animals. There are notable exceptions to this, however, found in the texts of precepts and behavioral guidelines that Daoists produced throughout the centuries. For example, *The 180 Precepts of Lord Lao*, a code of conduct for Daoists of the Celestial Masters tradition states a number of prohibitions against harming nonhuman animals. One should not fish or hunt, and thus not harm or kill living beings. One should not dig up hibernating animals and insects. One should not use cages to trap birds and animals. And one should not disturb birds and animals or the habitat they live in.[104] In other instances, Daoists put forth religious and theological reasons for avoiding nonhuman animal harm. For example, some Daoists in the Celestial Masters and Complete Perfection orders were vegetarian as a religious practice of purification. They avoided meat so their diet corresponded to the deities in the celestial world, and believed abstaining from meat helped one to become immortal.[105]

Nonhuman animal ethics in Daoism focuses more on avoiding harmful actions than on a prescriptive ethic. This has led to some debate whether non-intervention is a passive position that obstructs direct action to help nonhuman animals that are endangered, violated, or suffering from inhumane conditions. Underlying this difficulty is the Daoist acceptance of life, death, change, and destruction as part of nature.[106] But defining nature or what is a natural process in the contemporary industrialized world is a difficult contested question. Others argue that the individualistic self-cultivation of Daoism leads to indirect or non-interventionist actions that help nonhuman animals from a distance.[107] Contemporary Daoists are actively formulating clearer positions regarding nonhuman ethics and what kind of obligations we have to nonhumans.

Chapter summary

Mario Wenning's "Heidegger and Zhuangzi on the nonhuman: towards a transcultural critique of (post)humanism" is one of the comparative chapters in this volume, offering a comparative study of German philosopher Martin Heidegger and Daoist philosopher Zhuangzi. As Wenning notes, Heidegger's work has been taken up extensively by environmental philosophers,[108] and has also been explored repeatedly for its affinities with Daoism and for the influence of Daoism upon it. In contrast to these studies, the first part of Wenning's chapter criticizes Heidegger for his crypto-humanism, and explores the limitations of his philosophy for a posthumanist environmental philosophy. Wenning then turns to Zhuangzi's Daoist philosophy *not* to show its influence on and complementarity with Heidegger's thought, but to provide an alternative to the latter. Daoism, Wenning suggests, provides a means of critiquing Heidegger's lingering attachment to humanism. Even more significantly, Wenning argues that the crypto-humanism of Heidegger is in fact symptomatic of twentieth-century Western thought, including dominant trends in Critical Animal Theory today. Thus, Wenning argues, a turn to Daoism offers an antidote, not just to Heidegger, but to Western ways of theorizing animal relations more generally. In particular, it offers a way of thinking about animal relations beyond the human–animal binary and beyond extensionist approaches to animal ethics that merely re-entrench this binary. In confronting Heidegger's critique of anthropocentrism with Daoism's appreciation of nature's imperfection, Wenning's chapter outlines a philosophical approach that is built on the idea of the perfection arising from an acknowledgment of human as well as nonhuman imperfection.

Notes

1 Some of the well-known texts include *Nature in Asian Traditions of Thought*, edited by J. Baird Callicott and Roget T. Ames and the series of volumes on Religion and Ecology (including *Hinduism and Ecology*, *Buddhism and Ecology*, *Daoism and Ecology*, *Confucianism and Ecology*, and *Jainism and Ecology*) edited by Christopher Chapple (a contributor to this volume), Mary Evelyn Tucker, and others.

2 Some critical animal scholars have recognized that using the term "animal" to refer to all other species of animals besides the human is problematic because it reinscribes this ontological divide and moral abyss, and yet continue to use the term because they find the phrase "nonhuman animals" unwieldy or inelegant. We prefer to use a somewhat unwieldy term, however, than to reinscribe the problematic human–animal distinction in our language. As happened with using the term "humankind" rather than "man," and with using "their" rather than "his" to refer even to singular subjects where the gender is unspecified, we think that the initial sense of awkwardness that comes with using the term "nonhuman animal" disappears with use and familiarity. Nevertheless, we recognize at least two problems with the term "nonhuman animal." First, as Derrida has pointed out, the term "animal"—and "nonhuman animal" as well—homogenizes or erases the differences between a vast array of creatures, from aardvarks to bats and from whales to chipmunks. Second, the term "nonhuman animals" continues to define all other animals besides humans entirely in terms of their non-identity with the dominant species, and thus humans remain the tacit center point in our ethical and political discussions of species. In this sense "nonhuman animals" is similar to the term "non-whites" to describe all racial and ethnic groups besides Caucasians, who thus continue to be defined (and agglomerated) entirely in terms of their non-identity with the politically dominant group.

3 *A Communion of Subjects*, edited by Paul Waldau and Kimberly Patton, is a seminal volume on nonhuman animals and religion that includes a number of excellent essays on Asian traditions.

4 The introductory sections include the traditions covered by the chapters in this volume. We recognize that this volume does not cover many other important Asian traditions, such as Sikhism, Zoroastrianism, Shinto, Islam, and various marginalized indigenous and village traditions, as well as significant geographical areas such as Southeast Asia. Further research on these areas will certainly be of great value. The absence of Islam is perhaps most conspicuous due to its vast popularity and influence on conceptions of nonhuman animals in South and Southeast Asia. However, due to various constraints we chose in this volume to follow the classical split between Asian and Western religions, in which Islam typically comes under the rubric of "Western religions," and decided to focus on the major religious traditions that are typically discussed under the rubric of "Asian religions." Although this traditional split is common in Religious Studies and World Religions courses, we recognize that it is not unproblematic or this clear-cut in reality.

5 Dating ancient Indian texts and religious movements is a matter of great speculation, but most scholars believe the earliest Upaniṣads, such as the *Chāndogya Upaniṣad* and *Bṛhadāraṇyaka Upaniṣad*, were composed prior to the Buddha or Mahāvīra. Others, such as the *Śvetāśvatara Upaniṣad*, probably post-date the birth of Buddhism and Jainism.

6 Though it must be noted that some people today who identify as Hindu, Buddhist, or Jain do not believe in rebirth. Such theological beliefs were questioned even back in the nineteenth century in India by notable figures like Ram Mohan Roy of the Brahmo Samaj reform movement, who embraced a more secular rational approach. Thus, David Gosling questions if *karma* and rebirth can be a means to increase ecological awareness among educated Hindus. See David Gosling, *Religion and Ecology in India and Southeast Asia* (London: Routledge, 2001), 162.

7 Some South Asian traditions believe nonhuman animals do not make moral decisions. There are exceptions to this, particularly within Jainism, but generally the lack of moral consciousness or the lack of moral free will excludes other animals from transgressing morality and generating negative *karma*. Thus, a donkey does not deserve blame for kicking someone, or a tiger hunting prey does not accrue the karmic consequences of murder. Life as a nonhuman animal is negatively viewed as burning up or releasing negative *karma*, which is why their lives entail significant suffering.

8 Christopher Chapple, "Nonviolence to Animals in Buddhism and Jainism," in *Inner Peace, World Peace*, ed. Kenneth Kraft (Albany, NY: State University of New York Press, 1992), 53.

9 James P. McDermott, "Animals and Humans in Early Buddhism," *Indo-Iranian Journal* 32 (1989): 270–1, 276.

10 Louis Gomez, "Nonviolence and the Self in Early Buddhism," in *Inner Peace, World Peace*, ed. Kenneth Kraft (Albany, NY: State University of New York Press, 1992), 43–4.

11 Gomez, "Nonviolence and the Self," 45.

12 McDermott, "Animals and Humans," 274.

13 Chapple, "Nonviolence to Animals," 53.

14 In one story, a *nāga*, a type of celestial serpent, takes the form of a brahmin and joins the Buddhist monastic community. He is caught one night after revealing his natural serpent form while sleeping, and is subsequently expelled from the community. See Hermann Oldenberg, ed. *Vinaya piṭakam* [*The Basket of the Discipline*] (London: Williams and Norgate, 1879), 1:86–7, quoted in John Strong, *The Experience of Buddhism: Sources and Interpretations* (Belmont, CA: Wadsworth Publishing, 2008), 74–5.

15 Gomez, "Nonviolence and the Self," 40.

16 Duncan Ryūkan Williams, "Animal Liberation, Death, and the State: Rites to Release Animals in Medieval Japan," in *Buddhism and Ecology: The Interconnection of Dharma and Deeds*, eds. Mary Evelyn Tucker and Duncan Ryūkan Williams (Cambridge, MA: Harvard University Press, 1997), 150–1.

17 See Williams, "Animal Liberation, Death, and the State," 155. Williams notes that, for example in Japan, two-thirds of the fish and clams caught for the Hōjō-e ritual die before being re-released. He also explains that releasing them is not simply a sign of compassion but is intertwined with displaying political power, controlling land, or appeasing deities.

18 For more on this tension see Paul Waldau, "Buddhism and Animal Rights," in *Contemporary Buddhist Ethics*, ed. Damien Keown (Richmond, UK: Curzon Press, 2000).

19 McDermott, "Animals and Humans," 271.

20 Paul Waldau, *The Specter of Specieisism: Buddhist and Christian Views of Animals* (New York: Oxford University Press, 2001), 124. Waldau, in his "Buddhism and Animal Rights," 94–6, explains that Buddhists do conceive a vague hierarchy among other animals, but all nonhuman animals tend to be lumped together in the context of offences and punishments.

21 Vinaya 4-350, cited in Waldau, *The Specter of Speciesism*, 121; and Vinaya I. 218–20, cited in McDermott, "Animals and Humans," 274.

22 This is supposedly in response to the monk Devadatta's insistence on stronger ascetic practices. See D. Seyfort Ruegg, "*Ahiṃsā* and Vegetarianism in the History of Buddhism," in *Buddhist Studies in Honour of Walpola Rahula*, ed. Sōmaratna Bālasūriya (London: Gordon Fraser Gallery Ltd., 1980), 235.

23 Christopher Chapple, *Nonviolence to Animals, Earth, and Self in Asian Traditions* (Albany, NY: State University of New York Press, 1993), 22.

24 D. Seyfort Ruegg, "*Ahiṃsā* and Vegetarianism," 235; see McDermott, "Animals and Humans," 274 for Jain critiques of this qualification for meat eating.

25 Ruegg, "*Ahiṃsā* and Vegetarianism," 236.
26 Ruegg, "*Ahiṃsā* and Vegetarianism," 237. For Buddhist vegetarianism also see Peter Harvey, "Avoiding Unintended Harm to the Environment and the Buddhist Ethic of Intention," *Journal of Buddhist Ethics* 14 (2007): 1–34.
27 For a broader discussion on the significance of cows in Hinduism see Frank Korom, "Holy Cow! The Apotheosis of Zebu, or Why the Cow is Sacred in Hinduism," *Asian Folklore Studies* 59, no. 2 (2000): 181–203.
28 Laurie Patton has argued that the sacrifice and redistribution of the nonhuman animal reflects a Vedic understanding of ecological balance, human harmony with natural forces, and inherent processes in nature. See Laurie Patton, "Nature Romanticism and Sacrifice in Rgvedic Interpretation," in *Hinduism and Ecology: The Intersection of Earth, Sky, and Water*, eds. Christopher Key Chapple and Mary Evelyn Tucker (New Delhi: Oxford University Press, 2000), 43.
29 *Atharva Veda* 10.10.1, cited in Korom, "Holy Cow! The Apotheosis of Zebu," 187.
30 Bryan K. Smith, "Classifying Animals and Humans in Ancient India," *Man, New Series* 26, no. 3 (1991): 527–48. One could also argue the opposite, that the ritual order is the source dictating taxonomical divisions.
31 *Śatapatha Brāhmaṇa* 7.5.4.6, cited in Smith, "Classifying Animals and Humans," 534.
32 Bryan K. Smith, "Eaters, Food, and Social Hierarchy in Ancient India: A Dietary Guide to a Revolution of Values," *Journal of the American Academy of Religion* 58, no. 2 (1990): 180.
33 Wendy Doniger, "Reflections: Wendy Doniger," in *The Lives of Animals*, eds. J.M. Coetzee and Amy Gutmann (Princeton, NJ: Princeton University Press, 2001), 99.
34 Doniger, "Reflections," 99. For the same reason all five-nailed nonhuman animals are considered inedible due to their five-nailed resemblance to humans. Though there are five exceptions to the rule—the porcupine, hedgehog, monitor lizard, tortoise, and rabbit are edible—probably because they are significantly different from humans. See Manu, *Mānava-Dharmaśāstra*, 5.17, who adds the rhinoceros and animals with incisors in one jaw to the list of edible five-nailed animals.
35 For further details on this debate see J.C. Heesterman, "Non-violence and Sacrifice," *Indologica Taurinensia* 12 (1984): 119–27; Henk W. Bodewitz, "Hindu *ahiṃsā* and its roots," in *Violence Denied: Violence, Non-Violence and the Rationalization of Violence in South Asian Cultural History*, eds. Jan E.M. Houben and Karel R. Van Kooij (Leiden: Brill, 1999), 17–44; and Edwn Bryant, "Strategies of Vedic Subversion: The Emergence of Vegetarianism in Post-Vedic India," in *A Communion of Subjects: Animals in Religion, Science & Ethics*, eds. Paul Waldau and Kimberley C. Patton (New York: Columbia University Press, 2006), 194–203.
36 See Bryant, "Strategies of Vedic Subversion," for a discussion of ambivalence to *ahiṃsā* and sacrifice, and strategies to subvert and reinterpret sacrificial obligations in early Brahmanical texts. Also see Smith, "Eaters, Food, and Social Hierarchy." For South Asian philosophical approaches to the problem of ritual sacrifice see Jan E.M. Houben, "To Kill or Not to Kill the Sacrificial Animal (yajña-paśu)? Arguments and Perspectives in Brahmanical Ethical Philosophy," in *Violence Denied: Violence, Non-Violence and the Rationalization of Violence in South Asian Cultural History*, eds. Jan E.M. Houben and Karel R. Van Kooij (Leiden: Brill, 1999), 105–83.
37 See Smith, "Classifying Animals and Humans," 536, where he cites the *Aitareya Brāhmaṇa* 2.8 and *Maitrāyinī Saṃhitā* 3.10.2 as explaining that the sacrificial quality (*medhas*) passes from human to nonhuman animal to earth to plants. Such passages validate the merits of vegetable offerings by identifying them with the sacrificial animal and humans themselves, while at the same time prohibiting the sacrifice and consumption of those animals. Smith, in "Eaters, Food, and Social Hierarchy," 197, suggests that vegetarianism also subverts the hierarchy of social

ranking based on dominance through eating. Becoming vegetarian flattens the hierarchy of the human eater as superior to the eaten nonhuman animal.

38 Manu, *Mānava-Dharmaśāstra*, 6.39.

39 Manu, *Mānava-Dharmaśāstra*, 5.55, quoted from Patrick Olivelle, *Manu's Code of Law: A Critical Edition and Translation of the Mānava-Dharmaśāstra* (New York: Oxford University Press, 2005), 140.

40 It is interesting to note that humans can also be *vāhanas*. A man is the mount of Kubera, the god of wealth.

41 Manu, *Mānava-Dharmaśāstra*, 3.68, 3.70, 3.90, 3.92. In 3.68, Manu states that the five great sacrifices are done to expiate the unintentional death of beings in the fireplace, grindstone, broom, mortar and pestle, and water pot.

42 Frederick M. Smith, *The Self Possessed: Deity and Spirit Possession in South Asian Literature and Civilization* (New York: Columbia University Press, 2006), 585–6.

43 For example, in a well-known tale from the *Bhāgavatam*, the sage Jaḍabharata is reborn as a deer, but is fully cognizant of his identity and wisdom.

44 The *Yoga Sūtra* 3.17 states that yogis can gain the magical power of understanding the speech of nonhuman animals. The sages Cyavana and Kiṃdana in the *Mahābhārata* live with the fish and the deer respectively.

45 See Patrick Olivelle, "The Beast and the Ascetic: The Wild in the Indian Religious Imagination," in *Ascetics and Brahmins: Studies in Ideologies and Institutions*, ed. Patrick Olivelle (New York: Anthem Press, 2011), 91–100.

46 See Manu, *Mānava-Dharmaśāstra*, 12.54–69.

47 Lance Nelson, "Cows, Elephants, Dogs, and Other Lesser Embodiments of *Ātman*," in *A Communion of Subjects: Animals in Religion, Science & Ethics*, eds. Paul Waldau and Kimberley C. Patton (New York: Columbia University Press, 2006), 186.

48 See Lance Nelson, "The Dualism of Nondualism: Advaita Vedānta and the Irrelevance of Nature," in *Purifying the Earthly Body of God: Religion and Ecology in Hindu India*, ed. Lance Nelson (Albany, NY: State University of New York Press, 1998), 61–88; and Christopher Framarin, "*Ātman*, Identity, and Emanation: Arguments For a Hindu Environmental Ethic," *Comparative Philosophy* 2, no. 1 (2011): 3–24.

49 Kristi L. Wiley, "The Nature of Nature: Jain Perspectives on the Natural World," in *Jainism and Ecology*, ed. Christopher Chapple (Cambridge, MA: Harvard University Press, 2002), 39.

50 See Padmanabh S. Jaini, *The Jaina Path of Purification* (Berkeley, CA: University of California Press, 1979), 110; and Kristi L. Wiley, "Five Sensed Animals in Jainism," in *A Communion of Subjects: Animals in Religion, Science & Ethics*, eds. Paul Waldau and Kimberley C. Patton (New York: Columbia University Press, 2006), 251.

51 Jaini, *The Jaina Path of Purification*, 104.

52 Chapple, "Nonviolence to Animals," 51.

53 Flesh is a breeding ground for numerous smaller organisms. Consuming it would destroy these organisms. See Jaini, *The Jaina Path of Purification*, 169.

54 For example, in one story, King Yaśodara sacrifices a substitute rooster effigy made of flour. The repercussions of this sacrificial intention include enduring several rounds of traumatic nonhuman animal births. See Christopher Chapple, "Inherent Value without Nostalgia: Animals and the Jaina Tradition," in *A Communion of Subjects: Animals in Religion, Science & Ethics*, eds. Paul Waldau and Kimberley C. Patton (New York: Columbia University Press, 2006), 242–243.

55 Jaini, *The Jaina Path of Purification*, 173.

56 For a discussion of the ecological implications of *anekāntavāda*, see John Koller, "Jain Ecological Perspectives," in *Jainism and Ecology*, ed. Christopher Chapple (Cambridge, MA: Harvard University Press, 2002).

57 Jains divide nonhuman animals into those that are instinctive and those that are able to reason. See Jaini, *The Jaina Path of Purification*, 110.
58 Wiley, "Five Sensed Animals," 253.
59 See Paul Dundas, *The Jains* (New York: Routledge, 2002), 106–7.
60 Jaini, *The Jaina Path of Purification*, 143–8.
61 Wiley, "Five Sensed Animals," 250.
62 For a number of these stories, see Padmanabh S. Jaini, "Indian Perspectives on the Spirituality of Animals," in *Buddhist Philosophy and Culture: Essays in Honour of N. A. Jayawickreme*, eds. David J. Kalupahana and W.G. Weeratne (Colombo, Sri Lanka: N. A. Jayawickrema Felicitation Volume Co., 1987).
63 See Nathmal Tatia, "The Jain Worldview and Ecology," in *Jainism and Ecology*, ed. Christopher Chapple (Cambridge, MA: Harvard University Press, 2002), 11.
64 See Jaini, "Indian Perspectives," 175.
65 Roger Ames, "Human Exceptionalism versus Cultural Elitism," in *A Communion of Subjects: Animals in Religion, Science & Ethics*, eds. Paul Waldau and Kimberley C. Patton (New York: Columbia University Press, 2006), 312.
66 Ames, "Human Exceptionalism," 314.
67 Roel Sterckx, "Animal Classification in Ancient China," *East Asian Science, Technology and Medicine* 23 (2005): 33–4.
68 Ames, "Human Exceptionalism," 318.
69 Sterckx, "Animal Classification," 29.
70 Ibid., 29. Sterckx also points out other kinds of classifications such as lexicographic classification and ritual classification.
71 Ibid., 43. Sterckx also points out that such classification frameworks served as a way to project the organization of the nonhuman animal world within the bounds of human control during the Warring States and Han periods.
72 Roel Sterckx, *The Animal and the Daemon in Early China* (Albany, NY: State University of New York Press, 2002), 81.
73 Roel Sterckx, "'Of a Tawny Bull We make Offering': Animals in Early Chinese Religion," in *A Communion of Subjects: Animals in Religion, Science & Ethics*, eds. Paul Waldau and Kimberley C. Patton (New York: Columbia University Press, 2006), 263–4.
74 Ibid., 261–3.
75 For a window into this interaction in terms of nonhuman animal symbolism, see Hoyt Long, "Grateful Animal or Spiritual Being? Buddhist Gratitude Tales and Changing Conceptions of Deer in Early Japan," in *JAPANimals: History and Culture in Japan's Animal Life*, eds. Gregory M. Pflugfelder and Brett L. Walker (Ann Arbor, MI: University of Michigan Center for Japanese Studies, 2005), 21–58.
76 See Barbara R. Ambros, *Bones of Contention: Animals and Religion in Contemporary Japan* (Honolulu: University of Hawaii Press, 2012), 17–50.
77 Brett Walker, *The Lost Wolves of Japan* (Seattle, WA: University of Washington Press, 2005), 20.
78 Tongdong Bai, "The Price of Serving Meat: On Confucius's and Mencius's Views of Human and Animal Rights," *Asian Philosophy* 19, no. 1 (2009): 96.
79 Confucius, *The Analects of Confucius: A Philosophical Translation* (trans. Roger T. Ames and Henry Rosemont Jr.) (New York: Ballantine Books, 1998), 18.6.
80 Rodney Taylor, "Of Animals and Humans: The Confucian Perspective," in *A Communion of Subjects: Animals in Religion, Science & Ethics*, eds. Paul Waldau and Kimberley C. Patton (New York: Columbia University Press, 2006), 296.
81 Fan Ruiping, "How Should We Treat Animals? A Confucian Reflection," *Dao: A Journal of Comparative Philosophy* 9, no. 1 (2010): 82. For further information see Donald N. Blakeley, "Listening to the Animals: The Confucian View of Animal Welfare," *Journal of Chinese Philosophy* 30, no. 2 (2003): 137–57.
82 Ames, "Human Exceptionalism," 321–2.

83 Bai, "The Price of Serving Meat," 95.
84 Ruiping, "How Should We Treat Animals," 88.
85 Blakeley, "Listening to the Animals," 141–2.
86 Roel Sterckz, "Animals, Gaming and Entertainment in Traditional China," in *Perfect Bodies: Sports, Medicine and Immortality*, ed. Vivienne Lo (London: British Museum Research Publications, 2012), 36.
87 Mengzi, *Mengzi: With Selections From Traditional Commentaries* (trans. Bryan W. Van Norden) (Indianapolis, IN: Hacket Publishing Company, Inc., 2008), 9.
88 Bai, "The Price of Serving Meat," 94.
89 Taylor, "Of Animals and Humans," 301.
90 E.N. Anderson and Lisa Raphals, "Daoism and Animals," in *A Communion of Subjects: Animals in Religion, Science & Ethics*, eds. Paul Waldau and Kimberley C. Patton (New York: Columbia University Press, 2006), 279.
91 Sterckx, "Of a Tawny Bull We make Offering," 269.
92 Lao Tzu,*Tao-te-ching*, 42, quoted from Wing-Tsit Chan, *The Way of Lao Tzu (Tao-te ching)* (New York: Macmillan Publishing Company, 1963), 176 (Wing-Tsit's translation, my italics and style).
93 Anderson and Raphals, "Daoism and Animals," 286.
94 See Sterckx, *The Animal and the Daemon in Early China*; and Irving Goh, "Chuang Tzu's Becoming-Animal," *Philosophy East and West* 59, no. 1 (2011): 114.
95 Ames, "Human Exceptionalism," 313.
96 Anderson and Raphals, "Daoism and Animals," 278–9.
97 Goh, "Chuang Tzu's Becoming-Animal," 111.
98 Ibid., 125.
99 Anderson and Raphals, "Daoism and Animals," 281; Goh, "Chuang Tzu's Becoming-Animal," 124.
100 Zhuangzi, *Zhuangzi: The Essential Writings* (trans. Brook Ziporyn) (Indianapolis, IN: Hackett Publishing Company, Inc., 2009), 23. Also see *Zhuangzi*, 83, which recommends a bird live freely in the forest.
101 Ibid., 62.
102 Ibid., 75.
103 James Miller and John Patterson, "Sectional Discussion: How Successfully Can We Apply the Concepts of Ecology to Daoist Cultural Contexts," in *Daoism and Ecology: Ways Within a Cosmic Landscape*, eds. N.J. Girardot, James Miller, and Liu Ziaogan (Cambridge, MA: Harvard University Press, 2001), 238–9.
104 See Kristofer Schipper, "Daoist Ecology: The Inner Transformation. A Study of the Precepts of the Early Daoist Ecclesia," in *Daoism and Ecology: Ways Within a Cosmic Landscape*, eds. N.J. Girardot, James Miller, and Liu Ziaogan (Cambridge, MA: Harvard University Press, 2001), 81–4, 88; and Livia Kohn, *Cosmos and Community: The Ethical Dimension of Daoism* (Cambridge, MA: Three Pines Press, 2004), 137–44. It is interesting to note that *The 180 Precepts of Lord Lao* resembles earlier Confucian and Liji rules and may have been in part inspired by Buddhist traditions in China. See Anderson and Raphals, "Daoism and Animals," 169; and Kohn, *Cosmos and Community*.
105 Louis Komjathy, "Daoism: From Meat Avoidance to Compassion-based Vegetarianism," in *Call to Compassion: Religious Reflections on Animal Advocacy from the World's Religions*, eds. Lisa Kemmerer and Anthony J. Nocella II (New York: Lantern Books, 2011), 86–90.
106 Russell Kirkland, "'Responsible Non-Action' in a Natural World: Perspectives from the *Neiye*, *Zhuangzi*, and *Daode Jing*," in *Daoism and Ecology: Ways Within a Cosmic Landscape*, eds. N.J. Girardot, James Miller, and Liu Ziaogan (Cambridge, MA: Harvard University Press, 2001), 305.
107 See Lisa Raphals, "Metic Intelligence or Responsible Non-Action? Further Reflections on the *Zhuangzi*, *Daode jing*, and *Neiye*," in *Daoism and Ecology: Ways*

Within a Cosmic Landscape, eds. N.J. Girardot, James Miller, and Liu Ziaogan (Cambridge, MA: Harvard University Press, 2001), 307–14.

108 See, for instance, Ladelle McWhorter and Gail Stenstad's anthology of essays, *Heidegger and the Earth: Essays in Environmental Philosophy* (Toronto: University of Toronto Press, 2009).

Bibliography

Ambros, Barbara R. *Bones of Contention: Animals and Religion in Contemporary Japan*. Honolulu: University of Hawai Press, 2012.

Ames, Roger. "Human Exceptionalism versus Cultural Elitism." In *A Communion of Subjects: Animals in Religion, Science & Ethics*. Edited by Paul Waldau and Kimberley C. Patton, 311–24. New York: Columbia University Press, 2006.

Anderson, E.N. and Raphals, Lisa. "Daoism and Animals." In *A Communion of Subjects: Animals in Religion, Science & Ethics*. Edited by Paul Waldau and Kimberley C. Patton, 275–90. New York: Columbia University Press, 2006.

Bai, Tongdong. "The Price of Serving Meat: On Confucius's and Mencius's Views of Human and Animal Rights." *Asian Philosophy* 19, no. 1 (2009): 85–99.

Blakeley, Donald N. "Listening to the Animals: The Confucian View of Animal Welfare." *Journal of Chinese Philosophy* 30, no. 2 (2003): 137–57.

Bodewitz, Henk W. "Hindu *ahiṃsā* and its Roots." In *Violence Denied: Violence, Non-Violence and the Rationalization of Violence in South Asian Cultural History*. Edited by Jan E.M. Houben and Karel R. Van Kooij, 17–44. Leiden: Brill, 1999.

Bryant, Edwin. "Strategies of Vedic Subversion: The Emergence of Vegetarianism in Post-Vedic India." In *A Communion of Subjects: Animals in Religion, Science & Ethics*. Edited by Paul Waldau and Kimberley C. Patton, 194–203. New York: Columbia University Press, 2006.

Callicott, J. Baird and Ames, Roger T., eds. *Nature in Asian Traditions of Thought: Essays in Environmental Philosophy*. Albany, NY: State University of New York Press, 1989.

Chapple, Christopher K. "Nonviolence to Animals in Buddhism and Jainism." In *Inner Peace, World Peace*. Edited by Kenneth Kraft, 49–62. Albany, NY: State University of New York Press, 1992.

Chapple, Christopher K. *Nonviolence to Animals, Earth, and Self in Asian Traditions*. Albany, NY: State University of New York Press, 1993.

Chapple, Christopher K. "Inherent Value without Nostalgia: Animals and the Jaina Tradition." In *A Communion of Subjects: Animals in Religion, Science & Ethics*. Edited by Paul Waldau and Kimberley C. Patton, 241–9. New York: Columbia University Press, 2006.

Confucius. *The Analects of Confucius: A Philosophical Translation*. Translated by Roger T. Ames and Henry Rosemont Jr. New York: Ballantine Books, 1998.

Doniger, Wendy. "Reflections: Wendy Doniger." In *The Lives of Animals*. Edited by J.M. Coetzee and Amy Gutmann, 93–106. Princeton, NJ: Princeton University Press, 2001.

Dundas, Paul. *The Jains*. New York: Routledge, 2002.

Framarin, Christopher. "Ātman, Identity, and Emanation: Arguments for a Hindu Environmental Ethic." *Comparative Philosophy* 2, no. 1 (2011): 3–24.

Goh, Irving. "Chuang Tzu's Becoming-Animal." *Philosophy East and West* 61, no. 1 (2011): 110–33.

Gomez, Louis. "Nonviolence and the Self in Early Buddhism." In *Inner Peace, World*

Peace. Edited by Kenneth Kraft. Albany, NY: State University of New York Press, 1992, 31–48.

Gosling, David L. *Religion and Ecology in India and Southeast Asia*. London: Routledge, 2001.

Harvey, Peter. "Avoiding Unintended Harm to the Environment and the Buddhist Ethic of Intention." *Journal of Buddhist Ethics* 14 (2007): 1–34.

Heestermann, J.C. "Non-violence and Sacrifice." *Indologica Taurinensia* 12 (1984): 119–27.

Houben, Jan E.M. "To Kill or Not to Kill the Sacrificial Animal (yajña-paśu)? Arguments and Perspectives in Brahmanical Ethical Philosophy." In *Violence Denied: Violence, Non-Violence and the Rationalization of Violence in South Asian Cultural History*. Edited by Jan E.M. Houben and Karel R. Van Kooij, 105–83. Leiden: Brill, 1999.

Jaini, Padmanabh S. "Indian Perspectives on the Spirituality of Animals." In *Buddhist Philosophy and Culture: Essays in Honour of N. A. Jayawickreme*. Edited by David J. Kalupahana and W.G. Weeratne, 169–78. Colombo, Sri Lanka: N. A. Jayawickrema Felicitation Volume Co., 1987.

Jaini, Padmanabh S. *The Jaina Path of Purification*. Berkeley, CA: University of California Press, 1979.

Kirkland, Russell. " 'Responsible Non-Action' in a Natural World: Perspectives from the *Neiye*, *Zhuangzi*, and *Daode Jing*." In *Daoism and Ecology: Ways Within a Cosmic Landscape*. Edited by N.J. Girardot, James Miller, and Liu Ziaogan, 283–304. Cambridge, MA: Harvard University Press, 2001.

Kohn, Livia. *Cosmos and Community: The Ethical Dimension of Daoism*. Cambridge, MA: Three Pines Press, 2004.

Koller, John. "Jain Ecological Perspectives." In *Jainism and Ecology*. Edited by Christopher Chapple, 19–34. Cambridge, MA: Harvard University Press, 2002.

Komjathy, Louis. "Daoism: From Meat Avoidance to Compassion-based Vegetarianism." In *Call to Compassion: Religious Perspectives on Animal Advocacy*. Edited by Lisa Kemmerer and Anthony J. Nocella II, 83–103. New York: Lantern Books, 2011.

Korom, Frank. "Holy Cow! The Apotheosis of Zebu, or Why the Cow is Sacred in Hinduism." *Asian Folklore Studies* 59, no. 2 (2000): 181–203.

Laotzi. *The Way of Lao Tzu (Tao-te ching)*. Translated by Wing-tsit Chan. New York: Macmillan Publishing Company, 1963.

Long, Hoyt. "Grateful Animal or Spiritual Being? Buddhist Gratitude Tales and Changing Conceptions of Deer in Early Japan." In *JAPANimals: History and Culture in Japan's Animal Life*. Edited by Gregory M. Pflugfelder and Brett L. Walker, 21–58. Ann Arbor, MI: University of Michigan Center for Japanese Studies, 2005.

McDermott, James P. "Animals and Humans in Early Buddhism." *Indo-Iranian Journal* 32 (1989): 269–80.

McWhorter, Ladelle and Stenstad, Gail, eds. *Heidegger and the Earth: Essays in Environmental Philosophy*. Toronto: University of Toronto Press, 2009.

Manu. *Manu's Code of Law: A Critical Edition and Translation of the Mānava-Dharmaśāstra*. Translated by Patrick Olivelle. New York: Oxford University Press, 2005.

Mengzi. *Mengzi: With Selections from Traditional Commentaries*. Translated by Bryan W. Van Norden. Indianapolis, IN: Hacket Publishing Company, Inc., 2008.

Miller, James and Patterson, John. "Sectional Discussion: How Successfully Can We Apply the Concepts of Ecology to Daoist Cultural Contexts?" In *Daoism and Ecology: Ways Within a Cosmic Landscape*. Edited by N.J. Girardot, James Miller, and Liu Ziaogan, 237–41. Cambridge, MA: Harvard University Press, 2001.

Nelson, Lance. "The Dualism of Nondualism: Advaita Vedānta and the Irrelevance of Nature." In *Purifying the Earthly Body of God: Religion and Ecology in Hindu India*. Edited by Lance E. Nelson. Albany, NY: State University of New York Press, 1998, 61–88.

Nelson, Lance. "Cows, Elephants, Dogs, and Other Lesser Embodiments of *Ātman*." In *A Communion of Subjects: Animals in Religion, Science & Ethics*. Edited by Paul Waldau and Kimberley C. Patton, 179–93. New York: Columbia University Press, 2006.

Oldenberg, Hermann, ed. *Vinaya piṭakam* [*The Basket of the Discipline*]. London: Williams and Norgate, 1879.

Olivelle, Patrick. "The Beast and the Ascetic: The Wild in the Indian Religious Imagination." In *Ascetics and Brahmins: Studies in Ideologies and Institutions*. Edited by Patrick Olivelle, 91–100. New York: Anthem Press, 2011.

Patton, Laurie. "Nature Romanticism and Sacrifice in Rgvedic Interpretation." In *Hinduism and Ecology: The Intersection of Earth, Sky, and Water*. Edited by Christopher Key Chapple and Mary Evelyn Tucker, 39–58. New Delhi: Oxford University Press, 2000.

Raphals, Lisa. "Metic Intelligence or Responsible Non-Action? Further Reflections on the *Zhuangzi*, *Daode jing*, and *Neiye*." In *Daoism and Ecology: Ways Within a Cosmic Landscape*. Edited by N.J. Girardot, James Miller, and Liu Ziaogan, 307–14. Cambridge, MA: Harvard University Press, 2001.

Ruegg, Seyfort D. "*Ahiṃsā* and Vegetarianism in the History of Buddhism." In *Buddhist Studies in Honour of Walpola Rahula*. Edited by Somaratna Balasooriya, 234–41. London: Gordon Fraser Gallery Ltd., 1980.

Ruiping, Fan. "How Should We Treat Animals? A Confucian Reflection." *Dao: A Journal of Comparative Philosophy* 9, no. 1 (2010): 79–86.

Schipper, Kristofer. "Daoist Ecology: The Inner Transformation. A Study of the Precepts of the Early Daoist Ecclesia." In *Daoism and Ecology: Ways Within a Cosmic Landscape*. Edited by N.J. Girardot, James Miller, and Liu Ziaogan, 79–93. Cambridge, MA: Harvard University Press, 2001.

Smith, Bryan K. "Eaters, Food, and Social Hierarchy in Ancient India: A Dietary Guide to a Revolution of Values." *Journal of the American Academy of Religion* 58, no. 2 (1990): 177–205.

Smith, Bryan K. "Classifying Animals and Humans in Ancient India." *Man, New Series* 26, no. 3 (1991): 527–48.

Smith, Frederick M. *The Self Possessed: Deity and Spirit Possession in South Asian Literature and Civilization.* New York: Columbia University Press, 2006.

Sterckx, Roel. *The Animal and the Daemon in Early China*. Albany, NY: State University of New York Press, 2002.

Sterckx, Roel. "Animal Classification in Ancient China." *East Asian Science, Technology and Medicine*, 23 (2005): 26–53.

Sterckx, Roel. " 'Of a Tawny Bull We make Offering': Animals in Early Chinese Religion." In *A Communion of Subjects: Animals in Religion, Science & Ethics*. Edited by Paul Waldau and Kimberley C. Patton, 259–72. New York: Columbia University Press, 2006.

Sterckx, Roel. "Animals, Gaming and Entertainment in Traditional China." In *Perfect Bodies: Sports, Medicine and Immortality*. Edited by Vivienne Lo, 31–8. London: British Museum Research Publications, 2012.

Strong, John. *The Experience of Buddhism: Sources and Interpretations*. Belmont, CA: Wadsworth Publishing, 2008.

Tatia, Nathmal. "The Jain Worldview and Ecology." In *Jainism and Ecology*. Edited by Christopher Chapple, 3–18. Cambridge, MA: Harvard University Press, 2002.

Taylor, Rodney. "Of Animals and Humans: The Confucian Perspective." In *A Communion of Subjects: Animals in Religion, Science & Ethics*. Edited by Paul Waldau and Kimberley C. Patton, 293–307. New York: Columbia University Press, 2006.

Waldau, Paul. "Buddhism and Animal Rights." In *Contemporary Buddhist Ethics*. Edited by Damien Keown, 81–112. Richmond, UK: Curzon Press, 2000.

Waldau, Paul. *The Specter of Speciesism: Buddhist and Christian Views of Animals*. New York: Oxford University Press, 2001.

Waldau, Paul and Patton, Kimberley C., eds. *A Communion of Subjects: Animals in Religion, Science & Ethics*. New York: Columbia University Press, 2006.

Walker, Brett. *The Lost Wolves of Japan*. Seattl, WA: University of Washington Press, 2005.

Wiley, Kristi L. "The Nature of Nature: Jain Perspectives on the Natural World." In *Jainism and Ecology*. Edited by Christopher Key Chapple. Cambridge, MA: Harvard University Press, 2002, 35–59.

Wiley, Kristi L. "Five Sensed Animals in Jainism." In *A Communion of Subjects: Animals in Religion, Science & Ethics*. Edited by Paul Waldau and Kimberley C. Patton, 250–5. New York: Columbia University Press, 2006.

Williams, Duncan R. "Animal Liberation, Death, and the State: Rites to Release Animals in Medieval Japan." In *Buddhism and Ecology: The Interconnection of Dharma and Deeds.* Edited by Mary Evelyn Tucker and Duncan Ryūkan Williams. Cambridge, MA: Harvard University Press, 1997, 149–162.

Zhuangzi. *Zhuangzi: The Essential Writings*. Translated by Brook Ziporyn. Indianapolis, IN: Hackett Publishing Company, Inc., 2009.

1 Being sentiently with others

The shared existential trajectory among humans and nonhumans in Jainism

Anne Vallely

Introduction

Jainism is renowned for its exquisitely intricate ethical code that extends far beyond the human, and its complex catalogue of beings, some so small as to be invisible to the human eye, but who are nonetheless important players in the drama of life and liberation. The animal—or more accurately, the nonhuman—plays a role of immeasurable importance in Jainism, a degree which is astonishing in comparison with most other traditions. For this reason, among those with an interest in the "animal question," or, more generally, in the relationship between religion and ecology, Jainism has been garnering considerable attention as a possible source of traditional wisdom about the place of humanity within the broader biotic community. But Jainism differs in striking ways from most of the traditions that are explored for this end. While Jainism offers a fascinating articulation of the human–nonhuman dynamic in which all life is treated as inviolable, it considers human beings as distinct from and superior to all other life forms. In addition, it does not seek engagement or communion with other beings but, instead, it ultimately seeks distance from them. Jainism parts company with mainstream environmental thought in its refusal to see human potential as realizable only in fellowship with the rest of nature. Instead it envisions human fulfillment as possible only in isolation from the world.

By treating the human as ontologically distinct and privileged, Jainism can be said to violate the new "post-human" ethos, which problematizes the very demarcation between human and animal. Jacques Derrida, for instance, in his book *The Animal That Therefore I Am*, argues that the labeling of living beings as "animal" is a form of violence and tantamount to "a crime."[1] Jainism unapologetically does just that.

The word "animal" has become problematic for many in the contemporary period because, among other things, it glosses over the great diversity of life in the service of differentiating that which stands ostensibly outside it: the human. It is often used in such a way as to point unquestionably to a condition from which humanity is categorically exempt and, it is argued, thereby permits us to think about and act toward real, live animals in ways that would be unethical if directed toward humans. It is now commonly argued, on many fronts—from evolutionary biology to moral philosophy—that the human/animal demarcation has no ontological basis and should be discarded and superseded by a less anthropocentric classification.[2] Jainism, however, would never make this claim. Jains unhesitatingly demarcate between the human and the animal, and place human beings in a category of their own, superior to animals. Indeed, the animal is subsumed within the broader nonhuman category that also comprises insects and plants. Whatever the merits and demerits of this categorization, it is important to note that it does not, in and of itself, encode an exploitative relationship. The animal in Jainism, though ontologically distinct, is on the same existential trajectory as the human, and its claims to life are no less valid than those of any other sentient being.[3]

Despite the existential gulf Jainism posits between humans and nonhumans, it recognizes the world in its entirety as alive, purposeful, intelligent, sensory, and responsive. It is this crucial recognition—perhaps more importantly than the distinctive ideological and ethical elaborations emerging from it—that has secured Jainism's robust and harmonious human–nonhuman encounter for the past three millennia. The Jain example—among many others—should give us pause about making broad indictments about terminology, no matter how laudable the motives. More vital and more fundamental for the creation of a harmonious "community of subjects" than terminological correctness,[4] or "getting it right" conceptually, ideologically, or even ethically,[5] is the embodied, sensory experience of being in the presence of others, and with others.

Most scholarly attention, my own included, has focused on the renunciatory dimensions of Jainism: its philosophical texts, ethical system, distinctive religious practices etc., all of which aim to limit involvement in worldly existence. These undoubtedly make Jainism unique among the world's religions, but by confining our discussion to ideology and to conceptually informed practices relating to Jain renunciation, we run the risk of leaving its phenomenological meaningfulness unexplored. And yet the primary impetus for Jainism's celebrated focus on nonviolence and its astonishing attention to the nonhuman is not ideological (or, therefore, ethical), but relational, insofar as it inheres in the far more fundamental experience of being sentiently with others. This chapter argues that embodied perceptions of the animate cosmos constitute the generative ground from which Jain philosophical and ethical reflections emerge. This Jain "way of being" might fruitfully be characterized as one of sympathy—not in the sense of being tenderhearted—but in the sense of the word that accentuates its receptive and responsive connotations: being Jain means being receptive, or alert, to the omnipresence of the activities of life, in order to be effectively responsive to the universal requirement of all beings. In brief, the Jain way of being with animals, and with the nonhuman more generally, is where the Jain imagination begins.

Background

Appearing on the historical scene sometime between the ninth and sixth centuries BCE, Jainism was part of a *śramaṇa* ("world-renouncing") movement that also gave rise to Buddhism. The *śramaṇa* movement arose at a time of social and economic upheaval in India, with the development of cities, commerce, and increased trade. It was also the time of the emergence of the sciences of logic, physics, the establishment of rules for empirical observation, and the systematization of the Indian philosophical tradition. These developments reflect the emergence of new conceptions of the self and of the material, incarnate world. The early *śramaṇa* groups, in particular, emphasized the opposing natures of self and cosmos. The self came to be seen as estranged in the world, in a suffering state of karmic bondage and yearning for spiritual release (*mokṣa*). The *śramaṇa* movement rejected the Brahmanical orthodoxy of the day and considered the Brahmins' preoccupation with cosmic and social order to be fundamentally flawed. All the elements that went into maintaining that order—the hierarchical caste system, the elaborate liturgy, the rituals, and above all the cult of animal sacrifice—were anathema to the renouncers.

Jainism is the oldest of humanity's still extant world-renouncing traditions. Its scriptures capture, in a distilled form, a sense of radical alienation from the world. Of course, the Jain community of today is far more than simply a "renunciatory tradition," and certainly within the social world of South Asia, it is better known for its impressive this-worldly successes, than its asceticism. Nevertheless, renouncers continue to be held in very high esteem, and the renunciatory ethos of traditional Jainism continues to inform virtually all aspects of the tradition.

The most basic teaching of Jainism states that life, in all its myriad expressions (human, animal, insect, plant, water, earth, air, fire beings, hell and heaven beings etc.), is endowed with an eternal quality that is noble and worthy of respect. Each eternal quality, called *jīva*, is a perfect entity, endowed with omniscience and the capacity for bliss. But each is equally estranged in the world, and in a state of suffering. The most fundamental existential quandary shared by all beings of the cosmos is the entanglement of the soul and matter (i.e., of *jīva* and *ajīva*). That soul (*jīva*) and matter (*ajīva*) are utterly enmeshed is what prevents the soul from achieving a state of bliss, a bliss which can only be experienced in a state of purity and separation from all that is matter. Jains do not posit an original state of separation from which there was a "fall," instead they assert that the *jīva–ajīva* entangled state is eternal, "without beginning."[6]

Jainism depicts the *jīva* as blundering on a lonely sojourn through endless time within a purposeless, violent cosmos. It is a cosmos indifferent to its machinations; no hand of God extends to assist the fortunate few. Instead, the *jīva* moves continuously, one life after another, in and out of birth categories, inhabiting diverse sensory expressions. And it alone, on its own efforts, must meticulously extricate itself out of the worldly mess. This would be a hopeless, desperate situation if it were not for the teachings of the Jinas (Spiritual

Victors)[7]—those perfected human beings who attained enlightenment by their own might, and then taught others the way to escape the cycle of birth and death (*saṃsāra*). Within a fixed and vast cycle of time, a series of twenty-four such Jinas appear to reveal the timeless truth about the nature of the soul and the path to salvation. Their teachings, through memorialization, application in everyday life, ritualization, and celebration, constitute the foundation of the tradition of Jainism.

Being sentiently

Jains assert that the teachings of the Jina are perfect; beyond courage and self-determination, they have provided us with all we need to attain salvation. But what is to come of those who do not or cannot hear the teachings of the Jina? Jainism postulates the existence of some 8.4 million species of life, most of which lack the capacity to receive the Jina's message; they are literally blind and deaf to it.

All living beings are born in one of four states of existence, or "birth categories," called *gati*s. The four *gati*s are humans (*manuṣya*), celestial beings (*deva*), hell beings (*nāraki*), and the composite category of animals, plants, insects, and microorganisms (grouped together as *tiryañca*). The human *gati* is accorded such overwhelming prominence because it is from this state alone that final liberation (*mokṣa*) can be attained. Even the celestial beings look down from their heavenly abodes in envy at the uniquely human capacity for self-transcendence. Despite its privileged position, the Jina does not preach to those of the human *gati* alone. More fundamental than birth category for hearing and comprehending the teachings of the Jina is the degree to which one participates sensorially in the world. Those who are endowed with five senses are privileged in this way, and they are present in all four *gati*s; the rest, ignorant of the Jina's teachings, live unaware of their existential plight.

Jainism postulates that each being occupies a fixed place in a cosmological hierarchy based on degrees of sensory perception and self-awareness. Worldly beings inhabit space and time and come to perceive their existence in *saṃsāra* through their senses. By contrast, those beings who have attained enlightenment no longer exist sensorially. Instead, they experience unobstructed perception and inimitable bliss through the soul itself, which is its nature. This experience of plenitude, unmediated as it is by sensorial differentiation, marks the successful completion of the existential trajectory directing all life and, as such, it is the goal of the renouncers, the enlightened humans who have given themselves over to the disciplines that enable them to transcend their sensory modes of existence. They alone can remain detached and dispassionate, observing the world without emotionally participating in it. The canonical Daśavaikālika Sūtra states, "Knowing that pleasing sound, beauty, fragrance, pleasant taste and soothing touch are transitory transformations of matter, the renouncer should not be enamored of them."[8] But the rest of us—that is, all embodied life forms—are essentially sensorial beings. Our senses produce our way of being in the world, allowing us to engage with others in purposeful ways. The passions that course through our human bodies—sadness, joy, trust, fear, anger, jealousy etc.—which cause us to be transported to great heights and plunged to great depths, belong to the world. It is through such moods, informed by the senses, that all beings participate in the world with each other.

At the bottom of Jainism's cosmological hierarchy are single-sensed beings, possessing only touch (examples of these are the elements of earth, water, fire, and air, as well as most plants). As one moves up the hierarchy, additional senses are possessed. Doubled-sensed beings possess taste and touch (e.g., worms). Three-sensed beings possess smell, taste, and touch (e.g., ants). Four-sensed beings possess sight, smell, taste, and touch (e.g., butterflies). At the top of the hierarchy are five-sensed beings in possession of hearing, sight, smell, taste, and touch. They are referred to in Jainism as *pañcendriya* (the five-sensed), and among them are celestial and hell beings, animals, and humans. They alone can hear, understand, and benefit from the Jina's teachings.

Although only the most sensorially differentiated of beings, the *pañcendriya*, may receive the message of the Jina, it is the simpler-sensed beings that receive a preponderance of attention owing to the special vulnerability they incur as a result of their ontological ignorance. To repeat a point made earlier, plants, the elements, and microorganisms constitute the simplest category of being, the single-sensed, which possess only touch. Importantly, Jainism identifies touch as indicative of the presence of the soul (*jīva*). Though these beings lack the capacity to see, hear, taste, and smell, their ability to feel uniquely through touch confers upon them the capacity to suffer. These most rudimentary beings are nearly completely devoid of self-awareness, but are arguably more present to Jain consciousness than higher-sensed beings because of the enormous challenges they pose for the Jain commitment to non-harm (*ahiṃsā*). Avoiding harm to one-sensed beings, while engaged in the normal activities of existence, is impossible. And yet harm to any one of them leads to the inflow of negative *karma*. Worldly life, therefore, by its very nature, presents us with a terrible bind, for the very condition of existence equates to the capacity for suffering. In other words, suffering is the basic existential condition. And to cause suffering or destruction to any life—no matter how simple—is, for Jains, the primary cause of one's bondage in *saṃsāra*.

The intelligibility of Jainism's elaborate ethical codes rests upon this premise, as does the ascetic imperative. If the world we inhabit did not constitute a living, suffering multitude, ascetic withdrawal would be less urgent. Harm to fellow human beings and animals can be fairly easily avoided, say Jains. But harm to the minuscule, even invisible expressions who suffer greatly is impossible in the absence of total, ceaseless vigilance. From this, one also begins to grasp the enormous challenge that Jainism poses, or even, one might argue, its "impossibility."[9]

Intentionally harming another carries the heaviest, darkest, and most deleterious karmic burden, but even unintentional harm is not without karmic consequence. Therefore, intentional nonharm toward all life is the goal of all

Jains—fervently pursued with utmost scrupulousness among the renouncers. Because all life forms are in the possession of a *jīva* (soul), it is the ultimate task and vocation of each to attain salvation. Each is also said to participate in the existential condition of estrangement (though not equally since simpler forms are less aware of their plight). The authoritative Jain philosophic text, the Tattvārtha Sūtra, composed by philosopher-renouncer Umāsvāti (second century BCE), asserts that sentience is the defining characteristic of the soul: "The soul is never bereft of sentience, however feeble and indistinct this may be in underdeveloped organisms."[10]

The shared condition of *jīva*s ideally gives rise to a type of sensory communitas, which is commonly expressed in the scriptural principle "parasparopagraho jīvānām,"[11] and translates as, "All life is bound together by mutual support and interdependence." Jainism achieves its heightened ethical concern and compassion for the nonhuman not through a desire for communion with other beings, but through a sense of a shared plight, and a shared existential trajectory, that leads to empathy and a commitment to nonharm (*ahiṃsā*). The Prayer of Forgiveness (*micchamī dukkaḍaṃ*), which forms a part of daily prayer,[12] encapsulates this Jain sense of being with others, as well as its desire for *ahiṃsā* in an animate, purposeful cosmos:

> I ask for forgiveness from all living beings;
> May all living beings grant me forgiveness.
> My friendship is with all living beings;
> I have hostility towards none.

The omnipresence of life evokes, among renouncers as well as householders (though not to the same degree), a heightened awareness of one's being with other beings. Jains learn from a very early age to be aware of the space one's body occupies, its potential for harming others, and the need for attentiveness. Vigilance is an especially dominant feature characterizing the relationship with simple-sensed beings. Expressed in terms of emotions, it might very well be apprehension. James Laidlaw emphasizes this characteristic vigilance in his description of Jain nonviolence as "an ethic of quarantine."[13] The world for Jains is a living moral theater in which the drama of existence plays out. Each living being inhabits its own distinctive subjective reality, but is also inextricably united in a shared existential trajectory. Reflecting this, Jainism's central creed, "Ahiṃsā Paramo Dharma" ("Nonviolence is the Supreme Religion") is a commitment to nonharm that extends well beyond one's own kin to include all sensory beings. It is an expression of heightened sensitivity—but also of apprehension—emerging from the experience of inhabiting a world that is manifestly and unmistakably occupied by others.

Vigilance is certainly the primary concern that underpins the extraordinary practices of Jain ascetics, such as the wearing of the mouth guard to avoid harm to insects as well as air-bodied beings, the sweeping of the ground to avoid harming insects on one's path, the avoidance of root crops whose harvest causes unnecessary violence to the earth, traveling only by foot, and never in the dark, to be able to encounter life attentively, etc. In addition to vigilance, being alert to the omnipresence of life should ideally evoke compassion toward all, but the ability to feel genuine empathy for troublesome insects and even the microscopic is generally assumed to be reserved for the spiritually advanced who can perceive the suffering state of every soul.

For Jains, the presence of others is not experienced as an occasion for "communion of subjects"[14] or what Thomas Berry poetically describes as a "cosmic liturgy."[15] Instead, the presence of others is often experienced as potentially suffocating, perilous, and as the cause of suffering. But being with others is also the condition for greatness, for it is only with mindfulness and compassion that enlightenment is gained.

Before moving on to discuss five-sensed animals, which play a special role in Jainism, it is worth noting that gods and demons are also important presences of whom Jains must take note. Gods and demons are of many types (occasionally appearing in animal form) and constitute part of the multitude of beings that inhabit the world with us. They are among the five-sensed, and are possessors of mind who must at some future time take birth in human form in order to embark on the path of liberation. Most have their own preoccupations and are unconcerned with human affairs, but some can be called upon to help, and some also seek to harm. It is important to note that the normative tradition of Jainism, with its focus on world renunciation and detachment, counsels against interactions with these worldly presences. Nevertheless, most Jains regularly interact with gods (e.g., mother goddesses, gods of locales, gods associated with particular temples), approaching them through prayer and ritual, in the hope of gaining assistance in some worldly matter (such as a cure for illness, desire for wealth, help in childbirth). Apotropaic magic is also regularly undertaken to propitiate or ward off evil presences. Because the world is full of multiple intelligences and competing wills, it can be capricious and volatile, as well as magnanimous. Seeking assistance from the gods, and protection from evil, is simply another way of engaging the presences with whom we inhabit the world.[16]

Animals and the inner circle

> The weight of his body felt heavier than before, suddenly it was a burden to carry. Once a powerful force, it was now a useless instrument of violence. So perfectly crafted for a life of killing, it mocked him now as he felt as a stranger in the world of saṃsāra, an arena where birth and death, consuming and being consumed, generate meaning. The words of the sadhus quietened his passions and made clear his path. He remained still and ate no more. And as he laid down his noble head, with his magnificent orange mane gently crowning his face, his eyes communicated an awareness of who he was. Dispassionately and in full awareness, the once majestic lion grew frail and died. He thereby freed himself, once and for all, from his animal body, and moved one step closer to final release.[17]

The lion, or, more precisely, the eternal soul that was embodied as the lion, whose destiny it was, in a future incarnation, to eventually become the great Jina Mahāvīra, experienced a profound spiritual awakening upon hearing the words of the *sadhus* (mendicants). Called *samyak darśana*, this spiritual awakening is the crucial first step to eventual liberation (*mokṣa*). And, as the story makes clear, it is an experience open to animals.

Needless to say, the condition of animals in Jainism is manifestly different from that for plants, insects, and microorganisms who share their birth category, or *gati* (namely, the birth category called *tiryañca*, which includes animals, plants, insects, and microorganisms). For one, they were present at the *samavasaraṇa*—those privileged gatherings in the presence of the omniscient Jina, at which he delivered enchanted sermons on the path of salvation. The *samavasaraṇa* is among the most popular themes in Jain narrative, painting, and sculpture. At these exquisitely built divine assembly halls, *deva*s (celestial beings) hover in delight above the Jina, and listeners sit in concentric circles around him: closest to the Jina are male and female renouncers, followed by lay devotees, and then animals. Elephants, lions, birds, and other beasts, sit in rapture as they listen to, and understand, the preachings of the Jina. Clearly, animals represent the inner circle of the tradition.

But animals are not equal to humans since they are far more under the influence of their bodily appetites. While all beings in *saṃsāra* are governed by their embodied natures, the determining force of animal bodies is nearly absolute. The animal body's appetites, its aversions, and its attachments, can overwhelm the *jīva* (soul) to such an extent that it usually lives out its life in total ignorance of the existence of its eternal and true nature. Of course this misfortune is true for all simple-sensed *jīva*s, and, tragically, it can also befall a human being. Animals are in that unusual state of possessing the possibility of attaining *samyak darśana* (spiritual awakening/correct vision), but are normally so karmically burdened that they do not realize it. Only a very few manage to be awakened to the truth.

The distinctiveness of animals' place in the cosmological hierarchy means that the relationship Jains have with them is also fundamentally different, and far more complicated, than it is with simpler-sensed beings. Rather than apprehension, the dominant attitudes are those of compassion and commiseration, emerging out of a shared condition of alienation. From this comes profound empathy, and an attentiveness to the pathos of animal existence that may be unrivaled. The animal's suffering is tantamount to our own suffering as we partake of the same sensory condition. The earliest of Jain scriptures, the Ācārāṅga Sūtra (*c.* third century BCE) states:

> That which you consider worth destroying is yourself.
> That which you consider worth disciplining is yourself.
> That which you consider worth subjugating is yourself.
> That which you consider worth killing is yourself.
> The result of actions by you has to be borne by you, so do not destroy anything.[18]

The Ācārāṅga Sūtra continues: "All breathing, existing, sentient creatures should not be slain, nor treated with violence, nor abused, nor tormented, nor driven away. This is the pure unchangeable Law."[19] And from Hemacandra's twelfth century Yogaśāstra: "In happiness and suffering, in joy and grief, we should regard all creatures as we regard our own self."[20]

Jainism insists that we are embedded in a world of competing subjectivities—some of which we see, hear, and touch, and none of which we can blithely ignore. The cries of geese, the howls of wolves, and the chirping of birds, are purposeful utterances no less so than human speech. And when the raven, dog, snake, and cat return our gaze, it is nothing short of an exchange of vision. Our shared condition of being with means, at its most basic, a condition of communication. To assert, as Jains do, that we inhabit the world sensorially is to understand the world as fundamentally communicative, speaking as it does to the existential trajectory shared by all beings.

Animals as heroic

The Jain narrative tradition contains a great many discussions of animals, and the roles that they play are diverse. Stories of animals who act with restraint, as in the story of the lion-who-would-become-a-Jina, discussed above, are not uncommon. Perhaps the best known of this genre are those of Mahāvīra and Candkauśik, and the Elephant and the Rabbit. Both recount narratives that can be rightfully called heroic, in the Jain sense of the word, with its associations of detachment and compassion. Candkauśik was a gigantic, violent, and terrifying cobra who had viciously attacked and killed a great many hapless villagers. His presence caused the land to turn barren and for villagers to live in great dread, for even his glare had the power to kill. When the Jina, Lord Mahāvīra, came upon the village, he paid no heed to the villagers' warnings to avoid the forest where the cobra dwelt. Instead, he chose a spot near Candkauśik's cave to meditate. The cobra was immediately outraged at the stranger's audacity, and approached with the intention to attack. To his surprise, the stranger seemed unperturbed, and did not move. Enraged, the snake viciously attacked. Still, Mahāvīra remained tranquil and continued to meditate. The cobra was stunned when he saw milk, instead of blood, ooze from his victim's body. Finally, in the absence of fear and anger, Mahāvīra opened his eyes and looked upon his attacker with compassion. Cowed, Candkauśik retreated. Suddenly, as if with a flash of awareness, he recalled his previous births and the reason for his punishment as a snake. He immediately vowed to renounce violence, and returned to his cave. When the villagers became aware of Candkauśik's docility, they took revenge on him for his past deeds, and tortured him mercilessly. Though he suffered greatly, he remained steadfast in his commitment to nonviolence. Eventually he died, and was reborn in heaven.

Contained within this story of the heroic snake is the idea that animal birth is punishment for past sins—a belief that is well established in Jainism. The Tattvārtha Sūtra states that deceitfulness and self-indulgence are among the main causes leading to animal birth.[21] As such, animals serve as warnings not to squander the precious gift of human birth, the only birth from which *mokṣa* is possible. It must be stated, however, that while human form is viewed as the positive result of a previous life of soft-heartedness and honesty, all incarnations—even human—are the fruits of some past sins (*pāpa*). In the absence of all wrongdoings, incarnate existence would not occur.[22]

The story of the Elephant and the Rabbit is equally well known. It tells how, long ago, a terrible fire broke out in a densely populated forest and quickly threatened to consume it. As the fire raged, the animals of the forest fled in fear and quickly congregated on a tiny oasis protected from the blaze. All the animals huddled together, and soon the oasis was over-crowded, leaving no space for the animals to move. Desperate to survive, they quietly endured. An irrepressible itch caused the Elephant to raise his foot to scratch himself. The moment he did this, a rabbit moved into it, and out of danger, perceiving the newly opened space to be a shelter from the flames. If the Elephant were to lower his foot, he would immediately crush the rabbit; to make it scurry would mean certain death in the fire. Instead, he held his foot aloft for three days, the time it took for the flames to cease and for the animals to return safely to the forest. Exhausted and in agony from his ordeal, the Elephant collapsed and died shortly after the rabbit's release. Due to his compassion and restraint, he was reborn as a prince in his next life.

In both stories, the animals behave courageously. Candkauśik does not retaliate when abused by the villagers, and chooses death over violence. The Elephant too, chooses to endure suffering rather than to cause harm. Their actions are heroic because they are informed by restraint and nonviolence, and by the transcendence of bodily desire. Adding to these accounts, the heroism of animals is regularly acknowledged in the Jain narrative literature. Indeed, all of the venerated omniscient teachers (Jinas) are known to have had animal existences in prior incarnations, and most (nineteen out of twenty-four) are iconographically represented by an animal symbol. For instance, Mahāvīra, the most recent of the twenty-four Jinas, is represented by a lion, an incarnation he inhabited during a previous birth.

Animals as sufferers

Although animals in Jainism are recognized as possessing self-awareness and intentionality, these capacities are at times eclipsed in the narrative literature, especially when suffering is at focus. Animals here are depicted primarily as beings who feel pain, experience fear, and lack understanding of their predicament. Akin to philosopher Tom Regan's "moral patients," they are contrasted with human beings, or "moral agents," who possess the ability to reason and act ethically, but don't always do so.[23] In this context, suffering animals are identified as being at the mercy of others, serving as passive foils for humans to demonstrate their ethical superiority. However, their suffering also possesses the power to evoke deep compassion, and to awaken a soul out of its slumber. The classic tale in this genre is that of the twenty-second Jina, Neminath:

> The entire kingdom had for weeks been joyfully preparing for the royal wedding of Prince Nemikumar. Finally the day arrived and, accompanied by cheers, the Prince ascended his chariot to join the marriage procession. It moved slowly down the decorated path, weaving its way through throngs of well-wishers. Suddenly, it came to a halt. Disorder erupted in the crowds, and confusion spread: What happened to the prince? Amidst the crowd, Nemikumar stood gazing upon hundreds of caged animals. He saw in their eyes only anguish and pain, and demanded to know why they were there. When he was told that they were going to be used for the wedding feast, he was overcome with sadness and compassion. He then experienced a spiritual awakening, and realized that all beings are like the caged animals suffering before him; we are all trapped in the world of saṃsāra and only by renouncing worldly existence can one ever be free from suffering. On the spot, he declared that he would not marry. Instead, he initiated himself into the path of renunciation, and in time gained enlightenment, becoming Jainism's twenty-second Jina, Neminath.[24]

Modern day Jain animal shelters (*pinjrapole*s) operate on the premise that the animals in their care are innocent sufferers, dependent for their wellbeing on human kindness. Care for such animals is considered to be religious behavior, resulting in good *karma* (*puṇya*). There are literally thousands of animal shelters throughout India, providing compassionate care and medical attention to injured and dying animals. Most of the animals present have been the hapless victims of human activities or devices—birds mangled in the blades of ceiling fans, animals hit by trucks, chickens diseased and injured in cages etc. Interesting to note, carnivorous animals (e.g., birds of prey) are not kept at *pinjrapole*s as their care would require Jains to violate their commitment to vegetarianism. Perhaps, too, carnivorous animals disrupt, to a certain degree, the idea of the "innocent" animal, upon which the *pinjrapole*s are based.

Finally, and importantly, compassionate care toward the suffering of others is also undertaken in clear recognition of the emotional bonds that can form between sentient beings, and that can endure over time. The central Jain principle *parasparopagraho jīvānām*, or "all life is bound together by mutual support and interdependence,"[25] (mentioned above in relation to simple-sensed beings), recognizes that empathy is the nature of the soul, and that therefore the soul moves through sense-incarnations, transcending the particularities of time and space. The story of Lord Pārśvanath illustrates the reciprocal nature of existence, and the bonds of friendship that can endure across time:

> One day, while walking through a forest, the Prince Pārśva came upon the renowned yogi Kamath, performing a fire ritual. Immediately, he could intuit the presence of two cobras trapped in the burning logs being used for the ritual, and he requested Kamath to help the snakes. Kamath, who perceived nothing but the burning logs, was greatly annoyed by the disruption, and ignored the request. He then watched in anger as Pārśva proceeded to

> remove a log from the fire, crack it open, and reveal two scorched, dying cobras. As they died, Pārśva recited the Namaskāra Mantra[26] over their bodies, causing them to be reborn in heaven, as the god Dharaṇendra and the goddess Padmāvatī. Years passed. Kamath died, and was reborn as Meghmali, the god of rain. Prince Pārśva renounced his kingdom to pursue the path of renunciation. One fateful day, while Pārśva sat in the quiet of the forest, deep in meditation, the rain god Meghmali looked down from his heavenly abode and recognized his former antagonist. Filled with anger once again, he decided to take revenge on him, and released upon him a torrent of violent rains. The waters began to swell around Pārśva but, because he was deep in meditation, he remained oblivious to the danger. The raging waters rose ever higher and soon threatened to drown him. From heaven, Dharaṇendra and Padmāvatī (the former cobras) witnessed the scene below and quickly descended to assist the former prince. The Goddess Padmāvatī formed a lotus under the seated Pārśva, raising him aloft from the gushing torrents, and Dharaṇendra spread his 1,000 headed cobra hood above Pārśva's head, shielding him from the deluge. Pārśva, cocooned in the protective embrace of the gods, continued in his meditation, and soon attained enlightenment. When Meghmali saw his wicked efforts were in vain, he became humbled and sought forgiveness.[27]

Lord Pārśvanath, the twenty-third Jina of Jainism, is always represented with the protective hood of the snake, serving as a reminder of the reciprocal nature of life, and of the enduring bonds of friendship between sentient beings.

Animals as worldly

Above all else, Jainism valorizes restraint and detachment, and understands nonviolence in those terms. Animals are most commonly understood as beings who lack restraint, and therefore represent the very antithesis of the Jain ideal. As I have argued in the last section, animals are among the "inner circle"—they are five-sensed beings capable of self-awareness and ethical behavior. They are understood in diverse ways, including as fellow sufferers, as powerful and even as heroic. But taken together, they are the most conspicuous and unambiguous expressions of "the worldly" which Jainism seeks to transcend. A common aphorism in Jainism asserts that "in the absence of religion, man is no better than the animal." By this, Jains mean that in the absence of self-discipline and nonviolence, nothing of substance distinguishes humans from the nonhuman. And those beings, be they human or nonhuman, who dwell contentedly in their creatureliness (i.e., the vast majority of them) are regarded as lacking self-awareness, as being alien to their true selves. Animals are, in the main, untroubled by the violence of existence, and participate in it enthusiastically, unproblematically destroying life to sustain their own. Yet despite this, as the heroic narratives highlighted above demonstrate, animals can by virtue of their animality provide the substance of powerful pedagogical allegories, which communicate the moral requirement of existence, that of non-violent mindfulness. On a more basic level, when the communicative utterances of the beasts—their howls, chirps, bleatings, and the like—are properly heard and understood, these utterances are seen to express this same moral requirement of existence.

Of course, Jainism acknowledges the inescapability of violence in the world since all embodied life depends upon the death of others. To live is to consume, to consume is to participate in a cycle of violence. This "law of the fishes" is, for Jains, purposeless and mechanical, but ultimately escapable in a state of *mokṣa* (final release from the cycle of birth and death). Jainism does not seek to change this state of affairs, it seeks only to show the way out of it. It accepts the world as it is, but refuses to find meaning in its workings.

To elucidate this point, it is instructive to contrast the distinctively Jain view with that of the ancient Vedic tradition, a tradition against which Jainism so negatively reacted, and against which it powerfully defined itself in opposition. The Vedic tradition, centered on the sacrificial cult, acknowledged and honored the profound connection between existence and violence, and the union between flesh and spirit. Serving as a ritual linkage, sacrifice was (and is) a kind of theater of reciprocity, showcasing the shared nature of life and death and the need for regeneration to arise from destruction. Significantly, it conceived (as much of popular Hinduism continues to conceive) of the self as cosmologically embedded, part and parcel of a meaningful cosmos, and subject to its laws and rhythms.

In the Vedic Puruṣa Sūkta, among the most celebrated poems of the *Ṛg Veda*, the creation of the cosmos out of the sacrifice of a giant man (Puruṣa) is described (*Ṛg Veda*, 10.9).[28] Its dismemberment gives rise to the stars, moon, oceans, and wind, to the world as we know it with its myriad life forms. The destruction of the giant initiated all subsequent creations. This famous poem of the ancient Indo-Aryans, like many ancient cosmologies, describes an understanding of human existence emerging out of sacrifice, and of the cosmos as dynamic, reciprocal, and sacrificial. Implied in it (and in all such cosmologies) is the idea that creativity and destruction are one, they are inseparable and integrally linked. It is both a description of, and a charter for, a cosmology of reciprocity.

Jain cosmology also makes use of a primordial giant Puruṣa, though in ways that are distinctive. Importantly, the giant is not sacrificed to create the cosmos, because, according to Jains, the cosmos has no origin, it has always existed. By denying a genesis, Jains remove the possibility of conceiving "the sacred" or some "purpose" within its workings. Instead, the Puruṣa is understood as an abstract depiction of cosmography, an illustrative representation of Jain metaphysics where the drama of animate life plays out within the zones of the giant's body. Our world is situated between his chest and bowels, i.e., between the heavens and the hells.

Diagramatically, and fittingly, we are in the belly of the giant, and here we are subject to the law of consumption. This mechanical process (the sacrificial arena in the Vedas) is where the dreadful cycle of death and rebirth is played out, without end, a meaningless drama of devouring and being devoured.

Sacrificial rituals seek communion between flesh and spirit; they seek the transformation and regeneration of the embodied self. Jainism rejected the entire apparatus of sacrificial ritual and the ontology upon which it is based, in favor of a different goal, namely, the dis-communion of flesh and spirit. Indeed, Jainism (like the other world-renouncing traditions) asserts that true regeneration is not possible within *saṃsāra*—all actions within *saṃsāra* are simply the mechanical churnings of the belly of the Puruṣa. True transformation is achievable only in the state of *mokṣa*.

For Jains, there can be no "loop holes" of acceptable violence. Participating in life means grasping and devouring the world, with the body as our primary instrument of consumption. One ideally should eat to sustain the body only so long as it serves the purpose of liberation. And not eating is a central religious practice for Jains: fasting is so basic that it is emblematic of the tradition. The word Jains use for "fast" is "upvas," which literally means "to be near the soul," underscoring the belief that the soul can only be known when one is uninterrupted by the worldly demands of the body. But animals, subservient to the dictates of the body, are quintessentially "eaters." Significantly, *mokṣa* is described as a state of "not consuming" (*anāhārī pad*), a state of bliss attainable only when one is outside the violent, and meaningless, cycle of eating and being eaten.

Animals are those beings who are part and parcel of the cosmic surroundings, bound by the reciprocal nature of life and death, and firmly situated within the cosmic cycle of death and regeneration. Lacking restraint, they act impulsively to satisfy each and every bodily desire, making no distinction between soul (*jīva*) and body. Their bodies are their only source of pleasure and fulfillment; effectively they are their bodies. As such, they serve as a type of negative witness to the truth of Jainism, which insists upon the experience of body and world estrangement as the first step to liberation.

The Tattvārtha Sūtra describes, here in especially bleak terms, the body as fundamentally alien to the *jīva*:

> Reflecting upon the filthy condition of the body strengthens dispassion and disgust for the body. The body is impure because it is produced by a mixture of father's semen and mother's blood, which are impure. It is impure because everything it consumes turns foul and putrid. It is impure because it is the receptacle of dirt, sweat, phlegm, bile, urine and feces. It is impure because it is impossible to change its foul smell by any kind of bath or cosmetic.[29]

Meditation upon the "otherness" of the body constitutes a core practice of ascetic discipline, and is basic to the renunciatory ethos of the tradition. While human birth is also the means to liberation, and therefore cherished, its "otherness" is the central and constant theme found throughout Jainism.

Animals' effective "oneness" with their bodies is anathema to the Jain ideal. Their obvious delight in participating in the world through their sensory way of being—smelling, tasting, feeling, hearing, moving—is precisely the seductive trap of *saṃsāra* that all humans must judiciously avoid.

Conclusion

Jainism unhesitatingly demarcates between the human and the nonhuman, and places the human in a category of its own, superior to all others. By its ontological privileging of the human, Jainism acknowledges the differences in the capacities of sentient life for self-transcendence, but insists that all beings inhabit a shared condition of existence and possess a shared potential for release, however incrementally obtained. Moreover, the tradition posits a strict requirement upon the human to be with the nonhuman conscientiously and nonviolently, as both a means to activate release at the human level of being, but also to further this potential already inherent in the nonhuman.

As argued throughout this chapter, this distinctively Jain way of being stems from the experiential reality of inhabiting a world that is concretely and patently inhabited by others; it takes for granted the experience of life as always and unavoidably in a state of being with others. The animate and intelligent life that encompasses us, that perpetually bombards us, and leaves its innumerable impressions on us every moment of every day, is, for Jains, taken as a given. This all-encompassing life—along with the myriad beings it contains—while certainly a given, is also the foundational source for an understanding of life's existential purpose. When one engages with all senses open and is fully attuned to life's complex stratifications—when one is deeply cognizant of the suffering nature of the simplest of beings most especially—it is at this point that an ontological "crossing over" is possible and release may be obtained.

The impetus for the Jain path is, therefore, not ideological but relational, arising from the fundamental experience of being sentiently with others. Most fundamentally, our condition of being with means a condition of engagement with all life; we are all inescapably participants in a world that communicates, each speaking a language that expresses our distinctive levels of being, but all of a voice expressing the final objective of our shared existential trajectory. Thus, whether speaking through the fabulous personifications of traditional lore, or speaking viscerally through the cacophonous cries of natural creatures, the nonhuman unites, in calling out to the enlightened human, reminding one of the timely need for release.

Notes

1 Jacques Derrida, *The Animal That Therefore I Am* (New York: Fordham University Press, 2008), 48.

2 For example, see: Carol Adams, *The Sexual Politics of Meat: A Feminist-Vegetarian Critical Theory* (New York: Continuum International Publishing Group, 2000); Marc Bekoff, *Nature's Purposes: Analyses of Function and Design in Biology* (Cambridge, MA: MIT Press, 1998); Mathew Calarco, "Another Insistence of Man: Prolegomena to the Question of the Animal in Derrida's Reading of Heidegger," *Human Studies* 28, no. 3 (2005): 317–34; Mary Midgley, *Beast and Man: The Roots of Human Nature* (Brighton, UK: Harvester Press Limited, 1979; London and Oxford, Routledge Classics, 2002); Derrida, *The Animal That Therefore I Am*; Gary Francione, *Animals, Property, and the Law* (Philadelphia, PA: Temple University Press, 1995); Tim

Ingold, *What Is an Animal?* (London: Routledge, 1994); Paul Waldau and Kimberley Patton, *A Communion of Subjects: Animals in Religion, Science & Ethics* (New York: Columbia University Press, 2006).

3 See Christopher K. Chapple, "Inherent Value without Nostalgia: Animals and the Jaina Tradition," in *A Communion of Subjects: Animals in Religion, Science & Ethics*, eds. Paul Waldau and Kimberley C. Patton (New York: Columbia University Press, 2006), 241–9; and Kristi Wiley, "Five-Sensed Animals in Jainism," in *A Communion of Subjects: Animals in Religion, Science & Ethics*, eds. Paul Waldau and Kimberley C. Patton (New York: Columbia University Press, 2006), 250–5.

4 To use Thomas Berry's compelling phrase. Thomas Berry, *The Great Work: Our Way Into the Future* (New York: Bell Tower, 1999).

5 Here I refer to the ethical as a codified elaboration of dos and don'ts.

6 Umasvati, *Tattvārtha Sūtra* [*That Which Is*] (trans. Nathmal Tatia) (New York City: Harper Collins Publishers, 1994), xxi.

7 Also called Tīrthaṇkaras (ford makers).

8 Sayyambhava Arya, *Dasavailkalika Sutra* (trans. Chand Kastur Lalwani) (Delhi: Motilal Banarsudass, 1973), 58.

9 James Laidlaw, *Riches and Renunciation: Religion, Economy, and Society Among the Jains* (Oxford: Oxford University Press, 1995), 21.

10 Umasvati, *Tattvārtha Sutra*, 39. The *Tattvārtha Sūtra* defines sentience as "awareness or consciousness," which is both knowledge and intuition.

11 Ibid., 131.

12 *Micchami Dukkadam* forms part of the daily prayer called *Pratikramana*. It is also ritually recited during the holiest day of the liturgical calendar, *Saṃvatsarī*, the final day of *Paryūṣaṇa*.

13 Laidlaw, *Riches and Renunciation*, 153–9.

14 Thomas Berry, "Prologue," to *A Communion of Subjects: Animals in Religion, Science & Ethics*, eds. Paul Waldau and Kimberley C. Patton (New York: Columbia University Press, 2006).

15 Berry, *The Great Work*, 19.

16 For a more detailed discussion, see Anne Vallely, "Ancestors, Demons and the Goddess: Negotiating the Animate Cosmos of Jainism," in *Health and Religious Rituals in South Asia: Disease, Possession and Healing*, ed. Fabrizio Ferrari (New York: Routledge Press, 2011), 64–78.

17 Mahavira's twentieth incarnation was of that of a lion. This passage is the author's fictive retelling of the end of this incarnation.

18 Surendra Bothra, *Ahimsa: The Science of Peace* (Jaipur: Prakrti Bharati Institute, 1988), 1X. English translation of passage in Ācārāṅga Sūtra.

19 Hermann Jacobi, trans., *Sacred Books of the East, Jaina Sutras Part II*, vol 22:36 (Oxford: Clarendon Press, 1884), 36.

20 Hemachandracharya, *The Yoga Shastra of Hemchandracharya: A 12th Century Guide to Jain Yoga* (trans. A.S. Gopani), ed. S. Bothara (Jaipur: Prakrit Bharati Academy; Mevanagar: Shri Jain Swetambar Nakoda Parswanath Tirtha, 1989), 38, couplet 2.20.

21 Umasvati, *Tattvārtha Sūtra*, 159.

22 Birth in the female form, for instance, is similarly attributed to past deceitfulness, while "virulent aggression and extreme possessiveness" ensure birth as a hell being. Ibid., 159.

23 Tom Regan, *The Case for Animal Rights* (Berkeley, CA: University of California Press, 2004), 151–6.

24 Author's retelling of a well-known tale. See for example, JAINA Education Committee, *Jain Story Book* (Raleigh, NC: Federations of Jain Associations of North America, 2005), 29–31.

25 *Parasparopagraho jīvānām*. Umasvati, *Tattvārtha Sūtra*, 131.

26 Jainism's most fundamental mantra.

27 Author's retelling of a well-known tale. See for example JAINA Education Committee, *Jain Story Book* (Raleigh, NC: Federations of Jain Associations of North America, 2005), 32–3.
28 Ralph T.H. Griffith, *The Hymns of the Rg Veda*, rev. ed. (1896; reprint Whitefish, MT: Kessinger Publishing, 2006), 10.9.
29 Umasvati, *Tattvārtha Sūtra*, 223–4.

Bibliography

Adams, Carol. *The Sexual Politics of Meat: A Feminist-Vegetarian Critical Theory*. New York: Continuum International Publishing Group, 2000.

Arya, Sayyambhava. *Dasavailkalika Sutra*. Translated by Chand Kastur Lalwani. Delhi: Motilal Banarsudass, 1973.

Bekoff, Marc. *Nature's Purposes: Analyses of Function and Design in Biology*. Cambridge, MA: MIT Press, 1998.

Berry, Thomas. *The Great Work: Our Way into the Future*. New York: Bell Tower, 1999.

Berry, Thomas, "Prologue." In *A Communion of Subjects: Animals in Religion, Science & Ethics*. Edited by Paul Waldau and Kimberley C. Patton, 5–10. New York: Columbia University Press, 2006.

Bothra, Surendra. *Ahimsa: The Science of Peace*. Jaipur: Prakrti Bharati Institute, 1988.

Calarco, Mathew. "Another Insistence of Man: Prolegomena to the Question of the Animal in Derrida's Reading of Heidegger." *Human Studies* 28, no. 3 (2005): 317–34.

Chapple, Christopher K. "Inherent Value without Nostalgia: Animals and the Jaina Tradition." In *A Communion of Subjects: Animals in Religion, Science & Ethics*. Edited by Paul Waldau and Kimberley C. Patton, 241–9. New York: Columbia University Press, 2006.

Derrida, Jacques. *The Animal That Therefore I Am*. New York: Fordham University Press, 2008.

Francione, Gary. *Animals, Property, and the Law*. Philadelphia, PA: Temple University Press, 1995.

Griffith, Ralph T.H. *The Hymns of the Rg Veda* (1896). Whitefish, MT: Kessinger Publishing, 2006.

Hemachandracharya. *The Yoga Shastra of Hemchandracharya: A 12th Century Guide to Jain Yoga*. Translated by A.S. Gopani. Edited by S. Bothara. Jaipur: Prakrit Bharati Academy; Mevanagar: Shri Jain Swetambar Nakoda Parswanath Tirtha, 1989.

Ingold, Tim. *What Is an Animal?* London: Routledge, 1994.

Jacobi, Hermann, trans. *Sacred Books of the East, Jaina Sutras Part II*, vol. 22:36. Oxford; Clarendon Press, 1884.

JAINA Education Committee, *Jain Story Book*. Raleigh, NC: Federations of Jain Associations of North America, 2005.

Laidlaw, James. *Riches and Renunciation: Religion, Economy, and Society Among the Jains*. Oxford: Oxford University Press, 1995.

Midgley, Mary. *Beast and Man: The Roots of Human Nature*. Brighton, UK: Harvester Press Limited, 1978; Oxford and London: Routledge Classics, 2002.

Regan, Tom. *The Case for Animal Rights*. Berkeley, CA: University of California Press, 2004.

Umasvati. *Tattvārtha Sūtra* [*That Which Is*]. Translated by Nathmal Tatia. New York: Harper Collins Publishers, 1994.

Vallely, Anne. "Ancestors, Demons and the Goddess: Negotiating the Animate Cosmos

of Jainism." In *Health and Religious Rituals in South Asia: Disease, Possession and Healing*. Edited by Fabrizio Ferrari, 64–78. New York: Routledge, 2011.
Waldau, Paul and Patton, Kimberley C., eds. *A Communion of Subjects: Animals in Religion, Science & Ethics*. New York: Columbia University Press, 2006.
Wiley, Kristi. "Five-Sensed Animals in Jainism." In *A Communion of Subjects: Animals in Religion, Science & Ethics*. Edited by Paul Waldau and Kimberley C. Patton, 250–5. New York: Columbia University Press, 2006.

2 Animal compassion

What the *Jātakas* teach Levinas about giving "the bread from one's own mouth"

Katharine Loevy

Levinas often returns to a paradigmatic scene of ethics—a scene of feeding a stranger the bread from one's own mouth. This image is fundamental to Levinas's philosophical reflections in *Otherwise than Being*, and it recurs as paradigmatic of the ethical event in Levinas's subsequent work. Enjoying one's bread is a figure for living from the world as the subject of enjoyment, and giving this bread to another is Levinas's preferred narrative for describing the transformation of the subject of enjoyment into ethical subjectivity, called forth in this regard by the approach of the other person.

An important dimension of the scene of giving the bread from one's own mouth is that the gift of bread is a gift of oneself. This identification of one's bread with oneself can be traced back to the nature of the subject as in the first instance a subject born of joyful consumption. In *Totality and Infinity*, Levinas provides an analysis of subjectivity according to which the subject first comes to be through enjoyment. The enjoyment of existence in the mode of sensibility, and hence in the mode of consumptive appropriation of the world, gives the subject its first experience of itself. It is thus out of enjoyment that the I emerges, or as Levinas writes, "the I is the very contraction of sentiment, the pole of a spiral whose coiling and involution is drawn by enjoyment."[1] Enjoyment is prior to the constitution of the subject, and the subject originally comes to be through the contraction into self that enjoyment produces.

The ultimate consequence of the emergence of subjectivity through enjoyment is that enjoyment is the necessary pre-condition for the emergence of ethical subjectivity. The future of this account by the time we get to *Otherwise than Being* is that enjoyment and the wounding of the subject that characterizes for Levinas the subject undergoing its transformation into ethical subjectivity are mutually implicating. Enjoyment in a very physical and embodied sense is constitutive of subjectivity, and hence offering to another what one enjoys is potentially traumatizing and eviscerating. Only a subject born of enjoyment can also be a subject for whom ethicality is wounding, and it is in this sense that the gift of one's bread can be the gift of oneself. As Levinas writes in *Otherwise than Being*, "one has to first enjoy one's bread, not in order to have the merit of giving it, but in order to give it with one's heart, to give oneself in giving it."[2]

In this notion of giving oneself when giving one's bread, what we do not find in Levinas is any indication that the things we enjoy can themselves be other living beings deserving of ethical consideration. I am thinking in this regard of nonhuman animals, and of the way in which Levinas's deployment of the figure of "bread" potentially veils the animals that we eat or that we endanger or harm through agricultural and other practices by which food is made available. In my transformation into ethical subjectivity, I become aware of the potential cost to others of my existence. I become aware, in other words, of having usurped a place in existence that could have gone to someone else. Yet I become aware of this only in relation to other human beings who could have emerged in and through the same enjoyment and hence who could have taken my place. What is missing is an awakening to the presence of those beings whose bodies and lives provide the material support of the "bread" that I both enjoy and give.

Theorists of Levinas's treatment of the animal have made clear the ways in which Levinas's claims commit him to a much more robust engagement with animal others than he actually accomplishes.[3] Likewise, feminist engagements with Levinas's philosophy have demonstrated that those who occupy the position of what Levinas calls the "feminine" are compromised in their ability to appear as ethically commanding, and that this is in part because of the positioning of the "feminine" within rather than beyond the sphere of dwelling.[4] In what follows, I will be considering the degree to which we can understand Levinas's silences with regard to the claim of the nonhuman animal in terms of the position allotted to the animal within the sphere of dwelling insofar as the animal is covered over by the figure of "bread." Interior to the space of dwelling, and as an essential support of enjoyment, the animal as "bread" may be fundamentally unrecognized within Levinas's philosophy, and hence unrecognized in its potential capacity to interrupt enjoyment and to call forth the I into ethical subjectivity. And if this is the case, then nonhuman animals would stand as yet another class of effaced or forgotten others within Levinas's ethical vision—others who deserve ethical consideration, but who disappear because of their absorption into subjectivity-producing enjoyment.

In order to conduct this analysis, my approach will be to confront Levinas's characterization of the significance of the gift of bread with an alternative scene of giving—one in which the gift consists in one's literal body, and not simply in a gift of the food one eats and enjoys. This alternative scene aporetically expands the range of possible others that we could imagine as calling us forth into ethical responsibility, since it is a gift that is given so that another living thing is not caused to suffer and die in order to make possible a gift of food. As such, this scene dramatizes a wakefulness to the nonhuman animal who could otherwise be enjoyed by myself or someone else. This alternative scene thus highlights Levinas's silence with regard to those others who are at stake when I offer a gift of food as though it were a gift of myself. It enables us to return to Levinas's phenomenology of the subject of enjoyment and of ethicality, and to ask why the effacement of the animal through the figure of "bread" is never interrupted by an awakening to the animal as itself deserving of ethical consideration.

The *Jātaka* Tales

The alternative narrative that I will read alongside Levinas is drawn from two versions of the story of King Śibi and his ransoming of a dove, both of which emerge out of the Buddhist literary genre known as the *Jātaka* Tales. A dove has flown to the king in order to save itself from the hunter who stalks it, and the king grants the dove protection. But the king is reminded that the hunter is also his subject and hence also deserving of compassion. The hunter sometimes gives voice to this concern, since catching the dove will enable him once more to stave off starvation. In *Avadānakalpalatā* 55, the hunter's moral objection to the king's resolve to protect the dove is as follows:

> you should not show hatred to me out of affection for the dove.... As he is, so am I. What difference is there between us to you? Good people who are impartial toward all beings should not show compassion to one alone.[5]

In *Kalpanāmaṇḍitikā* 64, a version of the story in which the hunter is rather a hawk, we find the following exchange:

KING ŚIBI: ... when I made the vow to attain enlightenment, I accorded my protection to all beings.
HAWK: If your words are true, then quickly give me the dove. For if you cause me to die of hunger, you will no longer be showing compassion.
KING ŚIBI: I find myself in an extremely difficult situation.[6]

King Śibi faces a difficult situation because the interests of one vulnerable being are in direct conflict with the interests of another. His solution is to offer his own body in the dove's place. The classic image of this event is of the king cutting away the flesh of his thigh and placing it on a scale to weigh against the weight of the dove. We find an example of this image in a sculptural frieze from Gandhāra (second century CE) now held at the British Museum. In a wall painting in Cave I at Ajanta (late fifth century CE), King Śibi is shown lifting his entire body on to the scale (Figure 2.1).[7] The story of King Śibi's ransom of the dove presents us with an imaginative example of what a gift of oneself would look like if gifts of food were *not* immediately identified with gifts of the body. Likewise, it presents us with narratives in which nonhuman animals are beneficiaries of extreme acts of generosity and compassion.

A glance at the *jātaka* genre reveals that there are in fact many examples of stories in which a human being gives a gift of the body to feed or to otherwise protect animals. There are *jātakas* in which a man feeds a flock of hungry birds with his eye and then with his flesh. There are *jātakas* in which a prince, a brahmin, or an ascetic throws his body over a cliff or slits his own throat in order to feed a starving tigress about to eat her own cubs. The reverse is also the case: there are famous *jātakas* in which an elephant gives his body to feed human beings lost in the wilderness, and still others in which a hare jumps into a fire or into a pot of boiling water in order to feed a forest-dwelling ascetic. In some of

Figure 2.1 King Śibi steps on to the scale. Wall painting, Cave 1 at Ajanta, *c.* late fifth century CE (source: courtesy of Benoy K. Behl).

these stories, the giver's act is prevented or the giver's body is in the end restored, and in others the giver dies.[8] Regardless of the outcome, each story dramatizes in its own way an extreme act of generosity in the mode of giving one's own body as life-saving nourishment to someone else, and in these examples the act of compassionate giving crosses over the line that separates humans from nonhuman animals. These *jātakas* are a part of a religious, literary, and art historical genre within which the question of hunger is raised in relation to both human and nonhuman precariousness, and in which this precariousness is recognized in both the suffering of hunger and the violence of consumption.

The *jātakas* are notable in this regard as images of extreme generosity, and for this reason they speak to the images of generosity that Levinas imagines only for the inter-human. The image of an act of generosity wherein one offers *oneself* as the bread that feeds the starving other is past the limit of where Levinas's thought leads us, and Levinas does not develop any ethical scenarios in which a human being is ethically commanded by the hunger or the vulnerability to the violence of consumption of a nonhuman animal. But *why* do the *jātakas* outstrip even Levinas's extreme images of compassionate responsiveness and gift-giving in relation to the hunger of others, or, rather, what can we identify within interpretive frameworks more endemic to the *jātakas* that may serve to promote the development of these narratives? What is there to say about the cultural and religious contexts out of which the *jātakas* have elaborated these images of extreme generosity and compassion, and of generosity and compassion, moreover, offered to nonhuman animals?

Many of the *jātakas* are derivative of stories that pre-date Buddhism. The narrative tool for their incorporation into Buddhism is the notion that the historical Buddha achieved recollection of all his previous lives during the first part of the night of his enlightenment.[9] The *jātakas* are thus the stories of his previous lives as a *bodhisattva*, and hence as beings connected to one another through a chain of reincarnation that eventually produces Siddhārtha Gautama. While Siddhārtha, like all sentient beings, has an infinite number of previous lives, the previous lives chronicled in the *jātakas* are lives in which some act was accomplished that catapulted this series of beings further along the requisite spiritual path toward Buddhahood. The *bodhisattvas*' acts can thus go so far as to be fatal, and often do, without being the end of the story, and this is because the future enlightenment of the historical Buddha is on the horizon. In this regard, the acts portrayed can afford to be fatal, and are designed to be extreme so as to inspire awe and devotion.

The events of giving portrayed in the *jātakas* are thus exceptional, and this is to say that they are not meant to be imitated. Much of their meaning is derived from the fact that they are steps in the process toward the achievement of Buddhahood, and this is a process entered into only by certain spiritually advanced beings. These stories exalt Buddhist moral commitments to the values of compassion, forbearance, generosity, etc., but the concretization of each of these Buddhist ideals into brutal and extreme acts makes the *bodhisattvas* exceptional. The *jātakas* are to a certain degree rhetorically bound to seek out ever more extreme and inimitable enactments of Buddhist values in order to set the great heroes of the *jātakas* apart from all other sentient beings.[10]

An important feature of the *jātakas* is that they can have a significant and fairly direct relationship to practices of lay donation. It is relevant in this regard that the narrative time of the *jātakas* is in the past, and in an age before Buddhism has been established in the world. By contrast, the Buddhist layperson encountering these stories lives at a time when Buddhism is firmly established in the world, and hence his or her world can potentially include the Buddhist religious community, Buddhist holy sites, and many Buddhist ritual practices. The layperson thus lives in an age in which Buddhism makes available "fields of merit" according to which any gifts received by representatives of Buddhism are productive of amplified positive karmic merit.[11] The extreme acts of the *bodhisattvas* play an important role in bringing into existence Buddhism and its rich fields of merit through which lay donors can give a much more modest gift and nevertheless accrue a great deal of positive *karma*.

An interesting calculus thus relates the *bodhisattvas*' fulfillment of the Buddhist virtues and the lay donor's devotional giving to the "fields of merit" supplied by Buddhism. As Ohnuma explains: "The life of the Buddha can be replaced by the ritual of the Buddhist."[12] Referring to the *bodhisattva*'s acts as "perfections," Ohnuma writes:

> For "perfections" and "devotions" are, on some level, equivalent: the sort of ritual logic at work here means that every offering made, every act of devotion performed, no matter how small, is multiplied by the great field of merit in which it is bestowed—the resulting product calling to mind the magnificent past deeds of the Buddha himself.[13]

The inimitable acts of the *bodhisattvas* are reflected by the Buddhist laypersons' acts of donation. As James Egge writes, what we have is "giving as an act of detachment and generosity" on the part of the *bodhisattvas*, and acts of "meritorious sacrifice" on the part of the lay donors.[14] These two sets of acts are thus related to one another, but without being the same. The connection can then be amplified through location—lay donations can be received at the holy site where a *bodhisattva*'s acts are supposed to have occurred.

Acts of giving relevant to the *jātakas* thus operate within what are essentially two orientations toward the gift—one that belongs to the *bodhisattvas*, and one that belongs to everyone else. With regard to the *bodhisattva*, the meaning of the act of giving is that it is one more successful step toward fulfilling all of the Buddhist perfections. For everyone else, the meaning of giving is that one can acquire thereby a great deal of positive *karma* in this lifetime so as to be reborn into a better condition in the next lifetime.[15]

These two orientations are brought together in the art historical data that we find in the cave paintings at Ajanta, and a review of the relevant material from this site shows how the *bodhisattvas*' extreme acts and the lay donors' modest acts are mutually implicating. Over the doorway to the middle chamber of Cave 17 is painted the wheel of *saṃsāra* that depicts the various realms of rebirth. This door leads into a middle chamber painted with scenes of the previous lives of the Buddha, including some from identifiable *jātakas*. Entering into the last chamber, the visitor reaches an image of the Buddha (Figure 2.2). Stephen Teiser describes this progression through the space as follows:

> The wheel was positioned on the porch because it prepared the way for—and enticed the implied visitor into—the scenes portrayed inside the cave.... Passing through this exoteric, preambulatory space, the visitor proceeds through the parts of the temple narrating the gradual perfection of the Buddha-to-be over many lifetimes. The innermost space is the actual residence of the Buddha.[16]

In the exoteric space of the porch, the visitor confronts a door, and above the door is painted the wheel of *saṃsāra*. If the visitor passes through the door and into the first chamber, he or she confronts scenes from many of the *jātakas*, and hence scenes of a sentient being's movement beyond the wheel of *saṃsāra* in a

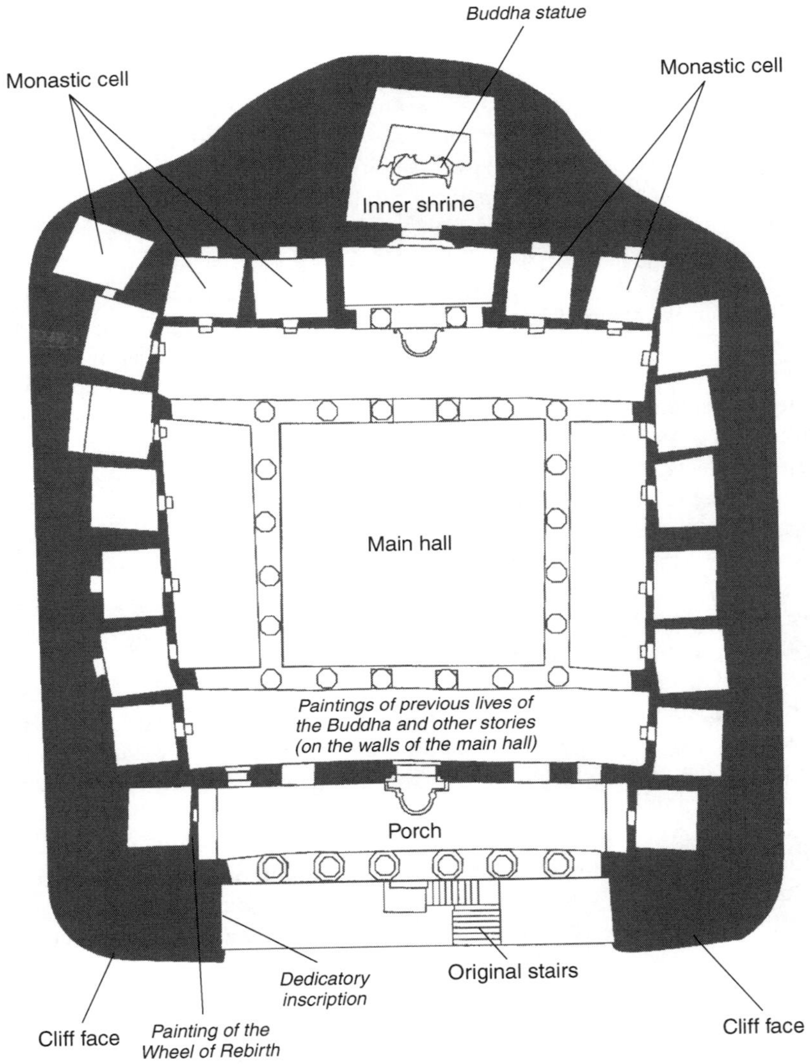

Figure 2.2 After Fergusson and Burgess, Cave Temples of India, fig. 33, right (source: drawn by Sorat Tungkasiri and Stephen F. Teiser).

process that requires multiple lifetimes. If the visitor passes through one more doorway and into the final and most remote chamber, he or she encounters the Buddha, and hence the embodiment of the possibility of enlightenment. According to Teiser, no Buddhas are present within the painting of the wheel of *saṃsāra* at the cave's entrance. Teiser thus concludes, "the painting on the porch, then, forms the perfect antithesis to the main shrine, where the Buddha himself resides."[17] The *jātakas* are thus the bridge between mortal entrapment in the endless cycles of rebirth, and release from these cycles through Buddhahood. And if the Buddha in the innermost chamber has escaped the workings of *karma* altogether, the Buddha is also that which provides for the "fields of merit" that allow the lay Buddhist to navigate the wheel of *saṃsāra* more successfully.

Insofar as images of the wheel of *saṃsāra* at Ajanta and elsewhere provide the layperson with comprehensive images of the workings of reincarnation, these images provide us with an essential clue as to why the *bodhisattvas* of the *jātakas* are sometimes portrayed as human beings who give gifts of their bodies in order to feed starving animals. Part of what has to be understood is what the wheel of *saṃsāra* teaches us about the spiritual status of nonhuman animals. Of the three "unfortunate rebirths" depicted on the most common versions of the wheel, one is the realm of hungry ghosts, one is the realm of the Buddhist hells, and one is the realm of animals. The implication, in other words, is that the spiritual status of animals is extremely low.

When it comes to "fields of merit, and hence to the karmic calculations appropriate to lay donation, animals are thus among the least desirable of all potential recipients of acts of meritorious giving. Ohnuma cites the *Dakkhiṇāvibhaṅga Sutta* of the *Majjhima Nikāya* in this regard. Within it, recipients are placed on a relative scale according to how productive they are as fields of merit for the donor. As Ohnuma reports,

> the Buddha tells Ānanda that giving to an animal produces ten times less merit than giving to an evil human being, which itself produces a hundred times less merit than giving to a virtuous human being, and so on—all the way up to arhats, pratyekabuddhas, and Buddhas as the most "productive" recipients of all.[18]

With such an economy at work, the gift of the *bodhisattva* stands apart not simply because it is an extreme gift, but because it is a gift that completely disrupts the logic of religious giving. Nonhuman animals are essentially worthless as fields of merit. This makes them inappropriate receivers for the donation of the layperson seeking to acquire karmic merit through acts of giving to a spiritually advanced being. Animal recipients are thus rhetorically desirable within the context of the *jātakas*, since a gift of the body *to an animal* amplifies the exceptional nature of the *bodhisattva*'s gift and proves the *bodhisattva*'s singular intentions.[19] The *bodhisattva*'s fulfillment of the perfection of generosity or compassion is untainted by the desire for karmic reward, because the animal recipient of the *bodhisattva*'s gift has no reward to offer.

Thus through the ideas of *karma*, of fortunate and unfortunate rebirth, of the *bodhisattva* path through multiple lifetimes, and of the historical Buddha's achievement of Buddhahood, the extreme gifts of the *bodhisattvas* to karmically worthless animal recipients is made sense of in relation to the modest gifts to superior recipients characteristic of the religious life of the layperson. This constellation of ideas and religious practice provides the rhetorical impetus and the interpretive framework for the *jātaka* of King Śibi's ransom of the dove, and for the many other *jātakas* in which human beings give gifts of the body for the sake of nonhuman animals. But if highlighting the exceptional character of the *bodhisattva* is the rhetorical impetus for portraying the *bodhisattva* as giving a gift of the body to nonhuman animals, it is nevertheless the case that these stories can also call certain features of Levinas's philosophy into question. Having situated the story of King Śibi's ransom of the dove within a more endemic interpretative framework, how might we read this *jātaka* as also a challenge to Levinas?

King Śibi is caught between the claims of the hunter and the claims of the dove. Let us imagine that the hunter occupies the position of Levinas's stranger at the door—the one whose knock at the door interrupts my dwelling and my enjoyment, and calls me forward into ethical subjectivity. If the hunter is the stranger, and if the bread that I am ethically beholden to give to the stranger is the dove, then what we see is King Śibi stopped in his tracks by the opposing ethical demands of the bread, and hence by the demand that he first account for what violence may be lurking in the potential gift. Alternatively, let us imagine that the dove is the stranger, in which case King Śibi answers the knock at the door and shelters the stranger from death, but finds that in so doing there is another other—the hunter—who is potentially compromised in the process, and whose ethical claims must be taken into account as well. If King Śibi is to respond to the call of both hunter and dove, what is left for him to do?

King Śibi refuses to give away the dove, but he also refuses to turn away the hawk or hunter. The option that remains open to King Śibi in this drama of extreme acts of compassion is to give the flesh of his own body as life-sustaining meat, and thereby to save both predator and prey with an act of self-sacrifice. And as extreme and unreasonable as King Śibi's solution is, his version of the gift of the body is one that does not assume that the gift of oneself can be accomplished through the gift of the body of someone else, and in this regard it reveals an essential ethical blind spot in Levinas's notion of bread. But to see the full extent of this *jātaka*'s contribution to the ethical project at stake in Levinas forgetting the animal, we must first take a closer look at why one finds in Levinas this notion that the gift of one's food is a gift of oneself.

Levinas's body aggregates

According to Levinas, ethical subjectivity emerges out of certain transformations in the subject of enjoyment that occur through the face-to-face encounter with another human being. Despite the overturning of the egoism of the I that ethical subjectivity entails, the subject of enjoyment is the essential precursor rather than the antithesis of ethical subjectivity. Through the process by which the subject comes to be on the basis of enjoyment, the subject of the ethical face-to-face has something to give. Likewise, as a result of the nature of the subject's self-relation in enjoyment, the subject gives itself when it gives its bread.

What is the relationship with the world, as constituted through enjoyment, such that the subject gives itself when it gives what it would have otherwise enjoyed? Levinas tells us that the constitution of the subject of enjoyment is possible because the world yields to the kinds of beings that we are—a yielding paradigmatically dramatized in consumption. Levinas describes this yielding in terms of his notion of "agreement." Insofar as the world is structurally amenable to its consumption in enjoyment, the world can serve as that from out of which the subject constitutes itself and lives. Levinas describes agreement as follows:

> The relationship of the I with the non-I produced as happiness which promotes the I consists neither in assuming nor in refusing the non-I. Between the I and *what it lives from* there does not extend the absolute distance that separates the same from the other. The acceptance or refusal of what we live from implies a prior *agreement* (agrément), both given and received, the agreement of happiness. The primary agreement, to live, does not alienate the I but maintains it, constitutes its *being at home with itself*.[20]

The subject of enjoyment is sustained as a subject in the mode of happiness, and happiness is produced through the agreement between the I and the non-I in the activity of "living from." As happiness, the I is supported and maintained in enjoyment. Thus the relationship of the I to the non-I is one in which the non-I is an essential support of the existence of the subject as such. The ethical implications are significant. The world that I enjoy does not stand in relation to me as an other, and hence the relationship of the I with the non-I of enjoyment is precisely *not* the relationship of the I with the concrete other of the ethical face-to-face.

Levinas uses the term "nourishment" to describe the dynamics of enjoyment. It is a word that he uses in the broadest possible sense with regard to what may nourish us, and hence it includes the nourishment we might receive, for example, from ideas. The structure of nourishment, whatever its source, is nevertheless consistent with biological processes of metabolism. As Levinas writes:

> Nourishment, as a means of invigoration, is the transmutation of the other into the same, which is in the essence of enjoyment: an energy that is other, recognized as other, recognized, we will see, as sustaining the very act that is directed upon it, becomes, in enjoyment, my own energy, my strength, me.[21]

In nourishment, what nourishes me is appropriated such that it becomes my strength and my energy. The expenditure of energy in my action of appropriation is thus transformed into a renewal of my capacity for action. In nourishment, what might appear as lost to the world in the depletions entailed by action is thus immediately recovered, and the subject, who, like Ulysses, ventures out into its engagements with the non-I, returns to and affirms only itself.[22]

The "other" of nourishment is thus not an other that appears as such, rather this other disappears into the subject's enjoyment, and hence into the subject's self-relation. That which supplies the material of enjoyment does not appear as independent of the I, but as reduced to the ways in which it excites and engages the subject's capacity for sensation such that, "in enjoyment the things revert to their elemental qualities."[23] Levinas identifies sensibility with enjoyment in this regard, and states that sensibility "establishes a relation with a pure quality without support, with the element."[24] The other of enjoyment is thus absent as a substantial other. "To live" according to Levinas, consists "in sinking one's teeth fully into the nutriments of the world, agreeing to (agréer) the world as wealth, releasing its elemental essence."[25]

Hence according to Levinas's phenomenology of the emergence of subjectivity, what is consumed is experienced as quality or element, and this reversion to quality as experienced by the non-I of enjoyment no doubt also applies when what is consumed and enjoyed is the body of a nonhuman animal. Just as we can soak up the rays of the sun without ever thinking of the sun as a discrete object, the same lack of awareness of the otherness of things is characteristic of all enjoyment, where enjoyment is the most basic mode of the subject's relation to the world, and of the subject's relation to itself through the world. In an important sense, we discover the distinctness of the beings we enjoy, if at all, only after and according to a different level of experience from the register of sensibility, which for its part sustains the self-relation of the egoist I through an immediate experience of the qualities of non-I in enjoyment.

Hence even at the most fundamental level of its existence, and as the condition of the possibility of it coming to be, the subject's self-relation is fully mediated through the world, and yet the world in this regard appears only as quality.[26] From the perspective of the subject of enjoyment, the ethical event whereby I give the world I enjoy to another can thus appear as a violation of me, since it is a violation of that which provides the material conditions of the possibility of my existence. To cut into the conditions of enjoyment is thus to cut into me, or as Levinas writes in *Totality and Infinity*:

> The presence of the Other is equivalent to this calling into question of my joyous possession of the world. The conceptualization of the sensible arises already from this incision in the living flesh of my own substance, my home, in this suitability of the mine for the Other.[27]

The other as Other, or as the other of the ethical face-to-face, calls into question my possession of the world, where dwelling is a matter of the subject's mastery of the world through labor and possession as a way of ensuring the possibility of enjoyment against an insecure future. But it is because of the nature of enjoyment as sensibility, and hence because of the way in which the subject is confirmed through its experience of the elemental quality of things, that being called into question vis-à-vis what I possess through dwelling is an "incision in the living flesh of my own substance." Through dwelling, the non-I achieves thing-like status insofar as what I possess are the qualities I enjoy made substantial as things that I can own and enjoy later. But these things that populate the space of dwelling are nothing more for me than the containers of my future enjoyment. Whatever they are for themselves (if anything), the things I possess in the mode of dwelling are more than mere quality, but not substantially other from me so as to call my possession and my enjoyment into question.

Through dwelling, the subject possesses the world, and hence has something to give. Through enjoyment, the subject's act of giving is a giving of oneself, or, as Levinas writes, enjoyment is that which "enables the wound to reach the subjectivity of the subject."[28] Both are essential precursors to the ethical scene in which I give the stranger at the door the bread taken from my own mouth, and in doing so give myself.

What the subject undergoes in giving is described by Levinas in a variety of ways, but we see the dynamics of subjectivity perhaps most clearly in Levinas's images of "coring out" and of "uncoiling," both from *Otherwise than Being*. Levinas uses the image of the "coring out" of the ego, such that "tearing away of bread from the mouth that tastes it" is "the coring out (*dénucléation*) of enjoyment, in which the nucleus of the ego is cored out."[29] This coring out is enabled by enjoyment because in order to be for the other—to "signify for the other"—Levinas argues that the subject must "be able to be complacent in itself" in the inward coiling of enjoyment, and as such the movement from complacency to being for another is something Levinas imagines in terms of the subject "unwinding its coils."[30] Whether through the image of "coring out," or through the image of "uncoiling," the ethical act is an eviscerating of subjectivity insofar as the material support of enjoyment, and hence of the subject itself, is that which the subject offers to the stranger at the door.

The nonhuman animal never shows up in the position of ethically commanding other, despite, for example, the potential for suffering.[31] Additionally, nothing Levinas says protects animals from providing the material basis for the "bread" in the scene of giving "the bread from one's own mouth." To the contrary, animal bodies are consumed and enjoyed as such, and this positions them directly within relationships of agreement whereby the independent thing disappears into the subject's enjoyment. Levinas's image of "bread" thus risks covering over the need to critically engage with the ethics of possession itself. To be sure, Levinas's account of the emergence of subjectivity through enjoyment, and his analysis of a world that appears as quality, give us phenomenological insight into the challenges that we face in awaking ethically to those whose bodies we possess and consume. But these challenges are not taken up by Levinas, and his lack of engagement in this regard is something that we can perhaps see reflected in him opting for the image of "bread."

The value of confronting Levinas's scene of giving "the bread from one's own mouth" with the story of King Śibi's ransom of the dove thus becomes clear. King Śibi is aware of the claim that issues from the animal that one eats. Levinas's subject, on the other hand, is interrupted by the human stranger at the door, but at no point awakens to the potential violence and suffering that may be involved in having something to give. Levinas does not discover in the world of enjoyment any resistance to agreement, or any alternative significance for the world of enjoyment except the alternative significance it acquires by becoming gift. The ethical issue arises insofar as this world can also include living things who take a perspective upon their own existence or who have the capacity to suffer. Each is a mode of resistance to agreement that persists even if these living things can also be absorbed into my enjoyment, on the one hand, or offered as a gift of myself to the human stranger at the door, on the other.

Conclusion

We have now taken account of those factors that promote the inclusion of animal recipients within *jātaka* gift-of-the-body narratives. We have also analyzed those aspects of Levinas's phenomenology of ethical subjectivity through which the effacement of the animal is sustained even at the level of the subject awakening to ethical responsibility. We are thus in a position to evaluate more fully what reading the *jātakas* alongside Levinas has taught us.

The lesson to be learned from the *jātaka* of King Śibi and the dove is not that we should embrace his solution. Indeed, an argument emerges from within the *jātaka* genre itself according to which acts like those performed by King Śibi are still too one-sided insofar as they extend consideration to *only* the dove and hunter or hawk. In giving a gift of the body, and hence in potentially or actually dying in the process, the *bodhisattvas* of the *jātakas* fail to respond to the solicitations for protection and support that issue from the *bodhisattvas*' families, and when the *bodhisattva* is a king, from the human and nonhuman inhabitants of his kingdom. Within the *jātaka* genre itself we find characters who voice opposition to the *bodhisattva*'s gift, and who sometimes offer explicit arguments for why the gift is more harmful than good because it only reflects the interests of a small fraction of those who will be affected.[32] And while within the *jātakas* the future enlightenment of the Buddha is the reason for the gift that trumps all counterarguments, engaging the *jātakas* without presuming the reality of either reincarnation or enlightenment makes clear nevertheless that it is ethically problematic for Levinas to assert that the gift of one's "bread" can be a gift of oneself.

Levinas's subject must thus become capable of being interrupted by those beings who are absorbed into enjoyment and who are possessed as a part of the subject's dwelling. In this regard, Levinas's ethical subject must somehow become capable of hearing the claim of the animal *as if* the animal arrives from beyond the sphere of dwelling and enjoyment while still remaining within it. What King Śibi shows us in his ability to respond to the hawk or hunter and also to the dove is that the independent beings who are susceptible to their absorption into my enjoyment can also be recognized by me in their otherness and in their ethical significance.

What may thus be lacking in Levinas's philosophy is a sufficient enough engagement with why we experience only certain others as ethically commanding. Levinas provides us with a richly embodied account of the emergence of ethical subjectivity, and he shows how we are brought forth into ethical subjectivity through finding ourselves face-to-face with concrete and ethically commanding others. Nevertheless, we may still need exposure to a relevant *jātaka* in order to be made aware of those potentially ethically commanding others that we have still managed to overlook or ignore. Does Levinas allow for this? For the concrete *education* of our ethical sensibilities? Can we not each play a part in introducing one another into the face-to-face encounter with beings whom we had failed up to that point to either notice or to properly consider? If this is the case, then the *jātakas* can expand our capacity to experience the ethical claims of others, thereby enabling us to include ever more forgotten others into the negotiations of justice.

Notes

1 Emmanuel Levinas, *Totality and Infinity: An Essay on Exteriority* (trans. Alphonso Lingis) (Pittsburgh, PA: Duquesne University Press, 1969), 118.
2 Emmanuel Levinas, *Otherwise than Being or Beyond Essence* (trans. Alphonso Lingis) (Pittsburgh, PA: Duquesne University Press, 1998), 72.
3 See Matthew Calarco, *Zoographies: The Question of the Animal from Heidegger to Derrida* (New York: Columbia University Press, 2008); Jacques Derrida, *The Animal That Therefore I Am* (ed. Marie-Louise Mallet, trans. David Wills) (New York: Fordham University Press, 2008); Christian Diehm, "Gaia and Il y a: Reflections on the Face of the Earth," *Symposium: Journal of the Canadian Society for Hermeneutics and Postmodern Thought* 7, no. 2 (2003): 173–83; Lisa Guenther, "*Le flair animal*: Levinas and the Possibility of Animal Friendship," *PhaenEx* 2, no. 2 (2007): 216–38; John Llewelyn, *The Middle Voice of Ecological Conscience: A Chiasmic Reading of Responsibility in the Neighbourhood of Levinas, Heidegger, and Others* (New York: St. Martin's Press, 1991); and David Wood, "Some Questions for My Levinasian Friends," in *Addressing Levinas*, eds. Eric Nelson, Antje Kapust, and Kent Still (Evanston: Northwestern University Press, 2005), 152–69.
4 See Silvia Benso, *The Face of Things: A Different Side of Ethics* (Albany, NY: State University of New York Press, 2000); Catherine Chalier, *Figures du féminin, lecture d'Emmanuel Levinas* (Lagrasse: Verdier, 1982); Tina Chanter, *Time, Death, and the Feminine: Levinas with Heidegger* (Stanford, CA: Stanford University Press, 2001); Lisa Guenther, *The Gift of the Other: Levinas and the Politics of Reproduction* (Albany, NY: State University of New York Press, 2006); Claire Elise Katz, *Levinas, Judaism, and the Feminine: The Silent Footsteps of Rebecca* (Bloomington, IN: Indiana University Press, 2003); Paulette Kayser, *Emmanuel Levinas: La trace du féminin* (Paris: Presse Universitaires de France, 2000); Christel Marque, *L'Utopie du Féminin: Une Lecture féminist d'Emmanuel Lévinas* (Paris: L'Harmattan, 2007); and Stella Sandford, *The Metaphysics of Love: Gender and Transcendence in Levinas* (London: Athlone Press, 2000).
5 Translated and quoted in Reiko Ohnuma, *Head, Eyes, Flesh, and Blood: Giving Away the Body in Indian Buddhist Literature* (New York: Columbia University Press, 2007), 122.
6 Ibid., 122.
7 For a discussion of the art historical iconography of King Śibi's ransom of the dove, see Edith Parlier, "La légende du roi des Sibi: Du sacrifice brahmanique au don du corps bouddhique," *Bulletin d'Études Indiennes* 9 (1991): 133–60. Parlier's account of some early versions of this image links the position of the dove on the thigh of the king and the king drawing his gift of flesh from his thigh as echoes of a much older Vedic sacrificial tradition.
8 This list is adapted from the appendix provided by Ohnuma. See Ohnuma, *Head, Eyes, Flesh, and Blood*, 273–83.

9 Ibid., 36.

10 There is anthropological evidence of people feeding their flesh to parents for medicinal purposes within the context of Buddhism in China, along with textual evidence of Buddhist sanctions against such practices. See Hubert Durt, "Two Interpretations of Human-Flesh Offering: Misdeed or Supreme Sacrifice," *Journal of the International College for Advanced Buddhist Studies* 1 (1998): 57–83 or 236–10.

11 According to Ohnuma, *Head, Eyes, Flesh, and Blood*, 59: "Buddhism, Hinduism, and Jainism all hold that religious gifts should generally be directed *upward* toward religiously worthy and superior recipients (such as monks, brahmins, Buddhas, and Jinas) because these gifts are productive of the greatest amount of merit (*puṇya*)."

12 Ibid., 43.

13 Ibid., 43. For this reason, Ohnuma sees the *jātakas* as importantly related to another Buddhist literary genre—the *avadānas*. As Ohnuma writes:

> by means of the *jātakas*, the bodhisattva is lauded and exalted for the magnificent lengths he went to during his previous lives—but by means of the *avadānas*, ordinary Buddhists receive the message that such magnificent lengths are now *unnecessary*, thanks to the presence of Buddhism in the world as a powerful field of merit.

And as Ohnuma continues:

> thus it is neither the *jātakas* alone nor the *avadānas* alone but only the two genres taken together that illuminate for the reader the ritual magic worked by Buddhism—a magic that allows pre-Buddha "perfections" to be replaced by post-Buddha "devotions."

14 James R. Egge, *Religious Giving and the Invention of Karma in Theravada Buddhism* (Richmond, UK: Curzon Press, 2002), 155, fn. 54.

15 See in this regard Egge, *Religious Giving and the Invention of Karma*, esp. 15–25.

16 Stephen F. Teiser, *Reinventing the Wheel: Paintings of Rebirth in Medieval Buddhist Temples* (Seattle, WA: University of Washington Press, 2006), 100–1. There are actually two doors to the middle chamber. The wheel of *saṃsāra* is painted over the left door.

17 Ibid., 101.

18 Ohnuma, *Head, Eyes, Flesh, and Blood*, 152–3.

19 According to Ohnuma, Buddhist literature in general portrays only beings such as Buddhas and *bodhisattvas* as donors of extreme gifts to worthless recipients. Nevertheless, there are some examples of such gifts being expected of laypersons. See Ohnuma, *Head, Eyes, Flesh, and Blood*, 60.

20 Levinas, *Totality and Infinity*, 143.

21 Ibid., 111.

22 The image of Ulysses is one that Levinas will sometimes deploy in his discussions of enjoyment. Levinas distinguishes between the trajectory of the subject of enjoyment with that of ethical subjectivity through a distinction between Ulysses's journey of return and the journey without return of the biblical Abraham. See, for example, Emmanuel Levinas, "The Trace of the Other," in *Deconstruction in Context*, ed. Mark C. Taylor (trans. Alphonso Lingis) (Chicago, IL: Chicago University Press, 1986), 345–59.

23 Ibid., 134.

24 Levinas, *Totality and Infinity*, 136.

25 Ibid., 134.

26 See Agata Zielinski's excellent discussion in *Lecture de Merleau-Ponty et Levinas: Le corps, le monde, l'autre* (Paris: Presses Universitaires de France, 2002).

27 Levinas, *Totality and Infinity*, 75–6.

28 Levinas, *Otherwise than Being*, 64.

29 Ibid., 64.
30 Ibid., 73.
31 With regard to what Levinas says about suffering in his essay "Useless Suffering," and with regard to the tenor of Levinas's overall philosophical project, commentators such as Matthew Calarco see in Levinas a failure on his part to live up to his own philosophical commitments when it comes to nonhuman animals. As Calarco writes, "although Levinas himself is for the most part unabashedly and dogmatically anthropocentric, the underlying logic of his thought permits no such anthropocentrism," Calarco, *Zoographies*, 55. See also Levinas, "Useless Suffering," in *Entre Nous: Thinking-of-the-Other* (trans. Michael B. Smith and Barbara Harshav) (New York: Columbia University Press, 1998), 91–102.
32 As Steven Collins makes clear in his discussions of Buddhist kingship, the question remains open as to whether there can be a king who is also a Buddhist. Collins is primarily addressing the incompatibility between the Buddhist absolute value of nonviolence and the exigencies of political rule. See Steven Collins, *Nirvana and Other Buddhist Felicities: Utopias of the Pali Imaginaire* (Cambridge: Cambridge University Press, 1998), 414–96.

Bibliography

Benso, Silvia. *The Face of Things: A Different Side of Ethics*. Albany, NY: State University of New York Press, 2000.

Calarco, Matthew. *Zoographies: The Question of the Animal from Heidegger to Derrida*. New York: Columbia University Press, 2008.

Chalier, Catherine. *Figures du Féminin, Lecture d'Emmanuel Levinas*. Lagrasse: Verdier, 1982.

Chanter, Tina. *Time, Death, and the Feminine: Levinas with Heidegger*. Stanford, CA: Stanford University Press, 2001.

Collins, Steven. *Nirvana and Other Buddhist Felicities: Utopias of the Pali Imaginaire*. Cambridge: Cambridge University Press, 1998.

Derrida, Jacques. *The Animal That Therefore I Am*. Edited by Marie-Louise Mallet. Translated by David Wills. New York: Fordham University Press, 2008.

Diehm, Christian. "Gaia and Il y a: Reflections on the Face of the Earth." *Symposium: Journal of the Canadian Society for Hermeneutics and Postmodern Thought* 7, no. 2 (2003): 173–83.

Durt, Hubert. "Two Interpretations of Human-Flesh Offering: Misdeed or Supreme Sacrifice." *Journal of the International College for Advanced Buddhist Studies* 1 (1998): 57–83 or 236–10.

Egge, James R. *Religious Giving and the Invention of Karma in Theravada Buddhism*. Richmond, UK: Curzon Press, 2002.

Guenther, Lisa. *The Gift of the Other: Levinas and the Politics of Reproduction*. Albany, NY: State University of New York Press, 2006.

Guenther, Lisa. "*Le Flair Animal*: Levinas and the Possibility of Animal Friendship." *PhaenEx* 2, no. 2 (2007): 216–38.

Katz, Claire Elise. *Levinas, Judaism, and the Feminine: The Silent Footsteps of Rebecca*. Bloomington, IN: Indiana University Press, 2003.

Kayser, Paulette. *Emmanuel Levinas: La trace du feminine*. Paris: Presse Universitaires de France, 2000.

Levinas, Emmanuel. *Totality and Infinity: An Essay on Exteriority*. Translated by Alphonso Lingis. Pittsburgh, PA: Duquesne University Press, 1969.

Levinas, Emmanuel. “The Trace of the Other.” In *Deconstruction in Context*. Edited by Mark C. Taylor. Translated by Alphonso Lingis, 345–59. Chicago, IL: Chicago University Press, 1986.

Levinas, Emmanuel. *Otherwise than Being or Beyond Essence*. Translated by Alphonso Lingis. Pittsburgh, PA: Duquesne University Press, 1998.

Levinas, Emmanuel. “Useless Suffering.” In *Entre Nous: Thinking-of-the-Other*. Translated by Michael B. Smith and Barbara Harshav, 91–102. New York: Columbia University Press, 1998.

Llewelyn, John. *The Middle Voice of Ecological Conscience: A Chiasmic Reading of Responsibility in the Neighbourhood of Levinas, Heidegger, and Others*. New York: St. Martin’s Press, 1991.

Marque, Christel. *L’Utopie du féminin: Une lecture féminist d’Emmanuel Lévinas*. Paris: L’Harmattan, 2007.

Ohnuma, Reiko. *Head, Eyes, Flesh, and Blood: Giving Away the Body in Indian Buddhist Literature*. New York: Columbia University Press, 2007.

Parlier, Edith. “La légende du roi des Sibi: Du sacrifice brahmanique au don du corps bouddhique.” *Bulletin d’Études Indiennes* 9 (1991): 133–60.

Sandford, Stella. *The Metaphysics of Love: Gender and Transcendence in Levinas*. London: Athlone Press, 2000.

Teiser, Stephen F. *Reinventing the Wheel: Paintings of Rebirth in Medieval Buddhist Temples*. Seattle, WA: University of Washington Press, 2006.

Wood, David. “Some Questions for My Levinasian Friends.” In *Addressing Levinas*. Edited by Eric Nelson, Antje Kapust, and Kent Still, 152–69. Evanston, IL: Northwestern University Press, 2005.

Zielinski, Agata. *Lecture de Merleau-Ponty et Levinas: Le corps, le monde, L’autre*. Paris: Presses Universitaires de France, 2002.

3 China's Confucian horses[1]

The place of nonhuman animals in a Confucian world order

Bao-Er[2]

Confucian hierarchy

Does it really matter what a Chinese philosopher thought about nonhuman animals over two-and-a-half millennia ago? I believe that it does, and in the following discussion outline my reasons for taking such a position.

Writing in 1997, Mark Elvin declared that China has lost two major worldviews since encountering the modern West in the course of the nineteenth century. First, "*Scriptural Confucianism*" which collapsed, he argues, as a self-reproducing system by the early years of the twentieth century, undermined initially by an attempt to intensify its religious character and by anguish at its *historical failure in the service of China. Second, by the start of the 1980s, "Maoist Communism"* was also strategically dead, destroyed, Elvin laments, by cynical and murderous abuse of its own noble ideals:

> Both in their time were powerful, intelligent, and inspirational interpretations of the world, even if inappropriate for China in any reasonable future. Both have also left residues, some of them fairly certainly dead, some perhaps seeds that may come to life again.[3]

Has Confucianism "come to life again?" And, if it has, is Confucianism likely to impact on our understanding of nonhuman animals?

Moral guidance

Chinese customs and traditional practices carry the imprint of a hierarchical life-world. During the latter stages of the Warring States period in China, Kongzi 孔子 (551–479 BCE), generally known in the West as Confucius, synthesized a selection of customary ideas into a functional social philosophy, one that could be realized through practice. Confucianism/Rujia Xueshuo 儒家学说 is essentially a code for living, later modified and further developed by disciples such as Mencius/Menzi 孟子 (372–289 BCE), Xun Zi 荀子 (312–230 BCE), and Zhu Xi 朱熹 (1130–1200 CE). Though it has been characterized at times as a religion, and in a number of important respects it certainly is (for example, ancestor worship), Confucianism has come to be understood in modern times as a philosophy of *moral guidance*.

What is it then that Confucianism might bring to the modern world and our understanding of nonhuman animals? Confucianism has a complex history but, essentially, relies on two primary ideas: *ren* 仁 and *xiao* 孝. *Ren* is concerned with a person's humanity, with the development of their internal essence, their virtuous benevolent self, how they might become more "humane." The character ren 仁 (composed of two radicals) represents the benevolence that links each person (radical on the left) with their neighbor (radical on the right).[4]

Xiao 孝 is concerned with the development of a person's filial relationships. The character captures within itself the hierarchical life-world of Confucianism in that it is composed of two radicals, the top radical means "elder," the lower radical "son"—elder over son.[5] For Confucianism, these two ideas are interdependent. It is everyone's duty to cultivate and nurture their "humaneness" by enhancing the quality and range of their human relationships. Where most religions generally search for answers to the ultimate questions by recourse to, or the lure of, a "paradise" somewhere else, Confucianism is committed to total engagement with, and participation in, society; where not only the present but also the past and future are truly immanent.

Confucianism situates the family-household at the core of a complex set of hierarchical relationships held tightly together by an intricate web of social and cultural rituals. Human relationships are fundamental to the Confucian philosophy. Whatever happens, the father, the senior member, the patriarch of the familial group must be deferred to, revered, and obeyed. If this fundamental rule of behavior is faithfully observed, social relationships fall harmoniously into line. Filial sons tend to be loyal subjects, content with the status quo and respectful of authority. In contrast, unfilial noncompliant sons are prone to political disaffection, readily mobilized for dissidence, rebellion, and even revolution. The maxim of imperial officials was: *da zhong da xiao*/大忠大孝, loyalty and filial piety above all else.[6]

"Filial piety" is Confucianism's keystone. If set in place correctly, filial piety is capable, at least theoretically, of resolving all of society's conflicts and contradictions. The reason for this extraordinary outcome is surprisingly simple. Every single individual in a Confucian society defines him or herself in terms of where they each stand as either superior or subordinate, senior or junior, in any and every socio-political situation. No one in imperial China, from the Emperor down, stood shoulder to shoulder with any other individual. Even the beggars on the street operated within a hierarchical structure. The son deferred to the father, wife to husband, second son to first son, concubine to wife, younger sister to older sister, student to teacher, first year student to second year student, second minister to first minister, and so on.

The prevailing system of ritualized norms served to confirm social realities in China on a day-to-day, hour-to-hour, and minute-to-minute basis. There was always a *deferree* and a *deferror* in every possible situation. That was the intrinsic nature of China's ritualized society. The China of today, despite (or partly because of) the communist interregnum of state-sponsored egalitarianism, based on an ideologically contrived notion of "comradeship," has certainly not managed to shake off this entrenched hierarchical worldview. While there may be a strong current of social Darwinism racing through China's Market Economy, there is also an equally strong interconnecting element of control. The intense experience over millennia of deferring to or being deferred to by others solely on the basis of one's social status has served to internalize in the Chinese people a strong cultural sense of inter-dependence, a reliance, especially in times of adversity, on relationships, connections, *guanxi* 关系. There is no uncertainty or doubt in such a regimen. Everyone knows their role in society and exactly what is expected of them, with the inevitable result that social and political stability—*harmonization*—cannot help but become the defining normative theme.

Environmental ethics

Where do nonhuman animals figure in the Confucian story? Significantly, the character for family, *jia* 家, consists of two radicals, a roof with a pig sheltering beneath. The implication being that the continued existence and flourishing of a family depends very much upon there always being sufficient nonhuman animals available to sustain its human members; without food and adequate shelter there can be no family, and without families there can be no organizations or philosophies,[7] no society or state.

The Confucian school of thought, as represented by Confucius, Mencius, and Xunzi, was particularly important, says Bell, in idealizing the order of *tian xia* 天下 (literally: the world under Heaven):

> [T]he Confucian conception of "tian xia" refers to an ideal moral and political order admitting of no territorial boundary – the whole world [is] to be governed by a sage according to the principles of rites [li 礼] and virtues [de 德]. This ideal transcends the narrowness of states.[8]

That sense of belonging, being part of something much larger, has the potential to extend out in all directions, so long as such order is based on a proper understanding of what is, and is not, "right behaviour" (*yi* 仪).

Fan Ruiping (2005) argues that while Confucianism encompasses a range of views concerning the environment, these views all take on a humanist viewpoint, in that they all hold that, "among all things in nature, only human individuals have high intrinsic values." Even if other entities have intrinsic values, for Confucianism, claims Fan, the "value of these entities" is necessarily ranked lower than human values.[9]

First, Fan identifies *ethical humanism*, an individualistic form where it is morally acceptable for a human individual to treat other entities in whatever way he or she judges appropriate. This is a strong form of anthropocentrism. Fan gives the example of a human torturing a dog. This is morally permissible so long as the subject dog is not the property of another human being. Should the tortured dog in fact be the property of another then any injury to the dog becomes morally significant simply because the act itself directly affects another human being.

Second, there is *contractual humanism*, which Fan sees as a medium strength anthropocentric form that reflects the fact that humans exist in groups and therefore they must create uniform moral standards for the treatment of other beings. Fan provides the example of one society that deems the eating of dogs acceptable while another holds that it is wholly unacceptable. Such a clash of "moral standards" was played out very publicly when an international campaign led by Brigitte Bardot, the French actress and animal rights advocate, attempted to use the 2002 Fifa World Cup to pressure South Korea, as co-host, into stopping the eating of dogs in South Korea. The response was a cross-party group of South Korean MPs introducing a bill to legalize the sale and export of dog meat.[10] Such campaigns raise the question of how eating a dog or cat in South Korea or China is any different from eating a cow or pig in England, or a sheep or kangaroo in Australia?

Third, there is *religious or cosmic humanism*. Here reference is made to some external moral standards to determine how humans should treat other things, the "divine revelation." For Fan, this view is a weak form of anthropocentrism. Although it does affirm that only humans have high intrinsic values, it is in essence cosmocentric in that the place of humans is located in terms of considerations or realities that transcend humans as well as the environment, including nonhuman animals and plants.[11] It was a "cosmocentric" set of moral standards that underpinned Confucianism in China for more than two millennia, and it was this same cosmology that was so comprehensively overwhelmed by Western technology and culture in the nineteenth and early twentieth century.

In pre-modern China respect for what came before, or precedent, claims Levenson,[12] was a prime Confucian attitude that pervaded intellectual life. Precedence played a central role in determining the place of nonhuman animals in Confucian thinking:

> [A] disciple of Confucius, Zigong [子 贡], wanted to do away with the sacrificing of a lamb at a certain ceremony, Confucius said to him, "you love the sheep, but I love the ritual propriety [li 礼]" (3.17). In this case, Confucius actively defended the killing of animals, not out of material needs, but out of ritual needs.[13]

Ritual was the institutional tool that connected individuals not only with other individuals, families, and groups but also with what was "other," to the mysterious unseen that surrounded and impinged upon every part of their daily lives (for example, "fertility spirits," "door gods," and "the ancestors"). While Zigong had an interest in preserving the sheep from death, it is clear, argues Blakeley,[14] that "Confucius favors past precedence as the way to fulfill the requirements of the occasion. In effect, what is 'known' to be good form and serves as an effective, proper procedure settles the matter for him."

This is *cosmic humanism*, utilizing ritual to connect humanity with the divine. The life of the nonhuman animal is forfeit. Their very existence is subjected totally to the values assigned to them by humans, values cosmic humanism deems to be intrinsic. The nonhuman animal must be sacrificed so that humans can connect with the cosmos. Nonhuman animals are a vital element in the eternal human quest to make direct contact with the divine. There is no unconstrained exercise of a human's free will in the way the nonhuman animal is to be treated, as may be found in *ethical humanism* or even *contractual humanism*; the latter form is to be seen in the "socially sanctioned" farming practice of extracting bile from East Asia's Moon bears. Instead, with *cosmic humanism*, the nonhuman animal's fate is pre-ordained in ritual, not subject to the whims of individual will, or the socio-economic dictates of contractual obligations.

As an intelligent interpreter of the Chinese tradition, Confucius, says Fan,[15]

> inherited the ancient Chinese understanding of virtue (de) [德] as force, which the ancient kings acquired through their willingness to perform sacrifice rituals to the spirits of their ancestors and Heaven on behalf of their subjects. The rituals involved a personal relationship with the divine and not merely a causal interaction with impersonal cosmic objects.

Anthropologist Monica Wilson believes that rituals can reveal values of a society at their deepest level, "men express in ritual what moves them most, and since the form of expression is conventionalised and obligatory, it is the values of the group that are revealed." Wilson sees "in the stuff of rituals the key to an understanding of the essential constitution of human societies."[16] Do the humanistic principles and practices of past-Confucianism concerning nonhuman animals have a role to play in present and future Confucianism?

Confucian future

In August 1973, the Chinese communist party's mass campaign to "Criticize Confucius" began in earnest. Writing at the time of the campaign, John Ma asked:

> how successful [can] this movement ... be in changing the Chinese people's traditional concept of Confucius as a sage ... [it] is difficult to tell at the moment, but one thing is clear: thanks to this mass movement, many Chinese who have never read a single Confucian classic since the modernization of Chinese education must now study Confucian books carefully so that they will be able to criticize Confucius competently.[17]

Indeed, Mao Zedong 毛泽东, the moving force behind the campaign to eradicate Confucianism from the face of the earth may, unwittingly, have been primarily responsible for Confucianism's miraculous revival. It was just a short span of five years following the commencement of this campaign that China embarked on its most extraordinary "economic revolution" (1978)—a fundamental transformation, which witnessed the re-emergence of Confucianism in China (during the 1980s and 1990s) as a significant political and cultural force.

Throughout Chinese imperial history, Confucianism overcame many obstacles. On a number of occasions it has been hard pressed to stave off the challenges and transformative forces of invasion. Foreign invaders such as the Mongols and Manchus, foreign religions such as Buddhism, Islam, and Christianity, and pervasive foreign ideologies such as Marxism and Mercantilism, all made their distinctive contributions to Confucianism and left their mark on Chinese culture. Despite these massive onslaughts, Confucianism managed to weather storm after storm and to further develop by adapting quickly to difficult and highly volatile situations. In fact, time after time, Confucianism succeeded in turning the tables and culturally absorbing foreign invaders who, in many respects, appeared to become even more "Chinese" (or Confucian) than the Chinese themselves.

A process of conceptual readjustment began in China during the final two decades of the twentieth century. The process involved an ideological realignment between Chinese Marxism, on the one hand, and a set of populist Confucian principles, on the other. Beginning in 1980 with a conference in Hangzhou on Confucian philosophy and culture and the formation of the China Confucius Foundation in 1984, official tolerance of and support for a Confucian renaissance steadily grew. The Confucius Foundation sited its head office in Beijing and a branch office in Qufu, the birthplace of Confucius in Shandong province.[18] In October 1989, there were official celebrations of Confucius's 2,540th birthday.[19]

> In these meetings, where high level government figures intervened, Chinese culture was claimed as quintessentially Confucian, and Chinese tradition and the current regime were presented as enlightened, progressive and open to the world. Confucianism was again exploited: the idea was that, by retaining and relying on the Confucian values of harmony and social discipline, China had traditional criteria for excluding decadent libertarian influences from the West, screening out the "spiritual pollution" already diagnosed as the source of the alleged unbridled disorders of Tiananmen.[20]

In 1994 President Jiang Zemin /江泽民 attended China's National Conference on Confucian Research. This very public act signaled an official change in government policy, and reflected a fundamental shift in thinking by the Chinese communist party leadership regarding the relevance of Confucianism and traditional culture to the future development of Chinese society.

All was not as it first seemed, however. Bakken argues that the Chinese style of modernization seems to follow a deeply rooted pattern of "controlled change," with tradition and modernity interlinked in a system of social control where "tradition" can also serve transforming purposes and "modernization" can mean stability and order.[21] He maintains that Chinese conformity is very often a surface conformity with individuals, more often responding to the dictates of the situation than the dictates of their own selves:

> Such behaviour is not necessarily construed as hypocritical behaviour; rather, it is a culturally sanctioned mechanism enabling the individual to maintain a *harmonious* relationship with the external world. Formalistic conformity has a ceremonial function in maintaining *social harmony* which was also the function of the classical li. Even the moral rules are not absolute, but follow a hierarchy of relations in which such rules are applied or neglected. Honesty, for instance, is sacrificed to preserve the greater value of *family harmony.*[22]

This means that individuals are not subject to serious pressures for consistency between inner and outer behavior.[23] This "psycho-social" disconnect in Sino-behavior patterns principally aimed at maintaining harmonious relations is not widely appreciated or properly understood, particularly in the West. Will this lack of a proper understanding prove significant in light of China's current attempts to develop its "soft power" base?

Soft power

Joseph Nye defines soft power as: "the ability to get what you want through attraction rather than coercion or payments."[24] In his report to the 17th Congress of the Chinese communist party on 15 October, 2007, President Hu Jintao 胡锦涛 claimed that cultural *soft power/ruanshili* 软 实 力 has two main purposes: (1) to enhance national cohesion and creativity and meet the demands of people's spiritual life, and (2) to strengthen China's competitiveness in the contest for comprehensive national power within the international arena.[25] The fact, says Li, that China sponsors "Confucius Institutes" throughout the world attests to the country's determination to expand its soft power:

> In today's world, interdependence is intensifying, calling for ever closer cooperation among nations. International cooperation depends on equality, mutual trust and mutual benefit. This growing urgency for international cooperation offers Chinese culture, which emphatically values "harmony," a valuable opportunity. The Chinese cultural stress on "harmony without suppressing differences" (He Er Bu Tong) [和 而 不 同] is likely to promote new thinking and a fresh approach to international relations, thus highlighting the cooperative advantages of Chinese culture. In the eyes of these optimists, "harmony" – laden Chinese culture can then proffer universal values to the outside world.[26]

In 2008, it was reported that the Chinese government spent more than 1.8 billion RMB to promote the Chinese language and culture around the world.[27] It has been stressed, says Li, that the Chinese diaspora is a good platform for promoting Chinese culture. "The Chinese government has also allocated significant funds in the past few years towards supporting, in partnership with various universities, the establishment worldwide of Confucius Institutes that promote educational programs on the Chinese language and culture."[28] It seems China-scholars have been gifted an environmental mission, whether they know it or not:

> Official reports state that part of the responsibility for promoting the influence of Chinese civilization throughout the world lies with scholars of philosophy, humanities and the social sciences. It is their mission to further discover and promote traditional Chinese cultural values with "harmony" at the core ... Chinese analysts claim that although in modern history Western civilization spearheaded industrialization, it cannot necessarily provide effective solutions to the various current challenges of environmental degradation, confusion in social ethics, and international and regional conflicts. Traditional Chinese culture, according to their view, stresses "giving priority to human beings" (yi ren wei ben), and is valuable in overcoming the Western obsession with omnipotent materialism, in resolving humankind's growing spiritual crisis, reversing the worsening natural environment and reining in escalating international conflicts.[29]

But which (if any) of Confucianism's anthropocentric humanist forms is capable of "reversing the worsening natural environment?" Of cleansing the poisoned-well that is now China? Not even Mao—in terms of his ill-conceived and devastating "Great Leap Forward" movement (1959–60), with its wholesale destruction of whole forests to feed backyard furnaces and the slaughter of entire bird species to preserve what inevitably became pest-infested grain—not even China's Great Helmsman had managed to cause the scale of lasting damage to the world's environment that Deng Xiaoping 邓小平 (1978) brought about with his deceptively simple entreaty to the Chinese people to sally forth and become "gloriously rich," As Hill notes, the adoption of this growth-first philosophy has led to "reports from the UN Food and Agriculture Organization, the World Bank, the World Resources Institute, and China's State Environmental Protection Administration (SEPA) all stress[ing] the gravity of China's environmental degredation."[30]

Confucius Institutes

In 2003/04, China began a program of establishing overseas education facilities aimed at promoting the Chinese language and culture. These institutions, which are called "Confucius Institutes"/*Kongzi Fayuan* 孔 子 学 院, acknowledge Confucius as China's foremost teacher. On its Confucius Institute website, as of July 2012, the University of Nebraska-Lincoln names 322 universities in 91 countries in its list of "Confucius Institutes Around the Globe."

Despite their name, Confucius Institutes were not initially intended to propagate Confucianism. Commentators such as Jocelyn Chey (a visiting professor at the University of Sydney and former diplomat), believe that Confucianism has been drafted into service and now forms the vanguard of China's global self-promotion campaign:

> Confucius has become a symbol of one of China's cultural diplomacy goals – to unite ethnic Chinese around the world and create a friendly environment for the conduct of international trade and diplomacy. The project to establish a network of cultural centres around the world borrowed the name of Confucius for this reason ... The CI program is administered by the National Office for Teaching Chinese as a Foreign Language (commonly known as Hanban),[31] which is linked to the Chinese Ministry of Education and governed by representatives of that ministry and several other government departments. It is chaired by a State Councilor – an indication of the importance attached to its "soft power" activities. The Hanban has published rules and regulations for the establishment of CI's on its website.[32]

Are Confucius Institutes promoting Confucian values? In October 2007, John Hearn, the Deputy Vice Chancellor of the University of Sydney,[33] believed they were. He noted that the worldwide objectives of the Confucius Institutes included the promotion of the philosophy of Confucianism as well as Chinese language and culture.[34]

In early 2009 the British Education Minister Jim Knight instituted a Confucian school program in the United Kingdom. Knight said:

> There is a lot we can learn from Chinese culture and Confucius ... Confucius said that alongside knowledge you should have time to think. It is not just about acquisition of knowledge but about respect for the importance of education and the family and that is something I would love to see engendered in our culture as well as it is in China.[35]

Jim Knight undertook a fact-finding trip to China to investigate why it is that Chinese students perform so well, when compared to indigenous British students. He visited the Headquarters of the Confucius Institute in Beijing where he discussed setting up "Confucius Classrooms" or centers of excellence in teaching Mandarin and Chinese culture in English state schools. He told the Sunday Times, "I want to develop Confucius classrooms ... these are cultures that strongly respect and value the family and strongly respect education."[36] What is it then that Confucianism can teach our children about nonhuman animals?

Confucian nonhuman animals

Donald Blakeley has identified sixteen passages in the Confucian Analects, which involve nonhuman animals.[37] From these passages certain Confucian standards of behavior can be discerned. More than anything else, Confucius is concerned with what it is that makes us human, and in pursuit of this quest he and Mencius unashamedly enlist nonhuman animals to best illustrate fundamental principles from which we may distil a *standard position* of the Confucian tradition on the topic of nonhuman animal welfare.[38]

Compassion

Bai Tongdong claims that Confucianism sees humans as having obligations to nonhuman animals, but that such obligations are all to do with the "compassion of human beings" rather than any "innate rights or qualities" that nonhuman animals may possess.[39] Where does this compassion come from? Is it to be found within the individual (ethical) alone, or as a result of the social (contractual), or else derived from an external source (religious/cosmic)?

Bai maintains that for the Confucian, human beings should be compassionate toward nonhuman animals not because nonhuman animals can reason or converse, not because they can suffer, and certainly not because they treat each other humanely, but rather because we human beings perceive their sufferings, the kind of sufferings that remind us of the sufferings of our own kind and, as human beings, we cannot bear to see these sufferings. Wolfe points out that the French philosopher Luc Ferry, a staunch liberal humanist, holds a strikingly similar view:

> "Animals," Ferry argues, "have no rights … but on the other hand we do have certain, indirect duties toward them, or at least 'on their behalf,' because the animal 'is (or should be) the object of a certain respect, a respect which, by way of animals, we also pay ourselves." In short, from the "indirect duty" point of view, the problem with the cruelty to animals is not that it is a violation of their basic interest in avoiding suffering and their basic right not to be treated as objects; it is rather that "the most serious consequence of the cruelty and bad treatment inflicted on them is that man degrades himself and loses his humanity," that cruelty "can affront or corrupt man's sensibility."[40]

Is Confucianism's concern for nonhuman animals based primarily on the belief that nonhuman animals simply remind humans of their humanity?

The story of the ox

> The king asked again, "Is such a one as I competent to love and protect the people?"
> Mencius said, "Yes."
> "From what do you know that I am competent to do that?"
> "I heard the following incident … from Hu He: –
> The king, said he, was sitting aloft in the hall when a man appeared, leading an ox past the lower part of it.
> The king saw him, and asked, 'Where is the ox going?'
> The man replied, 'We are going to consecrate a bell with its blood.'
> The king said, 'Let it go. I cannot bear its frightened appearance, as if it were an innocent person going to the place of death.'
> The man answered, 'Shall we then omit the consecration of the bell?'
> The king said, 'How can that be omitted? Change it for a sheep.' "

> Then Mencius said, "The heart seen in this is sufficient to carry you to the imperial sway. The people all suppose that Your Majesty grudged the animal, but your servant knows surely, that it was Your Majesty's not being able to bear the sight, which made you do as you did"...
> "Indeed it was because I could not bear its frightened appearance, as if it were an innocent person going to the place of death, that therefore I changed it for a sheep."[41]

Mencius's response is puzzling. Unlike the position taken by Confucius in the Analects, which is consistent with the *cosmic* humanist principle of priority being given to ritual over the life and welfare of the nonhuman animal, Mencius appears to be directly contradicting this fundamental tenet:

> Your conduct was an artifice of benevolence. You saw the ox, and had not seen the sheep. So is the superior man affected towards animals, that, having seen them alive, he cannot bear to see them die; having heard their dying cries, he cannot bear to eat their flesh. Therefore he keeps away from his cookroom.[42]

Closer examination reveals, however, that there may well be no real inconsistency in Mencius's position. The "existence of nonhuman animals" takes on significance only at those times when they are being perceived by a "humane" human being. When the nonhuman animal is being *seen and heard and smelt and felt* by the man leading the ox to slaughter, or by those at the sacrifice waiting for the ritual to begin, the nonhuman animal itself, though physically present, is "discursively *absent.*" The animal is purely a trope, a metaphor of sacrifice. However, when the "humane" king comes to perceive the ox, the ox himself becomes "discursively present." The king is then moved to save the ox from death and to substitute a sheep in the oxen's place, a nonhuman animal he has not seen. It seems the ring of compassion emanating from the king stops at what he can sense for himself, and goes no further—in effect, nonhuman animals, unless "discursively present" to a "humane" observer, will always be "discursively absent," their whole continued existence contingent on that which is deemed "humane."

Of course, this may not necessarily define the limits of Confucian compassion. Bai is very clear on this point.[43] If it is proven that an ox does suffer when being killed, the Confucian will claim it as being a "human concern." Bai sees that a key goal of Confucianism is to expand our natural compassion to eventually encompass everything in the universe, including nonhuman animals, and that this expansion of compassion is the basis for humane treatment of nonhuman animals and the enforceable obligations of human beings toward nonhuman animals. Though, at the same time, Bai does see that for the Confucian, both within various "human or animal rights" and between "human and animal rights," there is and will always be a hierarchical order. The consequence of this, believes Bai, is that many human needs, both physical and spiritual, will always necessarily override the wellbeing of nonhuman animals.

So, how does the Confucian deal with the meat in hamburgers or the "assorted" meats in a Mongolian hotpot? Does a Confucian's compassion extend that far, to the nonhuman animal they are eating right here and now? Bai declares that the Confucian never encourages people to become vegetarians, let alone vegans, and that the true Confucian only needs to keep their distance from the kitchen and the slaughterhouse. They do not even need to give up ritual ceremonies that involve the sacrifice of nonhuman animals.[44] It is vital that human relationships are developed and maintained and if this means retaining rituals involving *animal sacrifice* then the interests of the nonhuman animals are "naturally" subordinate to the interests of human beings. As anyone who has spent time in China knows, the coming together of a group of "associates" to share in a banquet, is more than just a meal, it is at times a complex socio-political ritual:

> A person thereby learns … to eat suckling pigs, bear paws, and a whole menagerie of other life forms, trained along the way not to be disturbed by the actual connection between the once-alive beings and their eventual destination as items for human consumption, ceremonial occasions, or uses in many other contexts.[45]

Propriety (*li* 礼), rightness (*yi* 仪), and understanding (*zhi* 智), says Blakeley, effectively guide judgment even when the initial sensibilities of humanity (*ren* 仁) might respond otherwise.[46]

The story of the ox should have been a straightforward account of *cosmic humanism*, where the death of the nonhuman animal links the human to the divine. The sacrificial object: "nonhuman animal" performs a vital functional role in the "humanization" of individuals by connecting them to a higher power. Except in this instance the ox did not die, it lived as a result of the intervention of the king. An anonymous sheep died in its stead. Surely this is an excellent example of strong *ethical humanism*, where the will of the individual (the king) holds sway regardless of the interests of the many. Yes the king acted out of *compassion*, but in so acting he effectively neglected the duty he owed to his people. He could just as well have acted out of *passion*, sparing the ox for some perverse carnal pleasure. The important point for Mencius, however, is that the king did act on the basis of his humanity, his *ren*, and since this is one of the four cardinal virtues[47] which Confucianism esteems as a life-goal, it is to be lauded not condemned.

Does this then mean that butchers cannot join the ranks of the Confucian elite? Bai acknowledges that there are problems with the Confucian position in this respect. Viewing the slaughtering of nonhuman animals is disturbing and the true Confucian should keep away from it. As it is regarded as a fact of life that nonhuman animals are slaughtered in order to meet the physical and spiritual needs of human beings, Bai then asks, who then is to do the slaughtering? What about the butcher's moral wellbeing? The butcher has to get used to the slaughtering scenes, and might well lose all compassion, which, according to the Confucian, would prove fatal to their moral cultivation, their very humanity.

It seems that compassion is an essential precondition (or ingredient) for moral cultivation, and from the start any search for humanness is crippled without it. Butchers are those, believes Bai, who from a Confucian viewpoint fail to develop their moral-self,

> if some butchers develop themselves and find slaughtering morally unbearable, they should leave their trade. The society also has a responsibility to help them. To expose them to slaughtering seems to be very bad for the development of their moral potential.[48]

Bai does suggest an alternative viewpoint though. He maintains that we may take the job of slaughtering as something comparable to the job of soldiering. Difficult as it sounds, a Confucian soldier still needs to kill and to be good at killing, although he is and should be pained by the slaughter. Bai maintains that the slaughtered nonhuman animals are perhaps more innocent than killed enemy soldiers, although killing a human being is of course much more serious to a Confucian than killing a nonhuman animal. In this scenario, says Bai, butchery becomes almost a quasi-religious activity itself, similar to butchery in the Jewish tradition. When all is said and done, however, even Bai thinks that this solution still looks rather artificial and opines: "unfortunately, it is the best I can come up with in defence of the Confucian position on animal rights. This problem is perhaps the price that we have to pay if we still wish to remain Confucian meat-eaters."[49] The Confucian solution appears to be that if an individual is to retain their humanity they must not be directly involved in taking the lives of nonhuman animals. They can achieve this by simply *staying out of the kitchen* and letting others demean their own humanity instead.

For Confucius, the reason that human beings place other beings below themselves in the hierarchical order is not, Bai argues, that human beings are superior to nonhuman animals but, rather, that human beings are naturally associated, and should be associated, with their fellow human beings. Human beings are naturally close to us, and this is reinforced by Confucius's tenet that we should start from what is near and close to us:[50] "Confucius said ruefully: 'Man cannot herd together with birds and beasts. So if I am not to get together with men, what else can I get together with?' "[51] Bai makes the point that Confucians put human beings first; for the Confucian, even if there were a highly intelligent and pain-sensitive pig, we would still take the interest of a not-so-bright human being first. So, for Confucius, the argument that since certain nonhuman animals have innate qualities that are comparable to human beings, they should be given equal rights does not work at all.[52]

Kinship love

Liu Qingping maintains that the theoretical defects and practical evils of Confucianism result mainly from the fact that it excessively exaggerates the importance of *kinship love* and takes it both as the ultimate foundation and as the supreme principle of human life. Correspondingly, he does not entirely negate the significance of kinship love or family life, but is a strong advocate for consanguineous affection taking its proper place in human life as a whole.[53] Liu claims that it is because Confucianism regards *kinship love* as the ultimate principle of human life, and prefers to sacrifice anything else to maintain this particular affection, that its universal ideal of loving all humans (*universal humane love*), cannot possibly be realized. And if this ideal of loving all humans cannot be realized then extending love to nonhuman animals is most certainly an unrealizable dream. It seems then that the fate of nonhuman animals in a Confucian world hangs very much on the distinction between "kinship love" and "humane love"—one being *love via association* and the other *love via universal ideal.*

The standard Confucian way, road, or *dao* 道 begins with the particular and then aims for the universal. Confucius and Mencius built a philosophical edifice, a way of life on the value of "kinship love" and from that foundation hoped to extend outwards to encompass all humanity, and even (at least in the case of Mencius) to go beyond and achieve a universal "humane love" of all things, including nonhuman animals. No matter what the ideal is, however, Confucianism will always, it seems, have an inherent associational limitation. There is always a need for a hierarchy. Whatever is the nearest in terms of kinship will inevitably be given priority when the hard choices need to be made. And unless nonhuman animals are somehow uplifted and brought nearer to human beings than they traditionally have been, they will remain on the outer rim of so called human-centric "kinship love." Never being brought into the fold of "universal humane love," as moral priority is necessarily accorded, by reference to more pressing kinship considerations. "Love or benevolence, as understood by Menzi," says Blakeley,

> is always expressed with a difference of degree. It is to be adjusted in composition ... according to the nature of the being or situation. It is not an appropriate exercise of ren to apply equal value to unequal objects or moral concern.[54]

Liu does suggest a way out of the dilemma facing Confucianism today. Through the "self-criticism of Confucianism," Liu proposes that Post-Confucianism can retain all of those important and valuable Confucian ideas, especially the two main pillars of traditional Confucianism, "filial piety" and "humane love," within its new framework:

> What it does is merely turn the old framework of traditional Confucianism upside-down; to make the universal dimension of humane love, which was secondary in the old framework, primary in the new one, and to make the particular dimension of filial piety, which was primary in the old framework, secondary in the new one.[55]

By doing this, argues Liu, Post-Confucianism will creatively transform traditional Confucianism from a particularistic doctrine into a universalistic ideal. He maintains that it will effectively resolve its profound paradox, prevent those evil consequences resulting from its fundamental spirit, and successfully continue the Confucian tradition in a new global age.

Unfortunately, Liu's solution does seem to have the aura of "wishful thinking" about it. Zhu Xi, says Blakeley, continued to refine the Confucian heritage. He maintained:

> all things have value, but not equal or unchanging value. The first part of this claim is egalitarian, that is, nothing is denied moral standing. But this must, secondly, be qualified and relativized. Proper treatment must be adjudicated ... treating others as they deserve to be treated must respond to individual value, interrelational value, and holistic value.[56]

For Confucianism, all animals, whether human or nonhuman, have moral value. The *standard position* for Confucianism is as follows:

> We love both plants and animals, and we can tolerate feeding animals with plants. We love both animals and men, and yet we can tolerate butchering animals to feed our parents, provide for religious sacrifices, and entertain guests ... there is a natural order. This is called righteousness. To follow this is propriety. To understand this order is wisdom.[57]

By implication, if you do not accept this worldview then you are not righteous, have no propriety, and are without wisdom. That is a very difficult set of negatives to counteract, especially in a society that is coming, or has come, to base itself on the following all-pervasive imperative: *maintain harmonious relationships at all costs.*

Conclusion

Those who want to universalize Confucian familism face, says Bell, an additional hurdle relative to universalist-defenders of Confucian concern for material welfare:

> The Confucian-inspired government has an obligation to promote material welfare because material welfare is necessary for the good life. This view is in principle, compatible with diverse conceptions of the good life. Confucian familism, however, is the good life. Such concerns, however, are rarely put in terms of the need to promote close relationships between adult children and their elderly parents. At best, then, Western-style Confucianism is likely to be "Confucianism lite", without emphasis on filial piety and the attendant restrictions on property rights and adult children'.[58]

Bell points out that contemporary Confucians typically reject such (apparent) classical Confucian values as the inherent superiority of men over women, the complete exclusion of commoners from the political decision-making process, the three-year mourning period for deceased parents, or the idea that "Heaven" somehow dictates the behavior of political rulers. A contemporary Confucian would not, however, reject *the subordination of nonhuman animals (in all respects) to that of humans*. Bell maintains that passages in *The Analects of Confucius* and *The Works of Mencius* that seem to lend themselves to these views have been either reinterpreted or relegated to the status of uninformed prejudices of the period, with no implications for contemporary societies.[59] Is there some hope, therefore, of reinterpreting the place of nonhuman animals in the modern Confucian universe?

Of course, there is always hope. Though the conceptual task is daunting, somehow contemporary Confucian theory needs to break through its own incredibly dense humanist barrier into a post-humanist era. If it cannot, then even in a "brave new" Confucian world I don't believe that nonhuman animals will ever come to assume more than a relative value. Always being evaluated in terms of how they affect or are affected by human beings, nonhuman animals will never really be recognized as having an inherent value all of their very own. If there is to be a fundamental change then Confucianism will need to find a way to value nonhuman animals in their own right, and to do that a radical re-appraisement of the intrinsic nature of Confucianism and its understanding of what it really means to become truly human must take place.

China's Confucian horses are certainly on the move. Only time will tell in which direction these modern-day "Trojans" will lead us.

Notes

1 This is an updated version of a paper delivered at the 2009 International Academic and Community Conference on Animals and Society: Minding Animals, Newcastle, Australia. I thank my co-researcher Dianne Hayles for her assistance with the review and update.

2 Is the principal solicitor and researcher at the Blue Mountains Legal Research Centre, PhD (Syd), LL.M (Hon I) (Syd).

3 Mark Elvin, *Changing Stories in the Chinese World* (Stanford, CA: Stanford University Press, 1997), 1.

4 Léon Wieger, *Chinese Characters—Their Origin, Etymology, History, Classification and Signification: A Thorough Study from Chinese Documents* (New York: Paragon Book Corp., 1965), 29.

5 William G. Stafford, "Seek a Loyal Subject in a Filial Son: Family Roots of Political Orientation in Chinese Society," in *Family Process and Political Process in Modern Chinese History*, ed. Ch'en Ch'iu-Kun (Taipei: Academia Sinica, 1995), 81.

6 Ibid., 943.

7 Which is also the second character of one of the terms (meaning home, organization, or philosophy) for Confucianism: *Ru Jia* 儒 家.

8 Daniel Bell, *Beyond Liberal Democracy: Political Thinking for an East Asian Context* (Princeton, NJ: Princeton University Press, 2006), 379.

9 Ruiping Fan, "A Reconstructionist Confucian Account of Environmentalism: Toward a Human Sagely Dominion Over Nature," *Journal of Chinese Philosophy*, 32, no. 1 (2005): 106.

10 Damien McElroy, "Korean Outrage as West tries to use World Cup to Ban Dog

Eating," *Telegraph*, January 6, 2002, accessed July 20, 2012 www.telegraph.co.uk/news/worldnews/europe/france/1380569/Korean-outrage-as-West-tries-to-use-World-Cup-to-ban-dog-eating.html.

11 Fan, "A Reconstructionist Confucian Account," 106.

12 Ibid., 30.

13 Tongdong Bai, "The Price of Serving Meat: On Confucius's and Mencius's Views of Human and Animal Rights," *Asian Philosophy*, 19, no. 1 (2009): 92.

14 Donald N. Blakeley, "Listening to the Animals: The Confucian View of Animal Welfare," *Journal of Chinese Philosophy* 30, no. 2 (2003): 140.

15 Fan, "A Reconstructionist Confucian Account," 110.

16 Monica Wilson and Leonard M. Thompson, eds. *The Oxford History of South Africa* (2 vols.) (Oxford: Oxford University Press, 1969), 6.

17 John T. Ma, "The Mass Campaign to Criticize Confucius in the People's Republic of China," *Chinese Law and Government* 8, no. 4 (1975–76), 8.

18 Theodore W. de Bary, ed. *Confucianism and Human Rights* (New York: Columbia University Press, 1998), xi.

19 Umberto Brescianni, *Reinventing Confucianism: The New Confucian Movement* (Taiwan: 永望文化事业有限公司, 2001), fn. 11.

20 Ibid., fn. 12.

21 Borge Bakken, *The Exemplary Society: Human Improvement, Social Control, and the Dangers of Modernity in China* (Oxford: Oxford University Press, 2000), 516.

22 Ibid., 516.

23 Ibid., 5.

24 Joseph S. Nye, *Soft Power: The Means to Success in World Politics* (New York: Public Affairs, 2004), x.

25 Mingjiang Li, "Soft Power in Chinese Discourse: Popularity and Prospect," *RSIS Working Paper* 165 (Singapore: S. Rajaratnam School of International Studies, Nanyang Technological University, 2008), 291. Li identifies four versions of "soft power": *ruan shili*, *ruan liliang*, *ruan guoli*, and *ruan quanli*. Li adopts *ruan shili* because it appears to be the most popular in China. Hu Jintao, "Report" (report at the CCP 17th Congress, October 15, 2007).

26 Ibid., 298.

27 "Confucius Institute of Hong Kong" website, accessed April 26, 2009 www.kongzixueyuan.hk/indexEng.html (no longer active).

28 Li, "Soft Power," 298.

29 Li, "Soft Power," 298.

30 Marquita K. Hill, *Understanding Environmental Pollution* (Cambridge: Cambridge University Press, 2010), 280.

31 Guojia Hanban 国家汉办 which literally means "Management of National Language."

32 Jocelyn Chey, "Chinese 'Soft Power' Cultural Diplomacy and the Confucius Institutes," *Sydney Papers* 20, no. 1 (2008): 39.

33 The University of Sydney hosts a Confucius Institute.

34 John Hearn, "Agreement brings Confucius Institute to Sydney," *Uni News*, 39, no. 14 (October 4, 2007), 1.

35 Sarah Knapton, "Chinese Culture to Revive English Education, says Minister," *Telegraph*, February 22, 2009, accessed May 15, 2009 www.telegraph.co.uk/education/educationnews/4780843/Chinese-culture-to-revive-English-education-says-minister.html.

36 Ibid.

37 Blakeley, "Listening to the Animals," 139.

38 Ibid., 138.

39 Bai, "The Price of Serving Meat," 913.

40 Cary Wolfe, *Animal Rites: American Culture, the Discourse of Species, and Posthumanist Theory* (Chicago, IL: University of Chicago Press, 2003), 38.

41 James Legge, *The Four Books: The Great Learning, the Doctrine of the Mean, Confucian Analects, the Works of Mencius* (Shanghai: International Publication Society, 1938), 5–16.
42 Ibid., 5–16.
43 Bai, "The Price of Serving Meat," 913.
44 Ibid., 913.
45 Blakeley, "Listening to the Animals," 148.
46 Ibid., 148.
47 The other three being performing *li* (ritual), exhibiting *yi* (righteousness), and exercising *zhen* (uprightness). Fan, "A Reconstructionist Confucian Account," 111.
48 Bai, "The Price of Serving Meat," 94–5.
49 Ibid., 94–5.
50 Ibid., 85–99.
51 Shixiang Bao and Lao An, *The Analects of Confucius* 儒 学 经 典 译 丛 Translated into Modern Chinese by Bao Shixiang and translated into English by Lao An (Jinan City 济南市: Shandong Friendship Press, 1998), 345 at 13.
52 Bai, "The Price of Serving Meat," 85–99.
53 Qingping Liu, "Confucianism and Corruption: An Analysis of Shun's Two Actions Described by Mencius," *Dao*, 6 (2007): 16.
54 Blakeley, "Listening to the Animals," 147.
55 Liu, "Confucianism and Corruption," 18.
56 Blakeley, "Listening to the Animals," 152.
57 Ibid., 153.
58 Bell, *Beyond Liberal Democracy*, 379.
59 Ibid., 379.

Selected bibliography

Bai, Tongdong. "Back to Confucius: A Comment on the Debate on the Confucian Idea of Consanguineous Affection." *Dao* 7 (2008): 27–33.

Bai, Tongdong. "The Price of Serving Meat: On Confucius's and Mencius's Views of Human and Animal Rights." *Asian Philosophy* 19, no. 1 (2009): 85–99.

Bakken, Borge. *The Exemplary Society: Human Improvement, Social Control, and the Dangers of Modernity in China*. Oxford: Oxford University Press, 2000.

Bao, Shixiang and Lao An. *Lun Yu* [论语 *The Analects of Confucius: An English Chinese bilingual edition*]. Translated into Modern Chinese by Bao Shixiang and into English by Lao An. Jinan China: Shandong Friendship Press 山 东 友 谊 出 版 社, 1998.

Bao-Er. "Chinese Family Structure and Values." *Centre for Asian and Pacific Law* (1999): 5–6.

Bao-Er. *China's Child Contracts: A Philosophy of Child Rights in Twenty-First Century China.* Sydney: BMLRC, 2008.

Bell, Daniel. *East Meets West: Human Rights and Democracy in East Asia.* Princeton, NJ: Princeton University Press, 2000.

Bell, Daniel. *Beyond Liberal Democracy: Political Thinking for an East Asian Context.* Princeton, NJ: Princeton University Press, 2006.

Bell, Daniel and Hahm Chaibong, eds. *A Confucianism for the Modern World.* New York: Cambridge University Press, 2008.

Blakeley, Donald N. "Listening to the Animals: The Confucian View of Animal Welfare." *Journal of Chinese Philosophy* 30, no. 2 (2003): 137–57.

Brescianni, Umberto. *Reinventing Confucianism: The New Confucian Movement*. Taiwan: 永望文化事业有限公司, 2001.

Chey, Jocelyn. "Chinese 'Soft Power' Cultural Diplomacy and the Confucius Institutes." *Sydney Papers* 20, no. 1 (2008): 46.

Confucius Institutes. "Constitution and By-Laws of the Confucius Institutes" (Provisional Version) (accessed March 23, 2009) http://english.hanban.org/kzxy_list.php?ithd=xyzc.

de Bary, Theodore, W. ed. *Confucianism and Human Rights*. New York: Columbia University Press, 1998.

de Bary, Theodore, W. *Asian Values and Human Rights: A Confucian Communitarian Perspective*. Cambridge, MA: Harvard University Press, 1998.

Elvin, Mark. *Changing Stories in the Chinese World*. Stanford, CA: Stanford University Press, 1997.

Fan, Ruiping. "A Reconstructionist Confucian Account of Environmentalism: Toward a Human Sagely Dominion over Nature." *Journal of Chinese Philosophy* 32, no. 1 (2005): 105–22.

Fan, Ruiping. "Consanguinism, Corruption, and Humane Love: Remembering Why Confucian Morality is Not Modern Western Morality." *Dao* 7 (2008): 21–26.

Fan, Wen-lan. "Confucius and the Confucian Theories He Created." *Chinese Law and Government* 8, no. 4 (1975–76): 3–10.

Hearn, John. "Agreement brings Confucius Institute to Sydney." *Uni News*, 39, no. 14 (October 4, 2007).

Hill, Marquita K. *Understanding Environmental Pollution*. Cambridge: Cambridge University Press, 2010.

Hsuan, Mo. "The 1974 'Criticize Lin Criticise Confucius' Campaign of the Chinese Communist Party." *Chinese Law and Government* 8, no. 4 (1975–76): 84–127.

Knapton, Sarah. "Chinese Culture to Revive English Education, says Minister," *Telegraph*, February 22, 2009 (accessed May 15, 2009) www.telegraph.co.uk/education/educationnews/4780843/Chinese-culture-to-revive-English-education-says-minister.html.

Legge, James. *The Four Books: The Great Learning, the Doctrine of the Mean, Confucian Analects, the Works of Mencius*. Shanghai: International Publication Society, 1938.

Levenson, Joseph R. *Confucian China and Its Modern Fate (A Trilogy)*. Berkeley, CA: University of California Press, 1968.

Li, Chenyang. "Does Confucian Ethics Integrate Care Ethics and Justice Ethics? The Case of Mencius." *Asian Philosophy* 18, no. 1 (2008): 69–82.

Li, Meng-Yu. "On the Traditional Chinese Notion of 'Harmony': Resources to the Intercultural Communication." *China Media Research* 5, no. 1 (2009): 55–8.

Li, Mingjiang. "China Debates Soft Power." *Chinese Journal of International Politics* 2 (2008): 287–308.

Li, Mingjiang. *Soft Power in Chinese Discourse: Popularity and Prospect*. Issue 165 of RSIS Working Paper. Singapore: S. Rajaratnam School of International Studies, Nanyang Technological University, 2008.

Liu, Qingping. "Confucianism and Corruption: An Analysis of Shun's Two Actions Described by Mencius." *Dao* 6 (2007): 1–19.

Liu, Qingping. "May We Harm Fellow Humans for the Sake of Kinship Love? Response to Critics." *Dao* 7 (2008): 307–16.

Ma, John T. "The Mass Campaign to Criticize Confucius in the People's Republic of China." *Chinese Law and Government* 8, no. 4 (1975–76): 7.

McElroy, D. "Korean Outrage as West tries to use World Cup to Ban Dog Eating."

Telegraph, January 6, 2002 (accessed July, 20, 2012) www.telegraph.co.uk/news/world-news/europe/france/1380569/Koreanoutrage-as-West-tries-to-use-World-Cup-to-ban-dog-eating.html.

McLaren, Anne E. "Reinventing 'Tradition' in the Shanghai Hinterland: The New Cultural Revivalism." *New Zealand Journal of East Asian Studies* 5, no. 1 (1997): 67–83.

Makeham, John, ed. *New Confucianism: A Critical Examination.* New York: Palgrave Macmillan, 2003.

Nye, Joseph S. *Soft Power: The Means to Success in World Politics*. New York: Public Affairs, 2004.

Stafford, Charles. *The Roads of Chinese Childhood.* Cambridge: Cambridge University Press, 1995.

Stafford, William G. "Seek a Loyal Subject in a Filial Son: Family Roots of Political Orientation in Chinese Society" In *Family Process and Political Process in Modern Chinese History*. Edited by Ch'en Ch'iu-Kun, 213. Taipei: Academia Sinica, 1995.

Tu, Wei-Ming. "Reconstituting the Confucian Tradition." *Journal of Asian Studies* 33, no. 3 (1974): 441–53.

Weatherly, Robert. "Harmony, Hierarchy and Duty Based Morality." *Journal of Asian Pacific Communication* 12, no. 2 (2002): 245–67.

Wieger, L. *Chinese Characters—Their Origin, Etymology, History, Classification and Signification: A Thorough Study from Chinese Documents*. New York: Paragon Book Corp., 1965.

Wilson, Monica and Leonard M. Thompson, eds. *The Oxford History of South Africa* (2 Vols.). Oxford: Oxford University Press, 1969.

Wolfe, Cary. *Animal Rites: American Culture, the Discourse of Species, and Posthumanist Theory.* Chicago, IL: University of Chicago Press, 2003.

Zhao, Dunhua. "A Defense of Universalism: With a Critique of Particularism in Chinese Culture." *Frontiers of Philosophies in China* 4, no. 1 (2009): 116–29.

4 Heidegger and Zhuangzi on the nonhuman

Towards a transcultural critique of (post)humanism

Mario Wenning

In recent years the message of humanism has been severely challenged. In spite of not going out of fashion completely, it seems to have entered a process of rapid decline. Animal welfare, environmentalist, and other movements that relocate the focus from *human perfection* to *protection from the human* look back on extraordinary careers. Even if the practices of human domination over nature continue at unprecedented speeds, within a few decades these formerly marginal subcultures have successfully managed to bring about a paradigm shift by setting up new normative standards. They have significantly contributed to the calling into question and subsequent fading of the two millennia old human fantasy of being at the center of the order of things. In this new context, the proclaimed project of self-taming by and of the human animal is diagnosed as utilizing barbaric means and treating allegedly uncultivated nonhuman life as standing reserve for human exploitation. In its radical versions, new misanthropic visionaries provide for a radical transformation, a Copernican turn that reverses the definition of what it means to be human: while the past has promised to save humans from remaining in or sinking back to natural barbarism, the present and future task consists in saving nonhuman life from the barbarization committed by and in the name of destructive humans. The former crown of civilization is degraded to being a parasite, which is functionally equivalent only to viral diseases. In their incapacity to establish a sustainable equilibrium, both humans and viruses spread by way of exploiting and thereby eradicating other forms of life and their habitat. In following the distant romantic ancestors, post- and antihumanists strive to reverse this occidental logic by privileging the natural and organic over the human and destructive. This methodological operation consists of assigning rights to the nonhuman and calling into question the domination exercised by the human. While such a strategic reversal does have the benefit of calling attention to problems concerning the previous exploitative default position, it also reenacts the initial one-sided logic of essential differences between the human and nonhuman where there might in fact be gradual transitions and overlaps. Zoocentrism and anthropocentrism, I want to argue, should thus not be conceived as radical alternatives, but as two sides of the same coin, the coin here standing for the shared operation of dividing the world according to onto- or zoo-political centers and attributing to these centers the possession or lack of essential capacities and special rights or limitations following from these capacities.

Martin Heidegger is often enlisted as an important resource for, and precursor of, environmental ethics and the zoological turn for understandable reasons.[1] He was one of the first Western philosophers to call attention to the exploitation of the world brought about by technological mastery. Yet there are also significant tendencies in his thought which call into question such interpretations. In the first part of this chapter I will thus raise doubts by showing that, while Heidegger does point out significant weaknesses in the humanist tradition, he is also suspicious of an anti- or post-humanist reaction to that tradition. His ontological determination of the nonhuman retains anthropocentric assumptions. These commit him to what I will call "crypto-humanism." Crypto-humanists conceal the anthropocentric premises underlying their philosophy by assigning humans the role of shepherds of, rather than masters over, nonhumans.

The second part of this chapter develops a transcultural critique of Heidegger's crypto-humanism by contrasting it with conceptions of the human–nonhuman relationship in the tradition of philosophical Daoism. This chapter thus contributes to the ongoing attempt to investigate the relationship between Daoist philosophy and Heidegger. However, rather than stressing the parallels and resonances, this chapter intends to uncover significant differences between the two accounts in conceiving of the human–nonhuman relationship.

The lure of humanism and Heidegger's crypto-humanism

Let us first recall the initial attraction of humanism to better understand the reaction against it. The philosophical project of humanism promised nothing less than the cultivation of the human animal. Classical humanism propagated the perfecting transformation from being a mere human, the unfinished or lacking animal, to becoming humane.[2] Self-perfection intends to relieve the *animal humanum* from its natural, i.e., animalistic, tutelage and transform it into *homo humanum*. In Western philosophy, humanists have attempted to lift the human species by its own bootstraps. All tutelage, it is claimed, after setting up humanity as the measure of all things, is self-incurred and what is self-incurred can also be overcome through practices of taming, reeducation, and self-fashioning. Increasingly these practices also draw on the auxiliary disciplines of bio-, info-, and nanological enhancement of the human body.[3] Transhumanism, the most recent stage of the striving to overcome the limits of humans by overcoming their constitutive mortality, is not the end but the ultimate culmination of the humanist project.[4]

By assigning humanity a task, the completion of which is relegated to the future, the ideal of progress and history was born. The human was thus seen as being at once medium, tool, and goal. It was the problem in terms of its prehistoric, beastlike, raw material and at the same time the solution to that very problem. This raises intricate questions: how was it possible to acquire that in-between location of being at once natural or animal prehistory, human presence, and trans-human future? How can one expect to use the same raw material—the natural, beastlike human—and replace it with the supernatural, Nietzschean fantasy of a self-fashioning superhuman (*Übermensch*)?

Various answers have been given to the question concerning the status of the link which provides a uni-directional bridge connecting and dividing animal and superhuman where the human constitutes beginning, passage, and goal. Most prominently, human beings have been proclaimed to be perfectible creatures in the "chain-of-being" *qua* their innate capacity to use propositional language. The ability to converse about matters near and far is equated with the capacity to replace an imperfect natural with a perfecting cultural shell. He, she, or that which does not share this linguistic capacity is relegated to a more primitive level on the evolutionary ladder. Rather than acknowledging a gradual continuity between the nonhuman and the human world, perfectionist projects and theories such as evolutionary biology have increasingly contributed to sedimenting the human self-image of being the crown of creation, of constituting a natural elite which has managed to transform its constitutive deficiency of being born prematurely into something other, more fit and allegedly superior to mere nonhuman nature. The nonhuman had to stand reserve for the project of human self-perfection, being exploited to serve as a resource for the project of humanism.

There can be no doubt that current discussions about the status of nonhuman life are deeply indebted to Heidegger's engagement with the nonhuman world, both the animate and the inanimate one.[5] In contrast to Heidegger's alleged environmentalism, there are at least two tendencies in his thought that point in opposite directions: the first concerns the ontological status he assigns to nonhuman life while the second consists in his critique of a reduction to conceiving of the human–nonhuman relationship primarily in ethical terms.

In his *Letter on Humanism*, first published in 1946, Heidegger responds to two dangers of contemporary approaches to thinking about what it means to be human and, by extension, what it means to be nonhuman.[6] The first danger is said to consist in reducing human beings to their biological conditions and thus equating them with their organic makeup. While Heidegger has good reasons to be skeptical of the tendency to conflate biological—today we would have to include neurobiological—modes of investigating the human condition, there is also a danger in assuming that science does not offer any valuable insights that could be taken up and interpreted by philosophical analyses.

The second danger that Heidegger identifies stems from the attempt to assign a metaphysical definition to the human being. Since Dasein is taken to be a being which is essentially unfinished and thus undefinable, any description of a specific essence seems illegitimate. While the first danger rests on the category mistake of investigating the human organism rather than the particular place inhabited by humans, the second problematic approach reifies what it means to be human. The reduction of the human to biology as well as the metaphysical determination of a specific human essence do not, Heidegger stresses, value humanity highly enough. The metaphysical prejudice of humanism thus does not consist in over privileging the human, but in misrepresenting the human's unique position within the world. The canonical Aristotelian definition of the human as *animal rationale*—to take the most prominent definition of the human in the history of metaphysics—is already problematic for two reasons. First, the translation of the Greek *zoon logon echon* (the animal possessing a capacity for discourse) into *animal rationale* (the rational animal) is all but innocent and constitutes a problematic metaphysical replacement of discourse or language with rationality. Second, the proclaimed animality (*animalitas*) constitutes a misleading attribution of genus.

If it is not rationality, what is the proper essence and dignity of the human being? Heidegger defines the human condition as an "ek-sisting," a stepping outside not only with regard to particular objects, but with respect to Being in general. What consequences does this have for the nonhuman world? To answer this question it is helpful to return to the early Heidegger. During the lecture course on the *Basic Concepts of Metaphysics*, which was delivered in 1929–30 at the University of Freiburg and includes his most detailed and influential discussion of the human–nonhuman relationship, Heidegger famously distinguishes three different entities and their respective ways of relating to the world: "1. The stone (the material world) is worldless; 2. the animal is poor in world; 3. humans are worldforming."[7] This tripartite division of entities into inanimate objects, animals, and humans, corresponding to the relational modes of worldlessness (*Weltlosigkeit*), world-deprivation (*Weltarmut*), and worldformation (*Weltbildung*), indicates that Heidegger sees the nonhuman world as essentially lacking (for the stone) and impoverished (for the animal). Both inanimate objects as well as nonhuman animals lack the capacity of entering into free and creative relationships with particular entities in the world. While stones simply fall under natural laws, animals such as lizards and bees relate to objects in the world and are thus already privileged when compared to the utterly relationless world of material objects. Drawing on the work of the biologist Jakob von Uexküll,[8] Heidegger does emphasize that the animal, in contrast to stones and, by extension, plants, stands in a relationship to the world. While the stone simply appears and cannot even lack a world, the animal has access to other beings. However, since the animal–world relationship is intrinsically non-discursive, governed by instincts and restricted in its capacities according to the specific domains and practical interests important for the survival of a given animal species (e.g., the lizard's search for the stone to bask in the sun or the bee's search for flowers before returning to his hive), animals are said to be deprived of experiencing objects *as* objects and the world *as* world. Animal organisms have capacities relating them to the environment (*Umwelt*), but they lack a free relationship to these capacities and, by extension, to the world (*Welt*), understood as the environment of all environments. It is due to these limitations, Heidegger contends, that animals are captivated or dazed (*benommen*). Due to the ontological difference distinguishing the human from the nonhuman, it is not possible for human beings to transpose themselves (*Sichversetzen*) into stones while transposing into the nonhuman animal world is essentially limited. Conversely, the "letting be" of beings which humans are capable of remains closed off to animals.

What is surprising about the lecture course is that Heidegger repeatedly refuses to construct hierarchical human–animal distinctions, locating each in a closed off category that stands in relationship to each other, yet, given even a charitable interpretation such as the one developed by William McNeill,[9] exposes them as hierarchical. Assuming that an open access to the world is considered to be a distinguishing criterion, nonhuman animals fall short of meeting the standard.

This does not mean that Heidegger privileges human beings in any straightforward moral sense. He emphasizes that human beings often deprive themselves of the capacity to engage in an open rather than dominating world-forming relationship. Paradoxically, this self-deprivation happens especially when the world is transformed into a mere object serving human goals, when it appears as enframed (*Gestell*) rather than open. Western rationality equates the human capacity of forming or building the world to that of cost–benefit calculation for the sake of technological mastery. When mastering the world in merely instrumental ways, humans fail to live up to the potential to experience the world independent of fixed and dominating rather than flexible and responsive means–ends relationships. As a consequence of his critique of this reduced form of occidental rationality, in his later writings, which are the reference point for those theorists enlisting him for anti-humanist purposes,[10] Heidegger gestures towards another beginning, a point of departure for a new form of thinking and world relationship. This altered world relationship would have to emphasize passivity over the activism springing from calculative thinking common in the history of Western metaphysics. To overcome the mastery of actively pursuing instrumental projects, Heidegger proposes equanimity (*Gelassenheit*), an attitude of caring (*Sorge*), and a primordial form of dwelling (*wohnen*). These forms of comportment are supposed to cultivate an appreciative sensitivity and responsiveness to the nonhuman, both the world-less inorganic as well as the world-deprived organic world.[11] These modes are distinctively human modes of appreciating their particular situatedness within and, at the same time, beyond the cage of nature.

The implication of these forms of comportment for human interactions with nonhuman animals is never fully developed. While Heidegger does focus on inanimate, worldless things and responsive ways of relating to them in lecture courses such as "On the Origin of the Work of Art" and "On the Thing,"[12] he is suspiciously quiet about responsive relationships between the human and the nonhuman, "world-deprived" animals. Heidegger's philosophical *Denkweg* could be characterized as the gradual replacement of anthropo- or *Dasein*-centrism with pastoral-centrism. The implication of making humans into the shepherds of, primarily, Being and, secondarily, inanimate objects and nonhuman animals, runs the risk of committing once again the original sin of humanism: as shepherding creatures, humans enjoy a privileged role as those who care for, oversee, and listen to a world inhabited by things and animals who are either worldless or deprived of world. While having declined the profession of director, now humans take their seat in the front row of the concert hall of

Being. As the guardians of speechless animals, only they can let them be, protect, and allow them to flourish.

In one last attempt to reanimate the promises of humanism in the form of a crypto-humanism, Heidegger draws on the entire arsenal of the history of Western metaphysics rather than daring to enter the promised new beginning. In "Letter on Humanism" he writes,

> it seems that the essence of the divine is closer to us than that of the alien living being [*Lebe-Wesen*]. Divine essence is closer to us in the sense of a distance of being, which as a distance is more familiar to our existing essence [*eksistenten Wesen*] than the hardly imaginable physical kinship to the animal. ... Being is essentially ... closer to the human being than any particular object [*jedes Seiende*], be it a rock, an animal, a work of art, a machine, be it an angel or God.[13]

It becomes apparent in this passage how Heidegger attempts to justify the elevation of the human to the status of a shepherd of the entirety of the nonhuman world. This hyperbolic reinscription of a privileging essence of being human, which sounds anachronistic in the present posthumanist *Zeitgeist*, repeats the claim that the nonhuman does not relate to Being as human beings do. Those creatures we might suspect to be familiar to us, turn out to be as distant from us as inanimate rocks or machines when compared to the far more proximate Being.

Heidegger justifies the human–nonhuman abyss with an eye to recovering the primordial meaning of defining humans as rational animals (*zoon logon echon*). In contrast to humans, who are in-the-world, nonhumans cannot engage in truth revelatory speech and are thus "worldless in their environment."[14] While humans enter the world in the form of a clearing in which different possibilities are revealed and manifest themselves to them in and through speech, animals are caged in by their environment. The ontic deficiency of being mute seemingly shared equally by all nonhuman animals makes them ontologically deaf to the voice of Being. To put the point sharply: nonhuman animals do not speak, therefore they do not listen, therefore they do not exist. The house of Being is a human house. Even if it was not made by them, only they provide the mood in which other animals can be captivated.[15]

Nonhuman animals are prevented entry to the existential concert for the sake of *Dasein* not only because they do not inhabit the house of language whose inhabitants are capable of world disclosure. Since nonhuman animals also lack a conscious relationship to their own mortality, they do not even die, but demise. Because they cannot relate to their death, they cannot run towards it, and thus fail to fulfill the preconditions of authentic existence. Heidegger does not leave any doubt that the question of Being, the *Seinsfrage*, is a distinctively human question, raised only by and for mortal beings capable of confronting and dying human deaths.

In addition to his banning of nonhuman animals from the symphony of Being, there is a second reason to be skeptical of the attempt to enlist Heidegger for the purpose of an anti-humanist ethics for saving the nonhuman world from humans. Not only was Heidegger resistant to developing explicit ethics, he also voiced reservations about the primacy of ethics to address the pathologies of the age. Ethics, as it is traditionally understood, assigns rights, and the concept of rights is deeply indebted to the metaphysical tradition. As Raymond Geuss argues in *Outside Ethics*, Heidegger's "constant goal was the permanent disabling of philosophy, and thus also of any philosophical ethics."[16] While aiming to recover an original experience of death and Being, Heidegger stresses that a turning to such authentic forms of existence is not, nor should be, in the power of any individual, group, or movement.

There are strong reasons to be skeptical about enlisting Heidegger for animal liberation movements as Frank Schalow has done.[17] Animal activism, one could claim from an anti-ethical and anti-activist stance developed by Heidegger, undermines the goal of preserving the environment by using calculative thinking and instrumental action and thus remaining inside the framework of Western rationality. By replacing an underestimation of humanity's destructive role with an overestimation of it, we witness an attempt to rescue moral agency for humanity. Humanity is once again described as worth preserving, and puts itself into the position of steering an animal liberation movement by way of deploying calculative strategies involving argumentation, shock effects, or other means of persuasion leading to forceful liberation.[18] Ethics, by definition, is a human pursuit, conducted by human beings. By assigning rights and personhood to the nonhuman, humanity (in the form of a group of people claiming to be its proper representation) makes itself into the only responsible judge and attorney of other creatures. In acts of retributive and restorative justice, animal liberators make the suffering of animal others into their own suffering, speaking for the animals rather than letting them be or letting them speak for themselves in their own ways.[19]

We have seen before that Heidegger's pastoral solution of caring for the nonhuman, while being more refined than the position of anti-humanist animal rights movements, also fails to escape this logic of assigning a privileged position to humanity. Heidegger distinguishes the human categorically (or ontologically) from the nonhuman. The rupture established between human life, animal life, and the inanimate material world is an absolute, abysmal one, making any true encounter or even comparison between these demarcated domains of Being impossible.[20] By way of driving a wedge between the proper essence of humans and the deprived world of nonhuman life, Heidegger bars himself from acknowledging existentially significant overlaps between them.

If we concede that such a deficient demarcation of ontological realms pervades not only Heidegger's thinking, but constitutes a generic feature of philosophical accounts in the Western canon, it could be helpful to turn to a tradition outside this canon. Perhaps an alternative account of the human–nonhuman relationship, allowing for human–nonhuman encounters, might thus be found. With Gadamer it could be argued that it is only in the confrontation and dialogue with the other that we learn to understand ourselves better.[21] Only by way of what

François Jullien calls a "detour through the East"[22] are formerly invisible blindspots revealed. However, the transcultural confrontation with radically different conceptual operations also opens up a constructive alternative of thematizing the human–nonhuman relationship.

Turning to the Chinese tradition of philosophical Daoism, I want to suggest, might open up a pathway, which does not start or end with identifying the weaknesses of Western metaphysics and gesturing to another beginning as Heidegger proposed. Rather than merely gesturing towards another beginning, the tradition of Daoism *embodies* a different, nonessentializing way of conceiving of the human–nonhuman relationship. As Eric Sean Nelson remarks about Daoism, "it is not the 'metaphysics of nature' that is so much at stake as it is an 'ethics of encounter' that does not exclude or trivialize the nonhuman."[23] We should add that such an "ethics of encounter" should not start from the ethical assumption shared by humanism, anti-humanism, and crypto-humanism, since Daoism is incommensurable with humanism, anti-humanism, and crypto-humanism. It constitutes a radical outside that provides an alternative to and points to blind spots of these seemingly oppositional, but at a deeper level complicit, strains of thinking the nonhuman.

The nonhuman in Daoism

A Daoist critique of Western conceptions of the nonhuman in general, and of Heidegger's crypto-humanism specifically, is particularly suggestive since Daoist thinking was not foreign to Heidegger. Recent scholarship has revealed that Daoism's importance for Heidegger's path of thinking should not be underestimated.[24] Not only did Heidegger spend a significant amount of energy translating sections of the *Daodejing* with one of his Chinese students during the summer of 1946 (the translation is now lost), he also recounts Daoist sayings in various writings, lectures, and letters, especially but not exclusively during the later period of his life. To mention just one of numerous recounted incidents, he referred to a Daoist story to illustrate that reflection, when properly understood, means "to awaken the sense for the useless."[25] It is not accidental that one of his guiding metaphors has been that of paths (*Wege*), alluding to the Daoist guiding concept of "the way" (*Dao*).

However, rather than stressing similarities, which has been the dominant tendency of recent approaches in comparative philosophy to Heidegger's Asian influences, a Daoist critique of Heidegger could point out blind spots in what I have been referring to as his "crypto-humanism," a humanism that assigns human beings the privileged and asymmetrical task of caring for the nonhuman by way of being their shepherds. First, such a transcultural critique helps us to better understand where Heidegger was reinscribing, rather than overcoming, certain prejudices of the specifically Western metaphysical tradition of humanism to which he remained bound despite his efforts to destruct this tradition from within.[26] Second, and more importantly, the Daoist alternative opens up a promising direction of constructively rethinking the human–nonhuman binary. A contemporary turn to Daoism overcomes the humanism–anti-humanism divide and the increasingly entrenched vocabulary of critical animal theory understood as an animal ethics.

While it is the case that early Chinese thought did not seek to categorically differentiate the human from the nonhuman as has been common in the zoological tradition from Aristotle through Lineaeus to Heidegger, it is misleading to assume that the construction of a harmonious cosmos with an amorphous human and nonhuman realm would thus be free of human domination over nonhuman animals. China's indigenous philosophical traditions do not prescribe that nonhuman animals should enjoy unconditional respect or even universal welfare. The proverb that the Chinese eat everything that can fly but airplanes and everything that has four legs but tables, reflects that the animal world is not attributed a special status that would protect it from satisfying human needs. In addition to being used for food, clothing, transportation, traditional Chinese medicine, and ritualistic sacrifice, the animal world figures prominently in tales and rituals. As Roel Sterckx has shown,

> the classic Chinese perception of the world did not insist on clear categorical or ontological boundaries between animals, human beings, and other creatures such as ghosts and spirits. The demarcation of the human and animal realms was not perceived to be permanent or constant, and the fixity of the species was not self-evident or desirable. Instead animals were viewed as part of an organic whole in which the mutual relationships among the species were characterized as contingent, continuous, and interdependent.[27]

Suffice it to say that there is no extensive debate in the classical Daoist and Confucian literature during the Warring States and Han dynasty periods about whether animals are or are not bearers of rights. At the same time, there is also no debate about distinct human rights privileging those over animal rights. The conception of rights could only emerge within Western traditions that assigned individuals as well as species a certain ontological position and rights ensuing from their position within the order of things. What is sometimes referred to as the pragmatic background of Chinese philosophy is an important reason for why there is no distinct form of animal ethics. The human–nonhuman relationship is part of the more general question of how the cosmos always already operates and how human beings can best adjust their lives to its dynamic rhythm. Rather than asking *what* an animal is and which rights he or she possesses, Warring States and Han writings pursue the question of *how* animals appear in specific, practical contexts. In the course of such "proto-phenomenological" (rather than ontological or ethical) investigations, it is taken for granted that human beings stand within nature and are not privileged in terms of possessing special rights and duties or assigning such rights and duties. The emphasis on cultivation and reaching normative excellence, which was propagated by the Confucian school, was seen with suspicion by the proto-Daoist, Zhuangzi, who lived during the fourth and third centuries BC.

Yet, despite the absence of anything resembling an animal ethics or an ontological determination of the relationship between humans and nonhumans, the presence of nonhuman animals, especially in the Daoist classics, is overwhelming. Standardly, these animals would be referred to as specific individuals engaged in specific actions and standing in specific relationships, rather than generic members of species with essential traits and properties. References to individual nonhuman animals serve to construct context-sensitive analogies to illustrate the working mechanisms of the cosmos and its myriad creatures. When the Daoist classics were written down during the fourth century BC, China was an extremely fertile land with a high level of biodiversity. The emphasis of the preserved texts is not on realistically rendering the fauna. It is thus no surprise that these texts are filled with laughing cicadas, mythical creatures like dragons, leviathans, the penumbra, the nine-tailed fox, a human-headed bird, the three-legged crow in the sun, rainbow serpents, giant wasps and ants, the phoenix, and the humanoid owl.[28] Animal depictions serve as imaginative projections and analogies to bring to light and come to terms with living experience, both human and nonhuman.

The four following stories about the interaction of human and nonhuman animals are taken from the fourth century BC *Zhuangzi* (莊子), which, in addition to the *Daodejing* (道德經), is the most important source of classical Daoist philosophy. The first one is the well-known story of the butterfly dream:

> Once Zhuang Zhou dreamt he was a butterfly, fluttering about joyfully just as a butterfly would. He followed his whims exactly as he liked and knew nothing about Zhuang Zhou. Suddenly he awoke, and there he was, the startled Zhuang Zhou in the flesh. He did not know if Zhou had been dreaming he was a butterfly, or if a butterfly was now dreaming it was Zhou. Surely, Zhou and a butterfly count as two distinct identities! Such is what we call the transformation of one thing into another.[29]

This story is seemingly similar to the passages of Descartes' *Meditations* on methodological doubt, in that a person is confronted by the difficulty of clearly distinguishing dream states from waking states.[30] However, this analogy fails upon closer examination. Whereas Descartes' doubt serves to erect the full certainty of an unquestionable and foundational rational (human) I, in the butterfly dream doubt is not dispelled. While Western philosophical traditions regard the dream as providing misleading illusions, the dream in ancient Chinese philosophical traditions makes a spiritual encounter possible.[31] Although Zhuangzi points out that butterflies and human beings are distinct, this distinction is not an ontological one. The experience of the dream leaves significant traces in who Zhuangzi takes himself to be. It is not only the doubt that he might be dreaming that is not dispelled; the doubt as to whether or not Zhuangzi could in fact be a butterfly and vice versa also persists.

As Hans-Georg Moeller emphasizes, drawing on Guo Xiang's commentary on this allegory, "the decisive turning point of the story is not remembering but forgetting."[32] All levels of experience, whether those in dreams or waking states, whether those of butterflies or human beings, are equivalent in terms of their internal claim to be taken seriously. The butterfly does not recall that it used to be Zhuangzi and the awakening Zhuangzi does not recall whether he is a dreaming butterfly or a philosopher. It is the forgetting of species difference that allows one to gain an insight into the dynamic nature of reality.

There is a distinct difference between the experiential field and capacities of philosophers and other human and nonhuman animals. As Graham Parkes has observed, the Zhuangzi makes ample use of animals who are not mammals in order to emphasize the larger degree of otherness in order to curb the temptation of anthropocentrism.[33] At the same time, there is a transition from one to the other field of experience, which is not perceived as a progression, regression, or transcendence. Rather, we witness changing forms of continuity and rupture. Nowhere does the text mention a static I which reflects on itself to then be transformed from dream to waking state.

The last line about the transformation of all things (*wuhua* 物化) attests to the omnipresence of change. Change is thought of outside the typical Western trichotomy of progress, regress, or circularity. Since there is no universal standard from which different episodes of change could be judged, irrespective of their specific contexts, change is not thought of as a convergence. The purpose is not to change into something or to reestablish an original state, but the change itself is taken to be a miraculous and adventurous passage from one form of living existence to another. This passage includes overlaps, ruptures, and jumps, as well as repetitions, continuities, and convergences.

In a second story, the dying Ziyu, when being asked if he resents his approaching departure, proclaims:

> Not at all. What is there to dislike? Perhaps he will transform my right arm into a crossbow pellet; thereby I'll be seeking out an owl to roast. Perhaps he will transform my ass into wheels and my spirit into a horse; thereby I'll be riding along—will I need any other vehicle?[34]

We might ask from where Ziyu's tone of contentment derives. For the Western reader, change itself does not seem to provide reasons to consider processes of change as processes necessarily invoking happiness in the creature undergoing these processes. Indeed Zhuangzi has been read as promoting a cheerful indifference with regard to what we would consider the threat of suffering, pain, and loss. The point of Ziyu is neither the "overcoming of the human" (Nietzsche) nor the "becoming animal" (Deleuze and Guattari) that Irvin Goh has suggested.[35] Both of these concepts remain within a teleological form of rationality typical of the West. Such forms of rationalizing are incapable of deriving fulfillment from the process rather than from the goal a process strives toward. In this as well as in many other stories, the reader or listener is reminded of the omnipresence of *ateleological* transformation processes, including living and dying.

As Roger Ames states:

> Zhuangzi's response to the misgivings one might have about "death" is that there is real comfort, and indeed even a religious awe, in the recognition that assuming the form of one kind of thing gives way to becoming another in a ceaseless adventure. Such a recognition presumably stimulates empathetic feelings and compassion for other creatures in a shared, continuous environment.[36]

There is neither an anxiety about nor a running towards death in Ziyu's story, nor even a sense of incompleteness due to being thrown into a world devoid of ends that would give it meaning. Rather, we witness a full absorption into the process of change in which neither the human nor nonhuman forms of existence enjoy preeminence. Every form of existence comes with a set of capacities it can perform and rejoices in exercising and sometimes cultivating these capacities. There is no linear process of change from or change towards, as there is no point of departure or final telos. The process is characterized by contingent transitions, states of being human, animal, plant, or inanimate object. Since there is no conception of a transcendent soul or a universal hierarchy of skills, the focus is on the process of transformation itself. Since this transformation is inexhaustible and connects different beings through the vital force, *qi* (氣), engaging in it rather than opposing it is considered to be delightful and energizing.

In the third story in which the nonhuman figures prominently, we are confronted with what is usually thought of as one of the most instrumental and horrific relationships between humans and nonhumans—that of butchery:

> The cook was carving up an ox for King Hui of Liang. Wherever his hand smacked it, wherever his shoulder leaned into it, wherever his foot braced it, wherever his knee pressed it, the thwacking tones of flesh falling from bone would echo, the knife would whiz through with its resonant thwing, each stroke ringing out the perfect note, attuned to the "Dance of the Mulberry Grove" or the "Jingshou Chorus" of the ancient sage-kings. A good cook changes his blade once a year: he slices. An ordinary cook changes his blade once a month: he hacks. I have been using this same blade for nineteen years, cutting up thousands of oxen, and yet it is still as sharp as the day it came off the whetstone. For the joints have spaces within them, and the very edge of the blade has no thickness at all. When what has no thickness enters into an empty space, it is vast and open with more than enough room for the play of the blade. That is why my knife is still as sharp as if it had just come off the whetstone, even after nineteen years.[37]

The story depicts the act of butchery achieved to its fullest. A seemingly instrumental activity of processing dead meat for the purpose of cooking and devouring is transformed into an art. The skill mastered by butcher Ding does not consist in dissecting an object and applying a method, but in intuitively becoming in tune with the body of the dead ox. By way of encountering the cadaver intuitively rather than scrutinizing it with his eyes only, Ding has learned to transform hacking into slicing and slicing into carving. Butchery was not a well-respected profession in ancient China anymore than it is today. It is all the more telling that the duke who visits the butcher is impressed by the latter's effortless mastery in cutting oxen and applauds him for having instructed him not only in the art of butchery, but in the art of nourishing life.

By forgetting himself and being fully absorbed in activity, the trained hand of cook Ding acts and reacts spontaneously and with a precision that avoids friction or loss of power and efficacy. Thus his knife does not lose any of its sharpness after nineteen years of service. It cuts and slices only in the empty spaces in between the bones, the natural joints that have been the moving centers of the ox and are now the focal points for the act of meat carving. The portrayed action presents an alternative to either instrumental objectification or ethically motivated empathy in relationship to the nonhuman. The butcher feels one with the ox, not in an ethical but in an aesthetic sense. Without will or intention, cook Ding imitates the effortless way of the Dao rather than implanting his will on the dead body. The butcher achieves the task Heidegger considered to be ultimately doomed to failure. He is capable of transposing himself into the dead body of the ox.

The fourth story, one which Heidegger knew well and recited as early as 1930,[38] is the story of the happiness of fish:

> Zhuangzi and Huizi were strolling along the bridge over the Hao River. Zhuangzi said, "The minnows swim about so freely, following the openings wherever they take them. Such is the happiness of fish." Huizi said, "You are not a fish, so whence do you know the happiness of fish?" Zhuangzi said, "You are not I, so whence do you know I don't know the happiness of fish?" Huizi said, "I am not you, to be sure, so I don't know what it is to be you. But by the same token, since you are certainly not a fish, my point about your inability to know the happiness of fish stands intact." Zhuangzi said, "Let's go back to the starting point. You said, 'Whence do you know the happiness of fish?' Since your question was premised on your knowing that I know it, I must have known it from here, up above the Hao River."[39]

In this fable there are again different levels of experience just as in the butterfly dream and the tale of the dying Ziyu. Zhuangzi and Huizi engage in an aimless walk along the bridge. Zhuangzi enters the experiential field of the fish and conveys to his friend that these fish must be happy since they swim around freely in the water. Here, unlike in the stories about the butterfly dream and the skilled butcher, we witness direct affective communication between human and nonhuman that is not, however, an empathy of a moral kind. What Zhuangzi experiences is a familiarity and a blending rather than a distinct exchange of information between the human and the nonhuman experiential fields.

There is an intended ambiguity in the Chinese characters serving as the title of this story. The happiness of fish, "yu zhi le," leaves open the question of whether what is intended is the joy of the fish or the joy which is brought about by seeing the fish swimming freely in the water. The intended ambiguity between the subjective and the objective genitive is a grammatical tool used to emphasize that the joy of the fish directly translates into Zhuangzi's joy without the two subjective fields communicating information in propositional language.

Zhuangzi's friend responds by doubting that human beings can know how fish feel since they are not fish. Zhuangzi dispels this doubt not by argument but by raising a counter question. His friend Huizi cannot know that he doesn't know what it is like to be a fish and his question already presupposes that Huizi knows that Zhuangzi knows. The point of the story is that Zhuangzi knows about the happiness of the fish not based on inductive reasoning but because he is doing something analogous to what they are doing even if he is not them. The character "you" (遊), which is used to refer to the act of wallowing or wandering at ease, occurs again in the case of the fish since it also means to swim and to play.[40] In this story we see that fish are not considered to be captivated or caged by the water that constitutes their environment. Neither is their experiential field closed off to humans because they cannot breathe under water. Rather, there is an intuitive communication or understanding between human beings and fish.

All four stories make a distinct point about the human–nonhuman relationship. The butterfly dream illustrates the nature of humans and butterflies and the irreducible transience of the world; the dying Ziyu illustrates that this transience is not to be seen as unfortunate, but as a delightful process; the anecdote about cook Ding carving an ox shows that intuitive knowledge and the principle of least effort provide for maximal competence; finally, the story about the happy fish emphasizes the potential for affective, non-inferential communication between nonhumans and humans.

These four stories do not present us with an ontology or an ethics. They do not establish a qualitative hierarchy between the human and the nonhuman. The relationship between species is interpreted as dynamic, contingent, and continuous while communicability in between species is possible due to an overlap of experiential horizons. Propositional language is not a necessary condition for such communication since it only marks one specific kind of communication.

Rather than privileging humans, the capacity of using language and discursive reason is interpreted as often standing in the way of unobstructed experience. This is expressed in the famous fish trap allegory: "words are there for the intent. When you have got hold of the intent, you forget the words."[41] The discursive and fixating addendum to the human mind is an obstacle which is in need of being limited at times if one wants to fully appreciate an irreducibly complex and transient reality. Daoism thus provides us not only with theories but with invitations to practically engage in various practices of unlearning rather than perfecting discursive reasoning. These practices range from engaging in art, humor, and idling to wandering and Tai Chi Chuan.

Neither Heidegger nor Daoist philosophers such as Zhuangzi develop an explicit ethics based on assigning rights to nonhuman beings. They were critical of normative discourse and saw it as a symptom of, rather than a solution to a problem. They identified this problem as an anthropocentric trust in assigning rather than acknowledging specific forms of significance in other living and dead things. Turning to a Daoist reading of Heidegger's late philosophy might help us to gain a more imaginative vocabulary to rethink the relationship between the human and the nonhuman in ways which are not from the outset couched in a humanist or posthumanist vocabulary. Rather than perfecting the world or developing pastoral strategies of caring, an encounter with the nonhuman might begin with the insight that humans, just like other animals, are at their best when they do not strive to be better.

Notes

1 Bruce V. Foltz, *Inhabiting the Earth: Heidegger, Environmental Ethics, and the Metaphysics of Nature* (Atlantic Highlands, NJ: Humanity Books, 1995). Also see George S. Cave, "Animals, Heidegger, and the Right to Life," *Environmental Ethics* 4, no. 3 (1982), 249–54 as well as Frank Schalow, "Who Speaks for the Animals? Heidegger and the Question of Animal Welfare," *Environmental Ethics* 22, no. 3 (2000): 259–71 as well as Craig Anthony Condella, "The Question concerning Ecology: Heidegger's Appropriation of Aristotle on the Way to an Environmental Ethic," dissertation Fordham University (2005).

2 Arnold Gehlen, *Der Mensch: Seine Natur und seine Stellung in der Welt* (Berlin: Junker und Dünnhaupt, 1940).

3 Peter Sloterdijk writes:

> humanity itself consists in choosing to develop one's nature through the media of taming, and to forswear bestialization. The meaning of this choice of media is to wean oneself from one's own bestiality and to establish a distance between yourself and the dehumanizing escalation of the roaring mob in the area.

Peter Sloterdijk, "Rules for the Human Zoo: A Response to the Letter on Humanism," *Environment and Planning D: Society and Space* 27, no. 1 (2009): 16.

4 Nick Bostrom, "A History of Transhumanist Thought," *Journal of Evolution and Technology* 14, no. 1 (2005): 1–25.

5 The following interpretation of Heidegger's account of the nonhuman world is indebted to: Matthew Calarco, *Zoographies: The Question of the Animal from Heidegger to Derrida* (New York: Columbia University Press, 2008); Stuart Elden, "Heidegger's Animals," *Continental Philosophy Review* 39, no. 3 (2006): 273–91; William McNeill, "Life Beyond the Organism: Animal Being in Heidegger's Freiburg Lectures, 1929–1930," in *Animal Others: On Ethics, Ontology, and Animal Life*, ed. H. Peter Steeves (Albany: State University of New York Press, 2000); and Frank Schalow, "Who Speaks for the Animals? Heidegger and the Question of Animal Welfare," *Environmental Ethics* 22, no. 3 (2000): 259–71.

6 Martin Heidegger, "Br i.e. füberden Humanismus," in Martin Heidegger, Wegmarken, ed. F.-W. von Herrmann (Frankfurt: Klostermann, 2nd edn., 1996), Gesamtausgabe (GA) 9, 313–64, translated by Frank A. Capuzzi and J. Glenn Gray as "Letter on Humanism," in Martin Heidegger, *Basic Writings* (New York: Harper & Row, 1977).

7 Martin Heidegger, *Die Grundbegriffe der Metaphysik: Welt-Endlichkeit-Einsamkeit*, Gesamtausgabe (GA) 29 (Frankfurt: Vittorio Klostermann, 1983), 263. Heidegger does not raise the question of where plant life is to be situated. In contrast to inanimate objects, it develops and, in a way, reacts to its world. As far as I can see, this lakuna in the tripartide division has not been discussed in the secondary literature, which has, by and large, been focusing on the human–animal distinction.

8 Jakob von Uexküll, *A Foray into the Worlds of Animals and Humans: With A Theory of Meaning* (trans. Joseph D. O'Neil) (Minneapolis, MN: University of Minnessota Press, 2011).
9 McNeill, "Life Beyond the Organism."
10 See Note 1.
11 Ute Guzzoni, *Der andere Heidegger: Überlegungen zu seinem späteren Denken* (Freiburg and Munich: Alber, 2009).
12 Martin Heidegger, "The Origin of the Work of Art," in Martin Heidegger, *Off the Beaten Track* (Cambridge: Cambridge University Press, 2002); Martin Heidegger, "The Thing," in Martin Heidegger, *Poetry, Language and Thought* (New York: Harper Row, 1971).
13 Martin Heidegger, "Brief über den Humanismus," 326–31.
14 Ibid., 326.
15 Simon Glendinning, "Heidegger and the Question of Animality," *International Journal of Philosophical Studies* 4, no. 1 (1996): 75–82.
16 Raymond Geuss, *Outside Ethics* (Princeton, NJ: Princeton University Press, 2005), 57.
17 Frank Schalow, "Who Speaks for the Animals? Heidegger and the Question of Animal Welfare," *Environmental Ethics* 22, no. 3 (2000): 259–71.
18 Eric S. Nelson, "Responding to Heaven and Earth: Daoism, Heidegger and Ecology," *Environmental Philosophy* 1, no. 2 (2004): 65–74.
19 Thanks to Chloë Taylor for pointing out parallels to arguments developed by contemporary critics of a rights-based approach to questions of animal ethics. These critics include Kelly Oliver, *Animal Lessons* (New York: Columbia University Press, 2009: 25–50), as well as Val Plumwood, "Nature, Self, and Gender: Feminism, Environmental Philosophy, and the Critique of Rationalism," *Hypatia* 6, no. 1 (1991): 3–27. Oliver and Plumwood rightly emphasize that in excluding people or groups of people based on their race or sex, tradition has typically depicted them "as animals." If animals are now seen and treated "as" or "like humans" in an effort to liberate them, the tradition of setting up "the human" as the normative yardstick is being continued. A typical strategy of analogizing animals and humans has been to categorize nonhuman animals according to whether or not they share specific traits considered to be essential to humans (e.g., sentience, rationality, goal-directedness, a sense of well-being, a capacity for anticipation and memory).
20 Matthew Calarco writes:

> The difference between the Being of human beings and that of animals marks a gap and a rupture that is utterly untraversable. In this sense, the animal's world can never be compared *with* the human world, only *to* the human world (and vice versa).
>
> (Calarco, *Zoographies*, 22)

21 Hans-Georg Gadamer, *Truth and Method*, 2nd rev. edn. (trans. J. Weinsheimer and D. G. Marshall) (New York: Crossroad, 2004).
22 François Jullien, *Detour and Access: Strategies of Meaning in China and Greece* (New York: Zone Books, 2000).
23 I would add that such an "ethics of encounter" is radically different from what is often understood by ethics, i.e., an occupation with outlining principles, rights, and duties. Daoist ethics, if one does want to use that term at all, begins with a phenomenology of what it means to be a natural being, which relates to other natural beings. Eric Sean Nelson, "Responding with Dao: Early Daoist Ethics and the Environment," *Philosophy East and West* 59, no. 3 (2009): 299.
24 Katrin Froese, *Nietzsche, Heidegger, and Daoist Thought: Crossing Paths In-Between* (Albany, NY: State University of New York Press, 2006); Reinhard May, *Heidegger's Hidden Sources: East Asian Influences on his Work* (London: Routledge, 1996);

Graham Parkes, ed., *Heidegger and Asian Thought* (Honolulu, HI: University of Hawaii Press, 1987).

25 Cited by Lin Ma, *Heidegger on East–West Dialogue: Anticipating the Event* (New York and London: Routledge, 2008), 122. Also see Otto Pöggeler, *Neue Wege mit Heidegger* (Munich and Freiburg: Karl Alber, 1992), 387–410.

26 Heidegger proposes two ways of deconstructing Western metaphysics. The one goes back to its very beginnings or even before those beginnings, while the other attempts a dialogue with traditions not standing in the history of Western metaphysics.

27 Roel Sterckx, *The Animal and the Daemon in Early China* (Alban, NY: State University of New York Press, 2002), 5.

28 E.N. Anderson and Lisa Raphals, "Daoism and Animals," in *A Communion of Subjects: Animals in Religion, Science & Ethics*, eds. Paul Waldau and Kimberley C. Patton (New York: Columbia University Press, 2006), 275–90.

29 Zhuangzi, *Zhuangzi: The Essential Writings* (trans. Brook Ziporyn) (Indianapolis, IN: Hackett, 2009), 2:48.

30 René Descartes, *Meditations on First Philosophy: With Selections from the Objections and Replies* (ed. John Cottingham) (Cambridge: Cambridge University Press, 1996).

31 Sterckx, *The Animal and the Daemon in Early China*, 215.

32 Hans-Georg Moeller, *Daoism Explained: From the Dream of the Butterfly to the Fishnet Allegory* (Perus, IL: Open Court Publishing Company, 2004), 47.

33 Graham Parkes, "Nietzsche and Zhuangzi: Ein Zwischenspiel," in *Komparative Philosophie: Begegnungen östlicher und westlicher Denkwege*, eds. Rolf Elberfeld, Johann Kreuzer, John Minford, and Günter Wohlfart (Munich: Fink Verlag, 1998), 216.

34 Zhuangzi, *Zhuangzi: The Essential Writings*, 6:39.

35 Irving Goh, "Chuang Tzu's Becoming-Animal," *Philosophy East and West* 61, no. 1 (2011): 110–33.

36 Roger Ames, "Human Exceptionalism versus Cultural Elitism," in *A Communion of Subjects: Animals in Religion, Science & Ethics*, eds. Paul Waldau and Kimberley C. Patton (New York: Columbia University Press, 2006), 313.

37 Zhuangzi, *Zhuangzi: The Essential Writings*, 3:3–3:4.

38 Pöggeler, *Neue Wege mit Heidegger*, 394.

39 Zhuangzi, *Zhuangzi: The Essential Writings*, 2:18.

40 Günter Wohlfart, *Die Kunst des Lebens und andere Künste: Skurrile Skizzen zu einem eurodaoistischen Ethos ohne Moral* (Berlin: Parerga, 2005), 176–9.

41 Zhuangzi, *Zhuangzi: The Essential Writings*, 114. See Jean Francois Billeter, *Lecons sur Tschouang-Tseu* (Paris: Editions Allia, 2009), 25–28 as well as Günter Wohlfart, Zhuangzi Lectures, 47–50, available at www.guenter-wohlfart.de.

Bibliography

Ames, Roger. "Human Exceptionalism versus Cultural Elitism." In *A Communion of Subjects: Animals in Religion, Science and Ethics*. Edited by Paul Waldau and Kimberley C. Patton, 311–24. New York: Columbia University Press, 2006.

Anderson, E.N. and Raphals, Lisa. "Daoism and Animals." In *A Communion of Subjects: Animals in Religion, Science & Ethics*. Edited by Paul Waldau and Kimberley C. Patton, 275–90. New York: Columbia University Press, 2006.

Billeter, Jean Francois. *Lecons sur Tschouang-Tseu.* Paris: Editions Allia, 2009.

Bostrom, Nick. "A History of Transhumanist Thought." *Journal of Evolution and Technology* 14, no. 1 (2005): 1–25.

Calarco, Matthew. *Zoographies: The Question of the Animal from Heidegger to Derrida.* New York: Columbia University Press, 2008.

Cave, George S. "Animals, Heidegger, and the Right to Life." *Environmental Ethics* 4, no. 3 (1982): 249–54.

Condella, Craig Anthony. "The Question concerning Ecology: Heidegger's Appropriation of Aristotle on the Way to an Environmental Ethic." Dissertation Fordham University (2005).

Descartes, René, *Meditations on First Philosophy: With Selections from the Objections and Replies*. Edited by John Cottingham. Cambridge: Cambridge University Press, 1996.

Elden, Stuart. "Heidegger's Animals." *Continental Philosophy Review* 39, no. 3 (2006): 273–91.

Foltz, Bruce V. *Inhabiting the Earth: Heidegger, Environmental Ethics, and the Metaphysics of Nature*. Amherst, NY: Humanity Books, 1995.

Froese, Katrin. *Nietzsche, Heidegger, and Daoist Thought: Crossing Paths In-Between.* Albany, NY: State University of New York Press, 2006.

Gehlen, Arnold. *Der Mensch: Seine Natur und seine Stellung in der Welt.* Berlin: Junker und Dünnhaupt, 1940.

Geuss, Raymond. *Outside Ethics*. Princeton, NJ: Princeton University Press, 2005.

Glendinning, Simon. "Heidegger and the Question of Animality." *International Journal of Philosophical Studies* 4, no. 1 (1996): 75–82.

Goh, Irving. "Chuang Tzu's Becoming-Animal." *Philosophy East and West* 61, no. 1 (2011): 110–33.

Guzzoni, Ute. *Der andere Heidegger: Überlegungen zu seinem späteren Denken.* Freiburg and Munich: Alber, 2009.

Heidegger, Martin. "Br i.e. füberden Humanismus." In Martin Heidegger, *Wegmarken.* Edited by F.-W. von Herrmann. Frankfurt: Klostermann, 2nd edn., 1996, Gesamtausgabe 9, 313–64, translated by Frank A. Capuzzi and J. Glenn Gray as "Letter on Humanism," in Martin Heidegger, *Basic Writings*. New York: Harper & Row, 1977.

Heidegger, Martin. *Die Grundbegriffe der Metaphysik: Welt-Endlichkeit-Einsamkeit*, Gesamtausgabe 29. Frankfurt: Vittorio Klostermann, 1983.

Heidegger, Martin. "The Origin of the Work of Art." In *Off the Beaten Track*. Edited and translated by Julian Young, 1–56. Cambridge: Cambridge University Press, 2002.

Heidegger, Martin. "The Thing." In *Poetry, Language and Thought*. Edited and translated by Albert Hofstadter, 161–84. New York: Harper Row, 1971.

Jullien, François. *Detour and Access: Strategies of Meaning in China and Greece*. New York: Zone Books, 2000.

Ma, Lin. *Heidegger on East–West Dialogue: Anticipating the Event.* New York and London: Routledge, 2008.

McNeill, William. "Life Beyond the Organism: Animal Being in Heidegger's Freiburg Lectures, 1929–1930." In *Animal Others: On Ethics, Ontology, and Animal Life*. Edited by H. Peter Steeves, 197–248. Albany, NY: State University of New York Press, 2000.

May, Reinhard. *Heidegger's Hidden Sources: East Asian Influences on his Work.* London: Routledge 1996.

Moeller, Hans-Georg. *Daoism Explained: From the Dream of the Butterfly to the Fishnet Allegory.* Perus, IL: Open Court Publishing Company, 2004.

Nelson, Eric Sean. "Responding to Heaven and Earth: Daoism, Heidegger and Ecology." *Environmental Philosophy* 1, no. 2 (2004): 65–74.

Nelson, Eric Sean. "Responding with Dao: Early Daoist Ethics and the Environment." *Philosophy East and West* 59, no. 3 (2009): 294–316.

Oliver, Kelly. *Animal Ethics*. New York: Columbia University Press, 2009.

Parkes, Graham, ed. *Heidegger and Asian Thought*. Honolulu, HI: University of Hawaii Press, 1987.

Parkes, Graham. "Nietzsche and Zhuangzi: Ein Zwischenspiel." In *Komparative Philosophie: Begegnungen östlicher und westlicher Denkwege*. Edited by Rolf Elberfeld, Johann Kreuzer, John Minford, and Günter Wohlfart, 213–22. Munich: Fink Verlag, 1998.

Plumwood, Val. "Nature, Self, and Gender: Feminism, Environmental Philosophy, and the Critique of Rationalism." *Hypatia* 6, no. 1 (1991): 3–27.

Pöggeler, Otto. *Neue Wege mit Heidegger*. Munich and Freiburg: Karl Alber, 1992.

Schalow, Frank. "Who Speaks for the Animals? Heidegger and the Question of Animal Welfare." *Environmental Ethics* 22, no. 3 (2000): 259–71.

Sloterdijk, Peter. "Rules for the Human Zoo: A Response to the Letter on Humanism." *Environment and Planning D: Society and Space* 27, no. 1 (2009): 12–28.

Sterckx, Roel. *The Animal and the Daemon in Early China*. Albany, NY: State University of New York Press, 2002.

von Uexküll, Jakob. *A Foray into the Worlds of Animals and Humans: With A Theory of Meaning*. Translated by Joseph D. O'Neil. Minneapolis, MN: University of Minnesota Press, 2011.

Wohlfart, Günter. *Die Kunst des Lebens und andere Künste: Skurrile Skizzen zu einem eurodaoistischen Ethos ohne Moral*. Berlin: Parerga, 2005.

Zhuangzi, *Zhuangzi: The Essential Writings*. Translated by Brook Ziporyn. Indianapolis, IN: Hackett, 2009.

5 The argument for *Ahiṃsā* in the *Anuśāsanaparvan* of the *Mahābhārata*

Christopher Framarin

Introduction

The *Anuśāsanaparvan* (*Book of Teachings*) of the *Mahābhārata* contains one of the most extensive discussions of vegetarianism and *ahiṃsā* (non-harm) in Indian literature (13.114–17). In this chapter, I assess the moral implications of this discussion. In the first section of the chapter, I argue that the passage entails that animals have moral standing. That is, the passage entails that there are possible circumstances in which human agents morally ought to consider animals in deciding what to do. In the second section, I argue that the passage entails that animals have *direct* moral standing, in virtue of their sentience. That is, the passage entails that there are possible circumstances in which human agents morally ought to consider animals *for their own sakes*—independent of their relations to other entities, including human beings—in deciding what to do, because they are capable of experiencing pleasure and pain. In the third section, I argue that the passage also implies that animals have direct moral standing because they are alive, and because they are capable of varying degrees of health, physical functioning, freedom from constraint, and so on.

The moral standing of animals

In chapters 114–17 of the *Anuśāsanaparvan* (*Book of Teachings*) of the *Mahābhārata*, *Bhīṣma* offers Yudhiṣṭhira an extensive argument in favor of vegetarianism and *ahiṃsā* (non-harm) toward animals more generally. The most salient reasons offered in favor of *ahiṃsā* toward animals are prudential. The agent who avoids *hiṃsā* (harm) toward animals attains pleasure, heaven, long life, health, strength, perfect physical form, safety, protection, praise, intelligence, beauty, wealth, fearlessness, auspicious marks, memory, and so on. The agent who causes *hiṃsā* to animals, in contrast, experiences pain, hell, death, disease, powerlessness, vulnerability, delusion, indolence, ruin, fear, and so on.

It might be tempting to conclude from this that all of the reasons to avoid harm to animals are strictly prudential. If this is right, then the passage denies that animals have moral standing. To say that an entity has moral standing is to say that there are possible circumstances in which agents morally ought to consider the entity in deciding what to do.[1] If there are possible circumstances in which agents morally ought to consider an entity in deciding what to do, then there are possible circumstances in which agents have moral reasons to consider the entity in deciding what to do. If all of the reasons to avoid harm to animals are strictly prudential, however, then there are no moral reasons to avoid harm to animals, and animals lack moral standing.

While no one, as far as I know, has advanced this interpretation of this passage in particular, a number of authors attribute it to other, related passages and texts. Lance E. Nelson, for example, claims that the *Bhagavadgītā*—which constitutes a portion of the *Bhīṣmaparvan* (Book of Bhīṣma) of the *Mahābhārata*—endorses *ahiṃsā* "out of concern for the private karmic well-being of the actor."[2] Klaus K. Klostermaier draws the same conclusion about the *Manusmṛti*: "Manu obviously does not think 'ecologically:' the rules which prescribe non-harming of living beings aim towards individual spiritual gain and not towards conservation of the environment."[3] Basant K. Lal defends the same position with regard to Hinduism more generally:

> The Hindu recommendation to cultivate a particular kind of attitude toward animals [namely, *ahiṃsā*] is based *not* on considerations about the *animal* as such but on considerations about how the development of this attitude is a part of the purificatory steps that bring men to the path of *mokṣa* [*sic*] [liberation].[4]

Swami Nirvedananda,[5] V.K. Bharadwaja,[6] Bryan G. Norton,[7] J. Baird Callicott,[8] Arvind Sharma,[9] Rita DasGupta Sherma,[10] Patricia Y. Mumme,[11] Bruce M. Sullivan,[12] M.K. Sridhar and Purushottama Bilimoria,[13] and others endorse this interpretation of various Hindu texts and traditions as well.

The most straightforward problem with interpreting the dialogue between Bhīṣma and Yudhiṣṭhira in this way is that the passage consistently characterizes *ahiṃsā* and *hiṃsā* in moral terms. Those who subsist on living beings are described as "morally blameworthy people" (*pāpāḥ … upajīvinaḥ*) (13.116.23),[14] exhibiting fundamental vices. "From killing a living being (*jantuṃ*) for the sake of the eater, that most vile person (*puruṣādhamaḥ*) accrues great demerit (*mahādoṣakaras*)" (13.116.44).[15] "The manner of meat-eating *rākṣasas* (demons) is dishonest, cheating, and violent" (13.116.27).[16] "There is no person meaner or crueler (*nāsti kṣudrataras … nṛśaṃsataro naraḥ*) than the person who desires to increase his own meat by means of the meat of others" (13.117.10).[17]

Additionally, the action of eating meat is itself described as *pāpa* (a moral wrongdoing), "the turning away from which produces very great merit (*sumahān dharmo*)" (13.116.46).[18] This suggests that the related word *doṣa*, which is used nearly a dozen times in the passage to characterize meat eating, the praise of meat eating, killing, and consenting to an animal's killing (13.115.10, 14, 116.26, 36, 39, 43, 44, 13.117.12, 19), implies not only fault, but moral fault in particular—moral demerit.

This implies that *ahiṃsā* and *hiṃsā* tend to produce merit and demerit, respectively, at least in part because they are (at least prima facie) morally right and wrong, respectively. This (moral) merit and demerit take the forms of various benefits and harms to the agents who performed the actions that produced them. The fact that an agent will experience these results constitutes a reason for the agent to avoid harm to animals. Hence the agent does indeed have a prudential reason to avoid harming animals. The prudential reason to avoid harming animals arises, however, at least in part because there is a pre-existing moral reason to avoid harming animals. Hence the passage attributes moral standing to animals.

Sentience as a basis for the direct moral standing of animals

It should be kept in mind that the claim that animals have moral standing does not entail that animals have direct moral standing. To say that an entity has moral standing is to say that there are possible circumstances in which agents morally ought to consider the entity in deciding what to do. To say that an entity has direct moral standing, however, is to say that there are possible circumstances in which agents morally ought to consider the entity for its own sake in deciding what to do. The alternative is that the passage attributes merely indirect moral standing to animals. To say that an entity has indirect moral standing is to say that there are possible circumstances in which agents morally ought to consider the entity in deciding what to do, not for the sake of the entity itself, but for the sake of other entities.

There are reasons, however, to think that the passage attributes direct moral standing to animals. As I've said, the passage claims that *ahiṃsā* and *hiṃsā* are (at least prima facie) morally right and wrong, respectively. As a consequence of these actions, an agent typically accrues merit and demerit, respectively.[19] And merit and demerit tend to take the forms of various benefits and harms to the agent. These connections can be diagrammed as follows:

(A)

ahiṃsā	merit	benefits to agent
hiṃsā	demerit	harms to agent

As I mentioned above, Bhīṣma offers a long list of benefits and harms that accrue to the agent as a result of *ahiṃsā* and *hiṃsā*. One of the most fundamental benefits that accrue to the agent is *sukha* (pleasure/happiness). One of the most fundamental harms that accrue to the agent is *duḥkha* (pain/suffering).[20] "The person who harms harmless creatures with a stick, wanting pleasure (*sukham*) for himself, he, having died, is not happy (*sukhī*)" (13.114.5).[21] "The person who treats all living creatures like himself, stick laid down, anger subdued, he, having died, becomes happy (*sukham*)" (13.114.6).[22] "And the person not eating any meat for one month, having avoided all pains (*sarvaduḥkāni*), he is happy (*sukhī*)" (13.116.62).[23]

Bhīṣma also repeatedly mentions heaven and hell as consequences of *ahiṃsā* and *hiṃsā*, which are normally characterized in terms of unalloyed pleasure and pain. "Those great souls who act according to this splendid, highest *dharma* characterized by *ahiṃsā*, they live in the highest heaven (*nākapṛṣṭhe*)" (13.116.72).[24] "The foolish person, who, by the paths of reverence, sacrifice, and Vedic rituals, kills a living being (*jantuṃ*) longing for its meat, he surely goes to hell (*naraka*)" (13.116.45).[25] So in many cases, the merit and demerit that agents accrue as a result of *ahiṃsā* and *hiṃsā* eventually take the form of pleasure and pain. The more general diagram (A) above might be adapted to read:

(B)

ahiṃsā	merit	pleasure
hiṃsā	demerit	pain

If the pleasure and pain that accrue to the agent as a result of *ahiṃsā* and *hiṃsā*, are suitable forms of merit and demerit, then pleasure has value, pain has disvalue, and pleasure is more valuable than pain. Pleasure is a suitable form of merit only if it has value, and pain is a suitable form of demerit only if it has disvalue. If pleasure were not more valuable than pain, then the fact that merit takes the form of pleasure, and demerit takes the form of pain, would be quite mysterious. So pleasure and pain have value and disvalue.

The value and disvalue of pleasure and pain are either wholly extrinsic, or at least partly intrinsic. The intrinsic value or disvalue of something is the value that it has as an end, independent of the further ends to which it is a means. The extrinsic value or disvalue of something is the value that something has as a means to further ends.[26] Hence, pleasure and pain have value and disvalue either wholly as means to further ends, or at least in part as ends.

If pleasure and pain have merely extrinsic value and disvalue, then their value and disvalue derive exclusively from some further end(s). The only seemingly plausible candidate for a further end from which pleasure might derive all of its value is the attainment of *mokṣa*. And the only seemingly plausible candidate for a further end from which pain might derive all of its disvalue is the postponement of *mokṣa*. This interpretation can be diagrammed as follows:

(B′)

ahiṃsā	merit	pleasure	*mokṣa*
hiṃsā	demerit	pain	postponement of *mokṣa*

I argue elsewhere, however, that this position is implausible.[27] To put the objection succinctly, if there are general correlations between pleasure, pain, the attainment of *mokṣa*, and the postponement of *mokṣa*, they are between pain and progress toward *mokṣa*, and pleasure and the postponement of *mokṣa*, rather than the reverse. An experience of pain tends to remind us of the inevitable suffering involved in the *saṃsāric* process, and thereby motivates us to escape *saṃsāra* and attain *mokṣa*. An experience of pleasure, in contrast, veils this fact about the cycle of rebirth, and thereby motivates the entity to remain within *saṃsāra*, and hence postpone the attainment of *mokṣa*.

Additionally, according to many texts and traditions, a pain experience lessens the negative karmic burden of the one who suffers it—and hence lessens a primary obstacle to the attainment of *mokṣa*. A pleasure experience, in contrast, does not have this benefit. Hence the following diagram is more accurate than B′:

(B″)

ahiṃsā	merit	pleasure	postponement of *mokṣa*
hiṃsā	demerit	pain	*mokṣa*

If this is right, then pain is more valuable than pleasure, and pleasure and pain are not suitable forms of merit and demerit, respectively. Hence the value and disvalue of pleasure and pain cannot derive exclusively from the intrinsic value of the attainment of *mokṣa* and the intrinsic disvalue of the postponement of *mokṣa*. Hence the value and disvalue of pleasure and pain are at least partly intrinsic.

This is not to say that pain is never counter-productive to the attainment of *mokṣa*. It might be that there are certain thresholds of pain, the crossing of which makes progress toward *mokṣa* more difficult, or even impossible. Nor is it to say that pleasure is never a means to the attainment of *mokṣa*. It might be that the pleasure that a student receives from Vedic study, for example, motivates him to further religious pursuits that are a means to *mokṣa*.

The point, however, is that in order for diagram B′ to be plausible, there must be relatively tight correlations between pleasure and progress toward *mokṣa*, on the one hand, and pain and the postponement of *mokṣa* on the other.[28] After all, if pleasure's value derives exclusively from the progress toward *mokṣa* that it causes, pleasure has no value at all in any case in which it does not cause progress toward *mokṣa*. In these cases, pleasure is not a suitable form of merit. The same can be said about pain and the postponement of *mokṣa*. If pain's disvalue derives exclusively from the postponement of *mokṣa* that it causes, then pain has no disvalue at all in any case in which it does not cause the postponement of *mokṣa*. In these cases, pleasure is not a suitable form of demerit.[29] Since the attainment and postponement of *mokṣa* are the only seemingly plausible candidates for further ends from which pleasure and pain derive their value and disvalue, the value and disvalue of pleasure and pain are at least partly intrinsic.

If the value and disvalue of pleasure and pain are at least partly intrinsic, however, then any sentient entity—any entity capable of pleasure or pain experiences—has direct moral standing, since there are possible circumstances in which human agents morally ought to consider the sentient entity for its own sake in deciding what to do—namely, those circumstances in which the agent might cause the entity pleasure or pain. The fact that an agent's action might cause an entity pleasure or pain constitutes a prima facie reason for or against performing the action.

The attribution of sentience to nonhuman animals is commonplace within Hindu traditions. Within the dialogue between Bhīṣma and Yudhiṣṭhira, Bhīṣma implies that animals are sentient when he says, "[t]hat called death, O Bhārata, is an aversion of all beings (*sarvabhūtānāṃ*). At the time of death, in that moment, trembling overcomes [all] beings (*bhūtānāṃ*)" (13.117.26).[30] If death is an aversion to all beings, then death is an aversion to animals. If animals are averse to death, and tremble at the time of death, then presumably animals are sentient. In another verse, *Bhīṣma* claims that the harmless agent "gives the gift of fearlessness to all beings (*sarvabhūteṣu*)" (13.116.20).[31]Again, if all beings are capable of fear, then presumably all beings—including nonhuman animals—are sentient.

Additional bases for the direct moral standing of animals

There is no reason to assume from the outset, however, that sentience is the only basis for the direct moral standing of animals. One seemingly promising basis for the direct moral standing of animals is their capacity to attain *mokṣa*.

Thus far I have argued that pleasure does not generally lead to *mokṣa*, and that pain does not generally postpone *mokṣa*. Consequently, the value of pleasure and the disvalue of pain cannot derive entirely from the value of these further ends. This is not to deny, however, that the attainment and postponement of *mokṣa* have intrinsic value and disvalue. Indeed, this claim is uncontroversial. All of the authors that I mentioned above who support a non-ethical interpretation of *ahiṃsā* toward animals claim that the attainment of *mokṣa* is not only intrinsically valuable, but the ultimate intrinsic good.[32]

One might argue, however, that if the attainment and postponement of *mokṣa* have intrinsic value and disvalue, respectively, then any entity capable of attaining *mokṣa* has direct moral standing, since there are possible circumstances in which human agents morally ought to consider the entity for its own sake in deciding what to do—namely, those circumstances in which the agent might affect the entity's prospects for attaining *mokṣa*.

Hindu texts and traditions tend to assert that animals are capable of attaining *mokṣa*. A passage from the *Āraṇyakaparan* (*Book of the Forest*) of the *Mahābhārata*, for example, says that a person,

> here in *saṃsāra* falls into wombs again and again. Due to ignorance, action, and desire, he moves about in a circle. He revolves in beings, from Brahmā to grass, being born over and over, in water, on earth, and in the air.
> (3.3.67–8)[33]

This implies that Brahmā, grass, and everything in between are reborn as human beings, and hence have the potential to attain *mokṣa*. If this is right, one might argue, then animals (and plants) have direct moral standing in virtue of their capacity to attain *mokṣa*—just as they have direct moral standing in virtue of their capacity for pleasure and pain.

That this is the view of the *Anuśāsanaparvan* in particular is supported by Bhīṣma's claim that "a [dharmic] person would not go to an animal birth, and would become a person of handsome form, certainly endowed with intelligence,

O Best of Kurus. He would attain great respect" (13.117.75).[34] This too suggests that animal lives constitute stations in the cycle of rebirth that an individual *ātman* might assume in the *saṃsāric* cycle. If animals can become human beings, however, and if human beings are often capable of attaining the intrinsically valuable end of *mokṣa*, then perhaps animals have direct moral standing in virtue of this capacity.

One problem with this view is that it is not clear that there are possible circumstances in which human agents might affect an animal's prospects for eventually attaining *mokṣa*. There are possible circumstances in which human agents might affect other human agents' prospects for attaining *mokṣa*. A person's parents teach him moral character and familial piety. A person's guru teaches him Sanskrit, the Vedas, the performance of rituals, and so on. All of these lessons potentially facilitate the attainment of *mokṣa*. Animals, however, cannot be benefited in these ways. Yet, the claim that an entity has direct moral standing in virtue of being capable of attaining *mokṣa* implies that there are possible circumstances in which human agents might affect the entity's capacity to attain *mokṣa*.

A second problem is that if human agents can affect an animal's capacity to attain *mokṣa*, then presumably they do this by increasing or decreasing the entity's likelihood of eventually attaining a human birth from which *mokṣa* can be attained directly. The most straightforward means by which an animal might attain a human birth, however, is by expending the demerit that caused the animal birth in the first place. This demerit is exhausted, however, by means of experiencing various forms of harm.

So even if human agents morally ought to consider animals for their own sakes in deciding what to do, this might not entail that human agents morally ought to count the fact that some action of theirs might benefit or harm (in any ordinary senses of these words) the entity as a prima facie reason for or against performing the action, respectively. On the contrary, it seems to entail that human agents morally ought to count the fact that some action of theirs might harm an animal as a prima facie reason in favor of performing the action.

Still, there might be bases for the direct moral standing of animals other than sentience. I chose pain and pleasure from an extensive list of benefits and harms that might accrue to the agent as a result of merit and demerit. They are only examples, however. Any other benefit or harm that might accrue to the agent as a result of merit or demerit also has value or disvalue, and any benefit or harm that has intrinsic value or disvalue is an additional basis for the direct moral standing of any entity capable of being benefited or harmed (directly or indirectly) by human agents in that way.

Consider, for example, the repeated claims that *ahiṃsā* and *hiṃsā* produce merit and demerit that take the forms of prolonged life and premature death. "*Hiṃsā* is certainly abandoned by those self-disciplined people with desires to attain … long life (*āyus*)" (13.116.8).[35] "Great self-controlled *ṛṣis* (seers) declared that the non-eating of meat is great. [It] produces … long life (*āyuṣyaṃ*)" (13.116.35).[36] "Since, O Splendid One, the lives of killers are also consumed [by their killing], therefore, he who desires his own existence (*bhūtim*) should abandon meat" (13.116.31).[37]

The diagram of these relations parallels diagram (B) above:

(C)

ahiṃsā	merit	life
hiṃsā	demerit	death

As in the case of pleasure and pain, if life and death are suitable forms of merit and demerit, then life and death have value and disvalue, respectively, and life is more valuable than death. This value and disvalue are either wholly extrinsic or at least partly intrinsic.

If the value and disvalue of life and death are wholly extrinsic, then perhaps the value and disvalue of life and death derive entirely from the intrinsic value and disvalue of pleasure and pain. This interpretation can be diagrammed as follows:

(C′)

ahiṃsā	merit	life	pleasure
hiṃsā	demerit	death	pain

This interpretation faces a familiar problem, however. In order for diagram C′ to be plausible, there must be relatively tight correlations between remaining alive and pleasure, and death and pain. Yet these correlations are dubious. Remaining alive causes pain rather than pleasure for any entity whose life is painful to begin with, and death is often painless. If the value of being alive derives exclusively from the value of the pleasure that being alive makes possible, then long life, or prolonged life, has no value at all in any case in which it does not lead to pleasure. Hence, in these cases, long life is not a suitable form of merit. Likewise, if the disvalue of death derives exclusively from the disvalue of the pain that being killed causes, then being killed has no disvalue at all in any case in which it is not painful. Hence, in these cases, being killed is not a suitable form of demerit. Hence the value and disvalue of life and death cannot derive exclusively from the intrinsic value and disvalue of pleasure and pain.

Another alternative is that the value and disvalue of life and death derive entirely from the intrinsic value of attaining *mokṣa* and the intrinsic disvalue of postponing *mokṣa*. Hence,

(C″)

ahiṃsā	merit	life	*mokṣa*
hiṃsā	demerit	death	postponement of *mokṣa*

Indeed, if this is right, then perhaps animals do indeed have direct moral standing in virtue of their capacity to attain *mokṣa*, since there are certainly circumstances in which human beings might affect an animal's longevity.

One reason to think that long life does indeed lead to *mokṣa* is that the *āśrama* system (stages of life) reserves the single-minded pursuit of *mokṣa* for those who have reached relative old age. If, instead, a person dies young, he is denied this opportunity.

The problem is that both the long life and premature death that an agent experiences as a result of *ahiṃsā* and *hiṃsā*, respectively, often do not occur within a birth that has this privilege. There is no guarantee that a person who causes sufficient *hiṃsā* to deserve premature death in a subsequent life will be born a human being at all, let alone a male twice-born Hindu.[38]

Outside these circumstances, there is little reason to think there is a correlation between life and death and the attainment and postponement of *mokṣa*, respectively. Hence the value and disvalue of life and death cannot derive exclusively from the intrinsic value of the attainment of *mokṣa* and the intrinsic disvalue of the postponement of *mokṣa*.

All of this suggests that the passage takes the value and disvalue of life and death to be at least partly intrinsic. If the value and disvalue of life and death are at least partly intrinsic, however, then any living being has direct moral standing, since there are possible circumstances in which human agents morally ought to consider the entity for its own sake in deciding what to do—namely, those circumstances in which the agent might affect the entity's longevity.[39]

A final reason to think that the disvalue of death does not derive from the disvalue of other ends is that the passage describes killing as a fundamental wrong, and life as a fundamental benefit. Bhīṣma says, for example, that "The one who captures, consents, butchers, buys, sells, prepares, or enjoys, every one of these is a killer" (13.116.47).[40] This suggests that it is the contribution that those who capture, consent, butcher, and so on make to the death of an animal that makes their actions morally wrong. The moral wrongness of these other actions derives from the moral wrongness of killing, rather than vice versa. Bhīṣma makes the point again when he says, "meat [arises] [only from] having killed a living being. *For this reason* [there is] fault in eating it" (13.116.26, my emphasis).[41]

Life, in contrast, is the greatest benefit that a human agent could bestow on an animal, or have bestowed upon him. "No gift in the past [was] greater than the gift of life. Nor will there [ever] be" (13.117.25).[42] If the value of life derives exclusively from the value of pleasure, and/or the value of the attainment of *mokṣa*, however, then pleasure and/or the attainment of *mokṣa* ought to be greater gifts. They are not, however. Hence life has intrinsic value, and death has intrinsic disvalue, and animals have direct moral standing both because they are sentient and because they are alive.

The case for the intrinsic value or disvalue of any of the remaining benefits and harms that Bhīṣma mentions is admittedly weaker. Some of the benefits that Bhīṣma lists have to do with physical health. "The person who does not eat meat, compassionate toward all creatures, [he is] unassailed by all creatures, long-lived, and healthy" (3.116.40).[43] "The person not eating any meat for one month, having avoided all pains, is happy, long living, and healthy" (3.116.62).[44]

"[A dharmic person], afflicted, will be released from misfortune. Fettered, he will be released from bondage. Weak, he will be released from disease" (13.116.74).[45]

It might be argued that the value of physical health derives exclusively from the value of pleasure, long life, and the avoidance of pain.[46] On the other hand, it might be argued that physical health is valuable as an end. Suppose, for example, that there are two dogs. One dog is in poor health as a result of eating unhealthy but delicious table scraps. The second eats only nutritionally balanced dry dog food. The first dog very well might be happier as a result of eating the unhealthy table scraps for which both dogs long. The first dog might also have just as long a life expectancy. Perhaps the fact that the first dog is unhealthy precludes her from engaging in certain dangerous behaviors, such as chasing raccoons that get into the yard. Yet there seems to be some sense in maintaining that the caretakers of the first dog morally ought to provide the dog with a healthier diet. This suggests that the value of health does not derive exclusively from the value of pleasure and long life.

Elsewhere Bhīṣma mentions strength and "perfect physical form" (*avyaṅgatām*), as benefits that accrue to the agent as a result of *ahiṃsā*. "The person who would avoid meat for the four months belonging to the rainy season attains the four prosperities of good name, long life, beauty, and strength" (3.116.61).[47] "*Hiṃsā* is certainly abandoned by those self-disciplined men with desires to attain beauty, and perfect physical form" (3.116.8).[48]

It might be that strength and perfect physical form are simply constituents of health, and hence do not constitute distinct bases of direct moral standing. At the same time, it seems possible to say that an eighty-year-old person is healthy, despite lacking both strength and perfect physical form. A person who has lost a limb—and hence lacks perfect physical form—might nonetheless be healthy and strong, and a person stricken with terminal cancer is not healthy, but might be strong and have a perfect physical form. If strength is valuable, it is surely not valuable solely as a means to long life and pleasure. Indeed, the correlation between these things is uncertain. And yet, the strong person is not necessarily healthier than the weaker person. So perhaps strength and perfect—or even adequate—physical form are valuable for their own sakes.

Another benefit that accrues to the agent as a result of *ahiṃsā* is freedom. "Fettered, he will be released from bondage" (13.116.74).[49] It might be argued that animals are not free in the same way that human agents are, and hence that animals cannot benefit from freedom. The freedom mentioned here, however, is not free will in any robust sense. It is a freedom from constraint—a freedom that all animals share.

Again, it might be argued that the value of freedom derives exclusively from the value of various further ends. Yet the claim that a polar bear is harmed as a result of being housed in the Lincoln Park Zoo in Chicago—even if her lifespan increases as a result (which it typically does), and even if the bear is spoiled, so that her overall pleasure greatly outweighs the pleasure of the typical polar bear living in the Arctic Circle—seems plausible.

The case for the intrinsic value and disvalue of other benefits and harms is even weaker. The benefits of safety, protection, and unassailability (3.116.13, 28, 32, 40, 3.117.23, 24), for example, probably derive their value exclusively from the avoidance of pain and death. Intelligence and memory (3.116.8) are reliable (although not sufficient) means to pleasure, the avoidance of pain, and the attainment of *mokṣa*. Perhaps their value derives entirely from the value of these further ends.

The question of whether the value and disvalue of these additional benefits and harms are intrinsic or extrinsic turns out to be much less significant than it might seem, however. If physical health, for example, is intrinsically valuable, then there are possible circumstances in which human agents morally ought to consider an animal for his or her own sake in deciding what to do—namely, those circumstances in which human agents might increase or decrease the animal's physical health. If, instead, physical health is merely extrinsically valuable, as a means to pleasure, the avoidance of pain, and longevity, then there are, nonetheless, possible circumstances in which human agents morally ought to consider the animal for his or her own sake in deciding what to do—namely, those circumstances in which human agents might increase or decrease the animal's physical health.

The only difference is that in the first case, the fact that the agent's action might increase or decrease the animal's physical health by itself counts as a prima facie reason for or against performing the action, respectively, whereas in the second case, it is the fact that the agent's action might increase or decrease the animal's physical health combined with the fact that the increase or decrease in the animal's physical health is a means to his or her pleasure, and so on, or pain, and so on, respectively, that counts as a prima facie reason for or against performing the action.

Another way to say this is to note that in the first case, human agents have a direct moral reason to avoid decreasing an animal's physical health, whereas, in the second case, human agents have an indirect moral reason to avoid decreasing an animal's physical health. In either case, however, the agent considers the animal for his or her own sake, since in either case, the direct moral reason is a fact about the being itself, rather than a fact about some other being. In the first case, the direct moral reason is the fact that the agent might increase or decrease the physical health of the animal. In the second case, the direct moral reason is the fact that the agent might cause the animal pleasure, pain, and so on.

Each benefit or harm that Bhīṣma lists, then, implies a prima facie moral obligation on human agents with regard to their treatment of nonhuman animals, so long as (a) the animals might be benefited and/or harmed (directly or indirectly) in that way, and (b) there are possible circumstances in which the actions of human agents might affect whether the animal is benefited or harmed in that way.

Most of the remaining benefits and harms that Bhīṣma lists, however, seem to meet both of these criteria. An animal might be benefited by beauty (13.116.8, 61, 75), memory (13.116.8), and fearlessness (13.117.21, 22) at the hands of human agents, just because human agents might bring about circumstances that do or do not compromise an animal's beauty, memory, fearlessness, and so on. It might even be that animals might benefit, either directly or indirectly, from great respect (13.116.75), a good name (13.116.61), and being remembered well (13.116.73) at the hands of human agents. This implies that human agents have moral obligations regarding these benefits. Moral virtue might be the only clear counter-example, since there is doubt about both whether animals can cultivate virtue and whether humans can act in ways that affect the cultivation of the moral virtue of an animal.

The result, then, is a robust conception of animal welfare, and correspondingly broad conceptions of *hiṃsā* and *ahiṃsā*. To act in a way that causes an animal pain or fear, shortens his or her life, compromises his or her health, strength, physical form, safety, beauty, memory, mobility, reputation, and so on constitutes at least prima facie harm to the animal. To act in a way that permits or brings about the pleasure, absence of pain, fearlessness, longevity, health, strength, good physical form, safety, beauty, memory, mobility, reputation, and so on of an animal constitutes at least prima facie non-harm to the animal.

Conclusion

In this chapter I have argued that the *Anuśasanaparvan* of the *Mahābhārata* ascribes moral standing to animals. The fact that harming animals is described as morally wrong by itself proves this.

I have also argued that the passage attributes *direct* moral standing to animals. Since the text counts pleasure and pain, life and death, and so on as suitable forms of merit and demerit, it attributes value and disvalue to them. Their value and disvalue cannot be derived exclusively from further ends. Hence animals have intrinsic value and disvalue. If they have intrinsic value and disvalue, then they are bases for the direct moral standing of any entity that is capable of pleasure, pain, life, death, and so on, so long as there are possible circumstances in which human agents might affect the entity with regard to pleasure, pain, life, death, and so on. Since this latter condition is also met, the passage attributes direct moral standing to animals.

Notes

1 Tom Regan says,

> by the expression *moral standing* I mean the following: X has moral standing if and only if X is a being such that we morally ought to determine how X will be affected in the course of determining whether we ought to perform a given act or adopt a given policy.

"The Nature and Possibility of an Environmental Ethic," *Environmental Ethics* 3, no. 1 (1981): 19, fn. 1. I add the words "there are possible circumstances in which" to my paraphrase of Regan's definition above in order to allow cases in which an entity has moral standing despite being contingently isolated from the effects of actual human actions. Also see Mark Timmons, *Disputed Moral Issues* (Oxford: Oxford University Press, 2007), 511.

2 Nelson says, "*ahiṃsā*, as a value, is articulated for the most part out of concern for the private karmic well-being of the actor." Lance E. Nelson, "Reading the *Bhagavadgītā* from an Ecological Perspective," in *Hinduism and Ecology: The Intersection of Earth, Sky, and Water*, eds. Christopher K. Chapple and Mary E. Tucker (Cambridge, MA: Harvard University Press, 2000), 142. The words "for the most part" are difficult to explain, however, given Nelson's view that only the attainment of *ātman/mokṣa* has intrinsic value.

3 Klaus K. Klostermaier, "Bhakti, Ahimsa and Ecology," *Journal of Dharma* 16, no. 3 (1991): 248.

4 Basant K. Lal, "Hindu Perspectives on the Use of Animals in Science," in *Animal Sacrifices: Religious Perspectives on the Use of Animals in Science*, ed. Tom Regan (Philadelphia, PA: Temple University Press, 1986), 200, emphasis in original.

5 Nirvedananda (Swami), *Hinduism at a Glance* (Calcutta: Ramakrishna Mission, 1979), 172.

6 V.K. Bharadwaja, "A Non-Ethical Concept of Ahimsa," *Indian Philosophical Quarterly* 11, no. 2 (1984): 171–7.

7 Brian G. Norton, "Environmental Ethics and Weak Anthropocentrism," *Environmental Ethics* 6, no. 2 (1984): 136.

8 J. Baird Callicott, *Earth's Insights: A Survey of Ecological Ethics from the Mediterranean Basin to the Australian Outback* (Berkeley, CA: University of California Press, 1994), 48.

9 Arvind Sharma, "Attitudes to Nature in the Early *Upaniṣads*," in *Purifying the Earthly Body of God: Religion and Ecology in Hindu India*, ed. Lance E. Nelson (Albany, NY: State University of New York Press, 1998), 51.

10 Rita DasGupta Sherma, "Sacred Immanence: Reflections of Ecofeminism in Hindu Tantra," in *Purifying the Earthly Body of God: Religion and Ecology in Hindu India*, ed. Lance E. Nelson (Albany, NY: State University of New York Press, 1998), 95.

11 Patricia Y. Mumme, "Models and Images for a Vaiṣṇava Environmental Theology: The Potential Contribution of Śrīvaiṣṇavism," in *Purifying the Earthly Body of God: Religion and Ecology in Hindu India*, ed. Lance E. Nelson (Albany, NY: State University of New York Press, 1998), 135.

12 Bruce M. Sullivan, "Theology and Ecology at the Birthplace of Kṛṣṇa," in *Purifying the Earthly Body of God: Religion and Ecology in Hindu India*, ed. Lance E. Nelson (Albany, NY: State University of New York Press, 1998), 262, fn. 1.

13 M.K. Sridhar and Purushottama Bilimoria, "Animal Ethics and Ecology in Classical India: Reflections on a Moral Tradition," in *Indian Ethics: Classical Traditions and Contemporary Challenges, Volume I*, eds. Purushottama Bilimoria, Joseph Prabhu, and Renuka Sharma (London: Ashgate, 2007).

14 All citations of the *Mahābhārata* refer to the Critical Edition: V.S. Sukthankar, et al., eds., *The* Mahābhārata *for the First Time Critically Edited* (Poona: Bhandarkar Oriental Research Institute, 1933–66).

15 *khādakasya kṛte jantuṃ yo hanyāt puruṣādhamaḥ/mahādoṣakaras.*

16 *kravyādān rākṣasān vidhi jihmānṛtaparāyaṇān//.*

17 *svamāṃsaṃ paramāṃsair yo vivardhayitum icchanti/nāsti kṣudrataras tasmān na nṛśaṃsataro naraḥ//.*

18 *bhakṣayitvā tu yo māṃsaṃ paścād api nivartate/tasyāpi sumahān dharmo yaḥ pāpād vinivartate//.*

19 I say "typically" to leave open the possibility that the liberated, desireless, or devoted agent does not accrue merit and demerit.

20 It is unclear whether the pleasure and pain described here are sensory pleasure and pain, attitudinal pleasure and pain, or both. I leave this question open in what follows.

21 *ahiṃsakāni bhūtāni daṇḍena vinihanti yaḥ/ātmanaḥ sukham anvicchan na sa pretya sukhī bhavet//.*

22 *ātmopamaś ca bhūteṣu yo vai bhavati puruṣaḥ* [*sic*]/*nyastadaṇdo jitakrodhaḥ sa pretya sukham edhate//.*

23 *atha vā māsam apy ekaṃ sarvamāṃsāny abhakṣayan/atītya sarvaduḥkhāni sukhī jīven nirāmayaḥ//.*

24 *tad etad uttamaṃ dharmam ahiṃsālakṣaṇaṃ śubham/ye caranti mahātmāno nākapṛṣṭhe vasanti te//.*

25 *ijyāyajñaśrutikṛtair yo mārgair abudhho janaḥ/hantāj jantuṃ māṃsagṛddhrī sa vai naraka … naraḥ//.*

26 As many authors have pointed out, the words "intrinsic value" and "extrinsic value" are notoriously ambiguous. See Callicott, *Earth's Insights*; Karen Green, "Two Distinctions in Environmental Goodness," *Environmental Values* 5, no. 1 (1996): 31–46; Elizabeth M. Harlow, "The Human Face of Nature: Environmental Values and the Limits of Nonanthropocentrism," *Environmental Ethics* 14, no. 1 (1992): 27–42; Christine M. Korsgaard, "Two Distinctions in Goodness," *Philosophical Review* 92, no. 2 (1983): 169–95; Katie McShane, "Why Environmental Ethics Shouldn't Give Up on Intrinsic Value," *Environmental Ethics* 29, no. 1 (2007): 43–61; John O'Neill, "The Varieties of Intrinsic Value," *Monist* 75, no. 2 (1992): 119–37. The definitions I give here are simply stipulations. I put aside the question of whether this value is objective (independent of the evaluations of valuers) or subjective (dependent on the evaluations of valuers).

27 Christopher G. Framarin, "The *Manusmṛti* and the Limits of Economic Value," Paper presented at the Tenth East West Philosophers Conference, University of Hawaii, Manoa, Honolulu, HI, May 16, 2011.

28 It might be argued that any improvement of an entity's chances in attaining *mokṣa* constitutes a benefit. If this is right, then pleasure might be a suitable form of merit even if the correlation between pleasure and the attainment of *mokṣa* are relatively weak, and pleasure only slightly increases the chances of the agent attaining *mokṣa*. Money, after all, might not lead to some further, intrinsically valuable end. Yet it is considered a form of reward, simply in virtue of the fact that it increases the agent's chances at attaining some further intrinsically valuable end. This isn't helpful in the present context, however, since it is not clear that pleasure even increases an entity's chances of attaining *mokṣa*.

29 One reply might be that merit takes the form of pleasure only when it is conducive to *mokṣa*. But then pain should be listed as a form that merit can take as well—with the understanding that merit takes the form of pain only when it is conducive to *mokṣa*—and pleasure should be listed as a form that demerit can take—with the understanding that merit takes the form of pleasure only when it is counter-productive to *mokṣa*. Yet only pleasure is listed as a form of merit, and only pain a form of demerit.

30 *aniṣṭaṃ sarvabhūtānāṃ maraṇaṃ nāma bhārata/mṛtyukāle hi bhūtānāṃ sadyo jāyati vepathuḥ//.*

31 *sarvabhūteṣu yo vidvān dadāty abhayadakṣiṇām/dātā bhavati loke saprāṇanāṃ nātra saṃśayaḥ/.*

32 I argue elsewhere that one possible explanation for the initial allure of the non-ethical interpretations of *ahiṃsā* is the ambiguity of the words "ultimate value." In one sense, they refer to what I have been calling intrinsic value—the value that something has as an end. In a second sense, they refer to the highest value—value that cannot be exceeded. It is a platitude in most Hindu texts and traditions that only the attainment of *mokṣa* has ultimate value, in the sense that its value cannot be exceeded. From this it does not follow, however, that only the attainment of *mokṣa* has value as an end. Christopher G. Framarin, "The Value of Nature in Indian (Hindu) Traditions," *Religious Studies* 44, no. 1 (2011): 43–61.

33 *evaṃ patati saṃsāre tāsu tāsviha yoniṣu/avidyākarmatāḥābhir bhrāmyamāṇo 'tha cakravat//brahmādiṣu tṛṇān teṣu bhūteṣu parivartate/jale bhuvi tathākāśe jāyamānaḥ punaḥ punaḥ//*Compare Śaṅkara's *Gītābhāṣya* 6.29–32.

34 *tiryagyoniṃ na gaccheta rūpavāṃś ca bhaven naraḥ/buddhimān vai kuruśreṣṭha prāpnuyāc ca mahadyaśaḥ//.*

35 *rūpam avyaṅgatām āyur buddhiṃ sattvaṃ balaṃ smṛtim/prāptukāmair narair hiṃsā varjitā vai kṛtātmabhiḥ//.*

36 *dhanyaṃ yaśasyam āyuṣyaṃ svargyaṃ svasty ayanaṃ mahat/māṃsasyābhakṣaṇaṃ prāhur niyatāḥ paramarṣayaḥ//.*

37 *yasmād grasati caivāyur hiṃsakānāṃ mahādyute/tasmād vivarjayen māṃsaṃ ya icched bhūtim ātmanaḥ//.*

38 A twice-born Hindu is a Hindu who has entered Vedic studentship. Traditionally, only male Hindus born in the top three social classes (*brahmaṇa, kṣatriya,* or *vaiśya*) are allowed to enter into Vedic studentship.

39 This implies that plants, too, have direct moral standing. In a book currently under review (*Environmental Ethics in Hindu Law, Literature, and Philosophy*), I argue that certain Hindu texts and traditions, including the *Anuśāsanaparvan,* claim that the direct moral standing of animals outweighs the direct moral standing of plants for a variety of reasons. This explains why it is better to eat plants than animals, even if it is prima facie wrong to kill plants.

40 *āhartā cānumantā ca viśastā krayavikrayī/saṃskartā copabhoktā ca ghātakāḥ sarva eva te//.*

41 *na hi māṃsaṃ tṛṇāt kāṣṭhād upalād vāpi jāyate/hatvā jantuṃ tato māṃsaṃ tasmād doṣo 'sya bhakṣaṇe//*The claim is not strictly accurate, since many animals die of natural causes.

42 *prāṇadānāt paraṃ dānaṃ na bhūtaṃ na bhaviṣyati/.*

43 *adhṛṣyaḥ sarvabhūtānām āyuṣmān nīrujaḥ sukhī/bhavaty abhakṣayan māṃsaṃ dayāvān prāṇinām iha//.*

44 *atha vā māsam apy ekaṃ sarvamāṃsāny abhakṣayan/atītya sarvaduḥkhāni sukhī jiven nirāmayaḥ//.*

45 *āpannaś cāpado mucyed baddho mucyeta bandhanāt/mucyet tathāturo rogād duḥkhān mucyate duḥkhitaḥ//.*

46 In a famous passage from the *Enquiries Concerning the Human Understanding,* Hume says, "ask a man *why he uses exercise*; he will answer, *because he desires to keep his health.* If you then enquire, *why he desires health,* he will readily reply, *because sickness is painful.*" David Hume, *Enquiries Concerning the Human Understanding* (Oxford: Clarendon Press, 1951), 293, emphases in original.

47 *caturo vārṣikān māsānyo māṃsaṃ parivarjayet/catvāri bhadrāṇy āpnoti kīrtim āyur yaśo balam//.*

48 *rūpam avyaṅgatām āyur buddhiṃ sattvaṃ balaṃ smṛtim/prāptukāmair narair hiṃsā varjitā vai kṛtātmabhiḥ//.*

49 *baddho mucyeta bandhanāt/.*

Bibliography

Bharadwaja, V.K. "A Non-Ethical Concept of Ahimsa." *Indian Philosophical Quarterly* 11, no. 2 (1984): 171–80.

Callicott, J. Baird. *Earth's Insights: A Survey of Ecological Ethics from the Mediterranean Basin to the Australian Outback.* Berkeley, CA: University of California Press, 1994.

Findly, Ellison B. *Plant Lives: Borderline Beings in Indian Traditions.* Delhi: Motilal Banarsidass, 2008.

Framarin, Christopher G. "The Value of Nature in Indian (Hindu) Traditions." *Religious Studies* 44, no. 1 (2011): 43–61.

Framarin, Christopher G. "*Ātman*, Identity, and Emanation: Arguments for a Hindu Environmental Ethic." *Comparative Philosophy* 2, no. 1 (2011): 3–24.

Framarin, Christopher G. "The *Manusmṛti* and the Limits of Economic Value." Paper presented at the Tenth East West Philosophers Conference, University of Hawaii, Manoa, Honolulu, HI, May 16, 2011.

Green, Karen. "Two Distinctions in Environmental Goodness." *Environmental Values* 5, no. 1 (1996): 31–46.

Harlow, Elizabeth M. "The Human Face of Nature: Environmental Values and the Limits of Nonanthropocentrism." *Environmental Ethics* 14, no. 1 (1992): 27–42.

Hume, David. *Enquiries Concerning the Human Understanding.* Oxford: Clarendon Press, 1951.

Klostermaier, Klaus K. "Bhakti, Ahimsa and Ecology." *Journal of Dharma* 16, no. 3 (1991): 246–54.

Korsgaard, Christine M. "Two Distinctions in Goodness." *Philosophical Review* 92, no. 2 (1983): 169–95.

Lal, Basant K. "Hindu Perspectives on the Use of Animals in Science." In *Animal Sacrifices: Religious Perspectives on the Use of Animals in Science*. Edited by Tom Regan, 199–212. Philadelphia, PA: Temple University Press, 1986.

McShane, Katie. "Why Environmental Ethics Shouldn't Give Up on Intrinsic Value." *Environmental Ethics* 29, no. 1 (2007): 43–61.

Mumme, Patricia Y. "Models and Images for a Vaiṣṇava Environmental Theology: The Potential Contribution of Śrīvaiṣṇavism." In *Purifying the Earthly Body of God: Religion and Ecology in Hindu India*. Edited by Lance E. Nelson, 133–62. Albany, NY: State University of New York Press, 1998.

Nelson, Lance E. "Reading the *Bhagavadgītā* from an Ecological Perspective." In *Hinduism and Ecology: The Intersection of Earth, Sky, and Water*. Edited by Christopher K. Chappelle and Mary E. Tucker, 127–64. Cambridge, MA: Harvard University Press, 2000.

Nirvedananda (Swami). *Hinduism at a Glance.* Calcutta: Ramakrishna Mission, 1979.

Norton, Brian G. "Environmental Ethics and Weak Anthropocentrism." *Environmental Ethics* 6, no. 2 (1984): 131–48.

O'Neill, John. "The Varieties of Intrinsic Value." *Monist* 75, no. 2 (1992): 119–37.

Regan, Tom. "The Nature and Possibility of an Environmental Ethic." *Environmental Ethics* 3, no. 1 (1981): 19–34.

Rolston III, Holmes. "Can the East Help the West to Value Nature?" *Philosophy East and West* 37, no. 2 (1987): 172–90.

Sadhale, Shastri G.S., ed. *The* Bhagavad-Gītā *with Eleven Commentaries, Volume 1.* Delhi: Parimal Publications, 2000.

Sharma, Arvind. "Attitudes to Nature in the Early *Upaniṣads*." In *Purifying the Earthly Body of God: Religion and Ecology in Hindu India*. Edited by Lance E. Nelson, 51–60. Albany, NY: State University of New York Press, 1998.

Sherma, Rita DasGupta. "Sacred Immanence: Reflections of Ecofeminism in Hindu Tantra." In *Purifying the Earthly Body of God: Religion and Ecology in Hindu India*. Edited by Lance E. Nelson, 89–132. Albany, NY: State University of New York Press, 1998.

Sridhar, M.K. and Bilimoria, Purushottama. "Animal Ethics and Ecology in Classical India: Reflections on a Moral Tradition," in *Indian Ethics: Classical Traditions and*

Contemporary Challenges, Volume I. Edited by Pursushottama Bilimoria, Joseph Prabhu, and Renuka Sharma, 297–328. London: Ashgate, 2007.
Sukthankar, V.S., et al., eds. *The Mahābhārata for the First Time Critically Edited.* Poona: Bhandarkar Oriental Research Institute, 1933–66.
Sullivan, Bruce M. "Theology and Ecology at the Birthplace of Kṛṣṇa." In *Purifying the Earthly Body of God: Religion and Ecology in Hindu India.* Edited by Lance E. Nelson, 247–68. Albany, NY: State University of New York Press, 1998.
Timmons, Mark. *Disputed Moral Issues.* Oxford: Oxford University Press, 2007.

6 Cutting the cat in one

Zen Master Dōgen on the moral status of nonhuman animals

James McRae

ばか猫や	baka neko ya	The foolish feline:
縛れながら	shibarare nagara	even though it is tethered,
恋を鳴く	koi o naku	it still cries for love.

Haiku by Issa[1]

Introduction

In the *Shōbōgenzō Zuimonki*,[2] Dōgen recounts a *kōan*[3] about Zen master Nansen (Nan-ch'üan), who found two groups of his monks arguing over a cat. He intervened and held the cat up, claiming that if no one could say anything to dissuade him, he would cut the animal in two. Dumbfounded, the monks watched as Nansen cleaved the cat before them. That evening, Nansen recounted the story for his fellow monk Jōshū, who responded by placing his sandal on his head and walking away. Nansen told Jōshū as he departed, "If you had been there, you would have saved the cat."[4]

This tale is perplexing since Buddhist doctrines such as non-injury (Sk. *ahiṃsā*; Jp. *fugai* 不害) and the cycle of rebirth (Sk. *saṃsāra*; Jp. *rinne* 輪廻) suggest that nonhuman animals are more worthy of liberation than laceration. This story raises two important questions about the role that nonhuman animals play in Zen ethics: what, if any, obligations do human beings have to animals and is it ever acceptable to injure animals for human benefit? The purpose of this chapter is to answer these questions by exploring the literature of the Sōtō Zen tradition, particularly the writings of Dōgen and his interpreters. The first section gives an overview of Zen ethics, the second section explores the general question of human obligations to animals, and the third section deals with how the doctrine of skillful means (Sk. *upāya*; Jp. *hōben* 方便) might provide exceptions to the precepts against harming animals. While Sōtō Zen is opposed to the unnecessary injury of any sentient being, some limited harm might be allowed in rare, extenuating circumstances to promote awakening and minimize suffering for humans.

An overview of Zen ethics

Zen Buddhism is a religious, cultural, and philosophical tradition with roots in India and China that has influenced Japan since the twelfth century. It represents a unique outgrowth of the Mahāyanā tradition of Indian Buddhism and many of its core ethical beliefs are grounded in Mahāyanā doctrines. Self-cultivation in Mahāyanā Buddhism is a process that involves the development of both wisdom (Sk. *prajñā*; Jp. 知恵 *chie*) and compassion (Sk. *karuṇā*; Jp. 慈悲 *jihi*. Enlightenment is not just an epistemological shift, it is also an ethical transformation.[5] Buddhist morality is founded upon compassion, which comes through the realization of wisdom. Since all things in the world are co-dependently interconnected (Sk. *pratītyasamutpāda*; Jp. *engi* 縁起), people's actions have consequences for every being around them, including themselves. Furthermore, since a person has no essential self, there is no absolute ego toward which selfish actions might be directed. When one realizes that one is part of an "extended web of interconnection,"[6] one feels an intense compassion and heartfelt unity with other beings: "Metaphysically, what we have is a field-like vision of the mutual interconnectedness of all non-substantial 'things' or seemingly independent centers of awareness, whereby each center is but a focus of awareness or consciousness in a seamless field of becoming."[7] This understanding of the self as a particular focus of a greater field of being parallels Hall and Ames' focus-field interpretation of the self in Chinese philosophy. Individuals are not distinct selves, separate from other people and their environment. Rather, they are "radically situated as persons-in-context," and thus fundamentally interdependent.[8]

It is not enough for a practitioner of Zen to have wisdom alone; compassion is also necessary for the attainment of enlightenment. Robert Carter describes the relationship of wisdom and compassion:

> *Nirvāna* is not just the result of metaphysical insight, nor is it a selfish, individual act. Rather, it is the cultivation of an ethical life, a life of compassionate and sympathetic identification; it is part of what enlightenment is all about.[9]

Compassion is a necessary part of enlightenment because it eradicates the egocentric thinking that is the cause of human conflict and suffering.[10] Dōgen endorses the Mahāyanā view that enlightenment involves the development of both compassion and wisdom through the dedicated practice of Buddhism.[11] This relationship is essential because the goal of Buddhism is the elimination of suffering, not just for oneself, but for all beings. According to the Four Noble Truths, all life is suffering, this suffering is caused by ignorance, and it is by overcoming this ignorance that one may overcome suffering. Zen enlightenment is accompanied by an ethical shift from conventional morality—such as the moral precepts for monks or laypersons—to compassion for all beings. This shift occurs because when one attains *satori* (悟り enlightenment), one sees all things, including the self, as impermanent (and thus attachment falls away), and one realizes the causal interpenetration of all beings. Immoral actions are performed out of selfishness and ignorance. Throughout the *Shōbōgenzō Zuimonki*, Dōgen stresses that one must cast aside the self in order to gain enlightenment.[12] By cultivating wisdom, one gains the ability to see things "as they are" (其儘 *sono mama*), at which point one realizes that there is no self and, thus, no distinction between oneself and other beings.[13] All of the false attitudes that have colored one's perceptions are stripped away, leaving a pure, untainted experience of the world. The negative emotions and ignorance that lead to immoral behavior fall aside and one sees that all things are fundamentally interconnected as part of a complex causal matrix. Nature and other beings are not something separate from oneself that need to be appreciated, but are rather part of the same causal continuum as oneself (since there is no such thing as *self*).[14] Therefore, wisdom and the realization of no-self lead to the destruction of selfishness and the development of compassion for all beings.[15]

In Chapter 10 of the *Shōbōgenzō*, Dōgen offers his own understanding of Buddhist morality in the *Shoakumakusa* passage:

諸悪莫作	*Shoakumakusa*	The nonproduction of evil
衆善奉行	*Shuzenbugyō*	The performance of good
自浄其意	*Jijōgoi*	The purification of one's own intentions
是諸佛教	*Zesshobukkyō*	This is the teaching of all Buddhas[16]

Here, Dōgen states that moral action is fundamentally related to self-cultivation. Evil actions arise through the impurity of one's intentions, which comes as a result of ignorance. When one experiences things as they are, the enlightened consciousness perceives reality without the least addition of intentionality or deliberative discrimination to color experience. Thus, one does not form attachments based upon the ignorant misinterpretation of one's experience. Since attachments are the source of evil actions, when one purifies one's own intentions and is free from attachments, one engages in the "nonproduction of evil" and the "performance of good." Dōgen's manner of framing ethics along these lines anticipates the contemporary ethical categories of nonmaleficence and beneficence.[17]

While deontology and other principle-based moral philosophies focus upon the "unbreakable nature of moral rules," Zen views all rules as "relative and circumstantial."[18] However, while Zen stresses compassion as the basis for moral action, it does have a place for rules. Zen morality consists of both a spontaneous compassion that comes from enlightenment and a set of "precepts, codes, virtues, and exemplars" that is part of the discipline of self-cultivation.[19] These precepts are not something to be idly broken by a Zen practitioner, but rather serve as a guide for one's actions until one cultivates the wisdom and compassion of enlightenment. Following Philip Kapleau, Carter compares the codes and precepts of Zen to the scaffolding that is used to construct a building and is then discarded when the work is completed. Before one has realized enlightenment, one needs the precepts to keep one's conduct appropriate, but, once enlightened, one will act appropriately out of a sense of compassion and will no longer need the precepts to guide one's actions.[20]

Dōgen argues that good and evil are not absolute categories, but rather depend upon the particulars of each situation. What is good in one context might be considered evil in another and vice versa.[21] He states that to "enter the Buddha Way is to stop discriminating between good and evil and to cast aside the mind that says this is good and that is bad."[22] When Dōgen refers to the transcendence of good and evil, he means that we should go beyond conventional, dualistic thinking to a morality that is based upon compassion for all beings. Although he states that we must cast aside the notions of good and evil, throughout the *Shōbōgenzō Zuimonki*, Dōgen repeatedly encourages Zen monks to do good and avoid evil.[23] He exhorts the monks, "concern yourself with saving and benefiting others, practice various forms of good, discard the evil actions of the past, and do not rest content with the present good but continue to practice throughout your life."[24] It is not morality itself that Dōgen wishes to abandon, only the conventional, absolutist morality of the laity.[25] Conventional morality is a hindrance to enlightenment because it is based upon absolute notions of the world that violate the Buddhist understanding of impermanence.[26] To say that something is always right or wrong is to say that there is an aspect of the world that is not subject to change. Unlike conventional morality, Zen ethics is capable of flowing with the continually shifting contexts to which it is applied. Thus, Dōgen states, "What the world considers good is not necessarily good": Buddhists must act upon a different set of principles if they are to perform good acts.[27]

Throughout the *Shōbōgenzō Zuimonki*, Dōgen demands that we discard evil and do good, so it is clear that these concepts still have meaning for him. He argues,

> Once we have thoroughly realized that all things are the Buddhadharma, then we know that evil is always evil and is far from the Way of the Buddha and the Patriarchs and that good is always good, and is linked with the Buddha Way.[28]

He further states that "[a]s long as you have a mind, you can distinguish between good and evil."[29] But how may we distinguish between good and evil if they are completely contextual and are not grounded on traditional morality? There must be some principle upon which we can base our actions in any context so that they will be sure to be good. For Dōgen, the morality of an act depends upon two factors: (1) the motivation that drives one to commit the act, and (2) the results of that act. Dōgen states that the good is that which does not arouse desire.[30] Since desire and craving are the cause of suffering, and the goal of Buddhism is to eliminate suffering, actions that are motivated by desire are immoral. Only actions that are motivated by compassion are morally good.[31] Again, since the goal of Buddhism is the elimination of suffering, the consequences of an act are important: evil acts are those that lead to the suffering of beings and good acts are those that lead beings to *satori* (the ultimate elimination of suffering). Thus, although the particular acts that a Buddhist commits will vary according to the specific demands of the context, good acts will always be those that are motivated by compassion and directed toward the elimination of suffering, and evil acts will always be those that are motivated by craving and likely to result in suffering. Because of this, it is possible for a moral pluralism to exist. Just as several different virtuosos might play the same piece of music in different ways and yet all play it well, different Buddhists might act morally in different ways and yet still act out of compassion to eliminate the suffering of all beings.

The cultivation of one's character through Zen is a lifelong endeavor. Until one is enlightened, it is important that one internalize the precepts of Zen so that one can meditate upon them and thereby "make morality altogether familiar."[32] Enlightened people have no need of the precepts because they understand the compassion that is at the root of morality. Students of Zen who do not yet have such an understanding should follow the rules so that they can imitate the conduct of an enlightened person.[33] Like Kierkegaard's knight of faith,[34] who must first pass through the ethical stage of development before he can teleologically suspend the ethical in a leap to the religious, Zen practitioners must internalize the precepts before they can cast these principles aside and act on the basis of spontaneous compassion.

General obligations to nonhuman animals

The debate about the ethics of nonhuman animals is grounded in the question of whether or not animals are morally considerable beings. To be worthy of moral consideration, something must be capable of being wronged in a morally significant way. Most ethicists, even those who endorse an anthropocentric perspective, agree that simple membership in *Homo sapiens* is not morally significant because it is an accidental characteristic with no moral significance. If humans deserve special moral consideration, it must come as a result of unique characteristics that nonhuman animals do not possess.[35] For example, Mary Anne Warren argues that personhood is based on attributes such as sentience, emotionality, reason, communication, self-awareness, and moral agency, all of which allow a being to take part in moral discourse. She articulates a "weak animal rights position" in which animals are not given the same rights as humans, but should nonetheless be protected from cruel treatment based on their status as sentient beings.[36]

To articulate Dōgen's perspective on animal rights, we must first articulate his criteria for moral significance and then determine whether human beings are deserving of special moral consideration due to their possession of morally significant attributes that they do not share with nonhuman animals. The ethics of the Mahāyanā tradition, which Zen inherited, are based on the principle of *ahiṃsā* (Jp. *fugai*), or non-injury, which is grounded in the epistemological shift that one experiences in *satori*:

> It [the enlightenment experience] is the reservoir of all things, and yet it itself is no-thing, is utterly without distinctions. It is an experience of

> profound compassion in that in it one comes to grasp that all is divine, and thus one is one's brother and sister, one is all animals, all living and all existing things, because all of these are but manifestations of the primal, the divine, and it is this seamless affinity and kinship that is recognized in awakening. One sees into one's own nature, and one finds there the pulse of the creative force of the universe itself. It is, therefore, the ground of all ethics.[37]

Interdependence means that one affects and is affected by one's context, such that one's self is radically contextualized.[38] When one realizes that all living things are mutually interdependent, one gains a profound sense of compassion for their well-being and will thus refrain from harming another sentient being unless it is absolutely necessary. Dōgen's writings contain numerous references to the value of nonhuman animals and the natural world. Dōgen states that "earth, grass, trees, walls, tiles, and pebbles all engage in buddha activity."[39] When discussing *uji* (being-time), Dōgen states, "The rat is time, the tiger is time, sentient beings are time, buddhas are time."[40] In his analysis of Zhaozhou's response of "*mu*" to the *kōan*, "Does a dog have buddha nature?" Dōgen states "What, in the end, are mountains, rivers, earth, human beings, animals, and houses?" The answer to this question is, of course, *mu* (無 nothingness).[41] There is *nothing* essential to any of these things that makes them truly separate from and superior to the rest of the world. All things are part of interdependent arising and thus everything has the buddha-nature. As a result, Dōgen urges his readers to develop a "kind mind" that shows parental care for all things. It seems that this applies not just to humans or animals, but to even non-sentient things as well. Dōgen states, "you should look after water and grain with compassionate care, as though tending your own children."[42]

The Buddhist tradition seems to support the notion that animals are deserving of moral consideration comparable to that given humans. Human beings can be reborn as some species of nonhuman animals, which means that there is a greater sense of interconnectedness that makes Buddhism decidedly non-anthropocentric. The first of the ten precepts (*jikkai*) prohibits the killing of all creatures, not just human beings, and the doctrine of non-injury (*ahiṃsā*) is an essential part of the Eightfold Path. The Buddha himself rejected animal sacrifice and the Indian Mahāyāna tradition explicitly forbids the eating of meat.[43]

Dōgen seems to endorse some level of equality among different forms of life. He speaks of "beneficial action" as working "to benefit all classes of sentient beings, that is, to care about their distant and near future, and to help them by using skillful means."[44] He specifically refers to the cases of Kongyu and Yangbao, who flourished after they showed kindness to caged and injured animals, respectively. Dōgen discusses a variety of different worlds in which sentient beings are manifest, ending with, "Wherever there is a world full of sentient beings, there is a world of buddha ancestors."[45] Dōgen repeatedly refers to the goal of Zen as the awakening of all "sentient beings," which can refer to either unenlightened human beings or all living things.[46] He states that "the thought of enlightenment is aroused even in the realm of hell, hungry ghosts, animals, and malevolent spirits," which indicates that all sentient beings take part in the same cycle of rebirth.[47] Dōgen states that humans and heavenly beings have a unique perspective on the world compared to animals, but implies that the views of "dragons and fish" might be closer to the true nature of things as impermanence.[48] He also compares the compassion and sympathy of a Buddha to the care that animals show for their own offspring without thought of extrinsic reward.[49] So it seems as though Dōgen values animals as much as human beings.

However, Dōgen's ethics are more ecocentric than biocentric. Deane Curtin argues that Dōgen takes a holistic perspective that is concerned with the welfare of *all* beings, not just the sentient ones. Dōgen identifies Buddha-nature with impermanence, which is a characteristic shared by all beings, including insentient things such as rivers and mountains. As Curtin puts it, "Mountains and humans abide together in their impermanence."[50] Instead of focusing on just sentient beings (*shujō* 衆生), Dōgen declares that it is the "whole-being" (*shitsū* 悉有) that is the Buddha-nature. This ascribes moral value to non-living things, which is consistent with a holistic, ecocentric perspective.[51] Ultimately, all things are the Buddha-nature and it is wrong to arbitrarily ascribe value to only part of our dynamic, interpenetrating reality.

Yet are *all* living things owed the same moral consideration as humans? What about plankton or bacteria? Even though nonhuman animals and even inanimate objects have moral worth in Buddhism, they seem to be not-quite-equal citizens in the ecological community when compared to human beings. Dōgen himself speaks of animals in unflattering terms, calling people who follow erroneous teachings "more stupid than animals who learn the buddha way."[52] He further states, "As long as you have a mind, you can distinguish between good and evil. … All human beings are born with this potential; this is not so of those born in the animal world."[53] Damien Keown clarifies the boundaries of moral consideration with the idea of "karmic life": "those forms of life that are sentient, reincarnate, and are morally autonomous."[54] Early Buddhist texts suggest that humans might be reborn as insects, but not as microscopic life forms such as bacteria or viruses, which lack nervous systems and volitional activity.[55] Within the cycle of *saṃsāra* (Jp. *rinne*), rebirth as a nonhuman animal is considered a punishment due to the *karma* accrued during one's existence as a human being. Human life has unique value because of humanity's ability to achieve enlightenment, but it is merely one stage in a larger cycle of rebirth that includes nonhuman animals. Yet monastic law draws a sharp distinction between the murder of a human, which is a major offense, and the killing of a nonhuman animal, which is only a minor offense.[56]

Traditionally, sentient beings (*shujō*) are reincarnated in one of six realms: hell, hungry ghosts, animals, fighting spirits, humans, or heavenly beings. The cultural origins of this belief date back to pre-Buddhist Hinduism, so it is unlikely that Dōgen interprets reincarnation according to these strict categories. Ultimately, these "realms" are just modes of existence within the same world. What is important is that all beings transmigrate in the same "dimension of generation-and-extinction."[57] Buddhist soteriology is thus non-anthropocentric:

all beings are part of the struggle for liberation. However, human beings are unique because our status as a "thinking animal" gives us self-consciousness, which allows us to recognize transmigration as a soteriological problem rather than a simple fact. Because humans do have a distinctive place—only we can realize enlightenment—Zen seems to have an anthropocentric focus within its larger ecocentric field of view.[58] Nonetheless, Buddhism transcends simple humanism and anthropocentrism because it views humans as part of a karmic process that includes other beings.[59] While our existence as thinking animals gives us special abilities that other beings do not share, it does not give us a special right to treat them any way we like.

Thus, it seems that Dōgen articulates a less-extreme view than the strong animal rights perspective advocated by philosophers such as Tom Regan, who grant all animals intrinsic value, and thus rights comparable to humans.[60] The Zen tradition would be decidedly uncomfortable talking about rights, since they imply permanent, universal values that do not change with context. However, Dōgen's perspective shares certain commonalities with the weak animal rights view articulated by Mary Anne Warren:

> The weak animal rights theory asserts that (1) any creature whose natural mode of life includes the pursuit of certain satisfactions has the right not to be forced to exist without the opportunity to pursue those satisfactions; (2) that any creature which is capable of pain, suffering, or frustration has the right that such experiences not be deliberately inflicted upon it without some compelling reason; and (3) that no sentient being should be killed without good reason. However, moral rights are not an all-or-nothing affair. The strength of the reasons required to override the rights of a non-human organism varies, depending upon—among other things—the probability that it is sentient and (if it is clearly sentient) its probable degree of mental sophistication.[61]

Dōgen would agree with Warren's first proposition: nonhuman animals should be allowed to pursue their own ends, particularly since their ends are interconnected with ours via the cycle of rebirth. He would also agree with her second proposition, that the sentience of a living being (its ability to suffer) makes it worthy of moral consideration. It is therefore prima facie wrong to cause suffering to a sentient being and any act that does so must be justified with an appeal to an overriding concern such as the promotion of enlightenment.[62] This is especially true when we consider the death of a sentient being (Warren's third proposition). However, it is questionable whether Dōgen would take "probable degree of mental sophistication" into account. On one hand, Zen ethics are based upon compassion, not rights, so the ability of an animal to function as part of a moral community is irrelevant, since even humans do not need to do this to be worthy of moral consideration (e.g., infants or coma patients). On the other hand, human beings have a special soteriological place in the cycle of rebirth because we—and we alone—are capable of distinguishing between good and evil and thus realizing *satori* (enlightenment).[63] Thus, if we replace "probable degree of mental sophistication" with "potential for achieving enlightenment," we find that Dōgen reaches the same conclusions as Warren: while animal cruelty is wrong, nonhuman animals might be harmed in certain circumstances in which doing so promotes the well-being of humans.[64]

So if human beings hold the most important position in the karmic cycle of rebirth, are we allowed to use animals for food or medical testing? Early Buddhist texts show Siddhartha Guatama eating meat and resisting attempts to make monks follow a vegetarian diet. Damien Keown argues that since meat-eating was so commonplace in the Buddha's time, following a strict vegetarian diet would have made it difficult for monks to get alms. However, the Mahāyāna tradition later forbids meat-eating because it injures sentient beings and hinders a monk's liberation.[65] Dōgen follows this tradition, advising Sōtō Zen monks to "eat and drink moderately."[66] He further states:

> monks should not concern themselves with that they have to eat. Just take what is there. If it is good, enjoy it; if it is bad, eat it without distaste. Just practice, eating enough to avoid starving, and maintain your life with the food provided.[67]

Monks should not worry about matters of taste and the desire to derive pleasure from food. Thus meat, which is not absolutely essential for survival and causes harm to sentient beings, should not be on the table for purely aesthetic reasons. Simply stating that one likes the taste of meat is not sufficient reason to cause injury to another sentient being and one should be mindful of one's attachment to the habit of meat-eating, which can cause one to stray on the path to enlightenment.

However, Dōgen does not demand of his monks a strict vegetarian diet. A monk might drink wine or eat meat because these are the only things offered him as alms by laypeople, but this does not necessarily mean he is attached to these things.[68] In the *Shōbōgenzō Zuimonki*, Dōgen recounts the tale of Fo-Chao, who gave a sick monk permission to eat meat. Supposedly, as the monk tried to eat the meat, a demon perched upon his head and surreptitiously devoured the flesh before the monk could put it in his mouth. Fo-Chao concluded that giving meat to monks recuperating from an illness was morally permissible because it was the demon, not the monk, who ate the meat. The meaning of the demon is open to multifarious interpretations. It might be meant literally or it could be a metaphor for the monk's sickness. In either case, it is clear that neither the carnivorous monk nor Fo-Chao accrued *karma* as a result of the action. Dōgen thus advises the *roshi* to "exercise judgment whether meat eating should be allowed or not."[69] However, certain forms of meat production such as veal and factory-farmed chicken are morally problematic because of the unnecessary suffering they cause to sentient beings. Zen practitioners must be constantly mindful of the extent to which the foods they consume promote awakening and minimize suffering.

While it is possible to live a healthy life on a purely vegetarian diet, ethicists such as Cohen have pointed out that our lives would be seriously compromised without modern medicine, which is dependent on animal testing.[70] Obviously, animal testing did not exist in Dōgen's Japan or Siddhartha Gautama's India, so Zen views on the subject must be inferred from the tradition's commentary on other uses for animals. Early Buddhist authors do not specifically condemn the use of nonhuman animals for human purposes, provided that there is no reasonable alternative.[71] Domesticating an ox for agriculture would be permissible, so long as the farmer treated the ox humanely and there was no other way to plough the field (e.g., a John Deere tractor). However, such domestication does not typically result in the death of the animal, while animal testing procedures like the Draize or LD-50 tests necessarily produce pain, disability, and death. Because human beings hold a privileged place in the cycle of rebirth, the restricted use of animals for medical testing might be permissible to create medicine to save human beings who might go on to become enlightened. However, animal testing for cosmetics would not be permissible, since things like men's hair-dye and baldness treatments represent attachments to ego and permanence. The overarching principle for the use of nonhuman animals is this: if there is a reasonable alternative that accomplishes the same goal, it is immoral to cause unnecessary suffering to a sentient being.

Hōben and exceptions to the principle of non-injury

But what do we make of Nansen's cat-cutting? *Roshi* Robert Aitken interprets this as a *kōan*, a puzzling story that is the focus of meditation and not meant to be taken literally. Like all *kōans*, the tale of Nansen and the cat invites varied interpretation. Sekida Katsuku interprets the story as a metaphor in which the cat represents the ego and its bifurcation symbolizes the severing of one's attachments to the self.[72] Douglas K. Mikkelson takes a similar approach, arguing that Nansen's action prompts his monks to experience the world via *hishiryō* (非思量 without thinking).[73] Dōgen seems to take this story literally, since he critiques the effectiveness of Nansen's teaching method. So what, if anything, could justify the cutting of the cat and what does Dōgen make of this explanation?

The term *hōben* (方便; Sk. *upāya*) is literally translated as "skillful means" and refers to the doctrine developed at length in the *Lotus Sūtra*, which Dōgen reveres as one of the most authoritative Mahāyanā texts. Collectively, *hōben* refers to all of the methods that *bodhisattvas* use to help sentient beings realize enlightenment.[74] For Dōgen, skillful means is the primary method through which the effectiveness of Buddhist teachings can be evaluated: they are efficacious insofar as they promote enlightenment.[75] The *Lotus Sūtra* illustrates this principle with the story of a man who returns home to find his house ablaze with his children still inside. When he tells them to leave, they refuse because they do not want to stop playing, so their father tells them a lie about a wonderful train of animal-drawn carriages outside, which motivates them to leave. In this case, the man is not guilty of maleficence because he told the lie to promote the children's well-being.[76]

Yet this case is uncontroversial. The lie is told to the children for their own benefit, so the harm to them is canceled out by the merit to them. Cutting the cat is different, since the harm is to the cat and the benefit is to the monks who witness the event. It seems that the cat has been wronged because it does not benefit from Nansen's lesson.[77] Though the two monks who claim to own the cat might be traumatized by the event, their concerns are severed along with their attachments (and their cat!), so there is really no lasting harm done to them. The controversial aspect of the doctrine of *hōben* is the fact that it allows a practitioner to commit acts that otherwise would be considered immoral without karmic consequence because the merit earned from liberating a sentient being would cancel out the *karma* accrued from violating the precept. Dōgen was careful to interpret this doctrine with a healthy grain of salt, since it can lead to a crass, act-utilitarian calculus in which the ends always justify the means. For Dōgen, practice and enlightenment are one, which means "the means and the end should be treated as a pair of foci in Dōgen's Zen."[78] Ultimately, Dōgen asserts that not all things are justified simply because they promote the ends of human beings. So, when might skillful means justify the injury of a nonhuman animal? To answer this question, we need to first examine this doctrine in detail and then revisit the meaning of the Zen story in which Nansen cuts the cat in half.

Keown describes *upāya* (skillful means) as the most important Mahāyanā ethical innovation because it allows the *bodhisattva* to commit otherwise immoral actions for the benefit of another human being. Keown distinguishes between two different kinds of *upāya*: one for unenlightened monks and the other for enlightened monks who have taken the *bodhisattva* vow. The first applies to the monk—the *bodhisattva* in training—who is allowed to commit minor offenses so long as they are performed solely in the interest of another person's salvation. The Mahāyanā tradition is pragmatic enough to recognize that the minor offenses that apply to monastic life often get in the way of action in the world that might promote the salvation of others. Because the *bodhisattva* has an obligation to aid sentient beings, there is a second form of *upāya* that allows a *bodhisattva* to commit the Ten Bad Paths of Action, the first of which is the killing of living beings. For example, the Buddha claimed that in a previous life, he killed an evil trader to save the lives of 500 innocent people. However, *upāya* does not mean that any act is permissible for a *bodhisattva*. Violating the precepts was permitted, provided two stipulations were met: the act must benefit others and it must have a pure motive. *Upāya* is part of the *bodhisattva* ideal: a *bodhisattva* actually has an *obligation* to commit an offense to promote the interest of sentient beings. Committing these acts does not force one to lose *bodhisattva* status because the *karma* that is accrued as a result of the action is immediately canceled out by the merit that comes as a result of benefiting sentient beings.[79]

So, can the doctrine of skillful means be used to justify Nansen cutting the cat? Dōgen does discuss skillful means in his writings and endorses a view of ethics that ultimately transcends the limitations of the precepts. In Zen, morality begins by following the precepts against killing, stealing, sexual misconduct, lying, etc. However, the goal of Zen is to cultivate a sense of compassion that will make morality familiar. The precepts are only guidelines that are grounded in an awareness of interdependent arising and compassion for all sentient beings. Upholding the precepts might *promote* virtue, but it is not the same thing as *being* virtuous. As Philip Kapleau puts it, enlightened people do not imitate the precepts; the precepts imitate them.[80] The five precepts against killing, stealing, lying, adultery, and intoxicants are not moral absolutes but rather resolutions that Buddhists undertake to change their habits. Thus, a precept should not be understood as "thou shalt not…" but rather as "I will not…"[81] Ultimately, once one has made these precepts familiar by changing one's habits, one becomes the kind of person who naturally does the right thing without having to appeal to the precepts. Like training wheels on a bicycle, the precepts help protect novices from falling until they can get a natural sense of balance that will keep them upright. This includes the precept against killing living beings; it is not an absolute law but rather a guideline for virtuous living.

Dōgen is a proponent of "face-to-face transmission," an intimate teacher–student relationship that cannot be reduced to a set of dogmatic principles.[82] The method that each *roshi* uses to teach his students will vary depending upon the needs of that particular student. No teaching methodology can be universally deemed wrong, as the context will always determine the efficacy of the methodology. Thus, cutting a cat in half might be justified if it were the most effective way to liberate one's students.

When discussing the story of Nansen cutting the cat in two, Dōgen advises the monk Ejō, "You know how to cut the cat in two with one sword, but you don't know how to cut the cat in *one* with one sword."[83] Cutting the cat "in one" might sound like a contradiction in terms—something like the "sound of one hand clapping"—but it is likely that Dōgen refers to the act of severing the monks' attachment to the cat while leaving the animal intact. He describes the phrase, "cutting of the cat," as a "pivot word" that promotes the realization of enlightenment.[84] The cat is the source of attachment for the arguing monks and the "cutting" represents the severing of attachments. "Cutting the cat in one" is a pivot word similar to Takuan Sōhō's paradoxical concept of the "life-giving sword": "the accomplished man uses the sword but does not kill others. He uses the sword and gives others life."[85] In this passage, Takuan is advising the great swordsman Yagyū Munenori about the proper use of violence: whenever possible, a good person should minimize the violence done to his opponent while simultaneously doing his duty. In some instances, this might involve killing his opponent, but a true master will inflict the minimum possible harm to accomplish his goals.

Similarly, Dōgen encourages Ejō to release the cat, which would have accomplished the same goal without harm. Dōgen states that "cutting the cat is an action of a Buddha" and "the action of the Buddha and the crime are separate, but they both occur at once in one action."[86] This refers to the doctrine of skillful means: the crime and its *karma* are separate from the action of the Buddha, who incurs no karmic consequence as a result of his action due to the fact that it promotes enlightenment among his monks. Even though killing the cat to promote enlightenment might be excused by *upāya*, Dōgen states that "while such a view is all right, it would be better not to hold it."[87] In other words, while it is acceptable to kill the cat to promote enlightenment, since "there are no fixed methods" in teaching, it would be better to find another way that did not harm a sentient being.

Upāya bears a close resemblance to the doctrine of double effect, which states that it is permissible to cause serious harm as an unintended side effect of an action that promotes a good end. An action with a good *intended consequence* and a bad *forseen consequence* is morally permissible, provided that the following conditions are met:

1 the action itself is not immoral (it is either good or neutral);
2 the agent intends the good effects, not the bad ones (though they are foreseen);
3 the bad effects are not a means to the end of the good effects; and
4 no better options are available to minimize harm to a greater degree.[88]

The classic example, given by Thomas Aquinas in the *Summa Theologica*, involves killing a man in self-defense. The intended consequences of the defender's actions are the protection of his and bodily integrity from an unjust attack, while the foreseen consequence is the likely death or serious injury of his attacker. However, Aquinas is careful to note that excessive force would violate the doctrine of double-effect: if I can simply run from my attacker or subdue him without injury, I would not be justified in killing him.[89] Takuan would agree: the life-giving sword demands that one choose the path that inflicts the least injury while still accomplishing one's goal.

The doctrine of double-effect can be used here to explain why Dōgen's actions are better than Nansen's. Dōgen hints at this line of thinking when he tells Ejō, "The action of the Buddha and the crime are separate, but they both occur at once in one action."[90] He criticizes Nansen for cutting the cat when he had another, viable option. Simon James argues that skillful means can only be invoked as a justification for precept violation when one has exhausted all of one's options,[91] which is identical to Condition 4 above. Table 6.1 illustrates how this doctrine applies to Nansen and Dōgen's approaches to dealing with the cat.

Nansen's actions cannot be justified by double-effect, since Condition 1 is violated (harming a sentient being) as is Condition 3 (cutting the cat is the means to the end of the monks' awakening). Granted, one might argue that skillful means render the precepts meaningless, since a *bodhisattva* may violate them at will, which legitimizes the use of such means to achieve the end of awakening. However, as Dōgen points out, since killing the cat is a crime, there might be a better option (Condition 4). Merely the threat of killing the cat would be enough to promote awakening. Threatening to kill the cat is morally neutral

Table 6.1 Double-effect and skillful means

Double effect conditions	*Nansen cutting the cat in two (killing the cat)*	*Dōgen cutting the cat in one (releasing the cat)*
1 Action itself is not immoral	✗ Killing a sentient being violates the first precept	✓ Threatening and releasing the cat violates no precepts
2 Agent intends good effects, not bad foreseen effects	✓ Nansen intends to enlighten his monks; the cat's death is foreseen	✓ Dōgen intends to enlighten his monks; the cat's death is neither intended nor foreseen
3 Bad effect not a means to the good effect	✗ The cutting of the cat is the cause of the monks' enlightenment	✓ There is no bad effect, since the cat is released
4 No better options	✗ Dōgen's option is better	✓ Dōgen's option is best

(Condition 1), because the cat cannot comprehend the threat, so it would not be in fear for its life. Dōgen would intend only good effects; bad effects would be neither foreseen nor intended. The bad effect (the cat's death) would not actually happen, so it would not be a means to an end (Condition #3); only the threat of cutting would be there, which is morally neutral. Finally, this would be the best option, since it would promote enlightenment without harming the cat (Condition 4). James interprets Dōgen's response to Nansen as a commentary on inherent enlightenment: because we *realize* our original enlightenment rather than *earning* it, "following the precepts is not a means to awakening, but a manifestation of awakening itself."[92] Thus, violations of the precepts are justified only in rare circumstances in which the enlightenment of sentient beings is at stake. For Dōgen, the doctrine of skillful means is not a karmic "get out of jail free" card. Killing sentient beings must only be done as a last resort when no other viable options present themselves.

Conclusions

Dōgen's ethics of nonhuman animals is grounded in wisdom of interdependent arising, which produces a sense of compassion for all beings, including nonhuman animals. While there are rules and precepts that prohibit the killing of living beings—human and nonhuman alike—the precepts are not unbreakable universal laws, but rather guidelines that promote the cultivation of the twin virtues of wisdom and compassion, which are the real ground of ethical conduct in Zen. Though all beings are part of the same karmic cycle of rebirth, human beings have a special soteriological status as thinking, moral beings, which means only we are capable of realizing enlightenment. This results in an ethic that is somewhat weaker than the strong animal rights view: while causing suffering to sentient beings is wrong, it may be done on those rare occasions when it promotes the awakening of human beings. This means that eating meat or using animals for medical testing might be justified, so long as there is no reasonable alternative available that would minimize suffering and maximize awakening more effectively. Even though skillful means might be used to justify violations of the precepts against killing, Dōgen argues that the only time a bad unintended consequence is justified is when the agent's motive is pure and there is no better option.

Zen prompts us to continually reevaluate the ways in which we both perceive and conceive the world. The purpose of a *kōan* is to discourage our everyday ways of thinking and push us to a higher level of understanding grounded in interdependent arising. Often, we choose to harm sentient beings, not because we have no other choice, but because we lack the imagination to create alternative solutions that minimize suffering to the greatest possible extent. The law of *karma* is always in effect: the infliction of wanton suffering upon sentient beings will become an impediment to one's awakening.[93]

Notes

1 Translation is the author's own.

2 The *Shōbōgenzō Zuimonki* (正法眼蔵随聞) is a collection of Dōgen's lessons on the practice of Zen. The title can be loosely translated as "The Simplified Eye of the True Law" and refers to the fact that this is a more accessible version of Sōtō Zen teachings than Dōgen's seminal work, the *Shōbōgenzō*. All references to this text in this chapter come from *A Primer of Sōtō Zen: A Translation of Dōgen's Shōbōgenzō Zuimonki* (trans. Reihō Masunaga) (Honolulu, HI: University of Hawaii Press, 1971).

3 *Kōans* (公案) are puzzling questions, statements, or tales designed to expose the flaws in a student's objective, discursive methods of reasoning, thereby pushing the student to a new mental schema characterized by a heightened awareness of interdependent arising that, over time, leads to *satori* (悟り enlightenment).

4 Dōgen, *Shōbōgenzō Zuimonki*, 8–9. Also see Robert Carter, *Encounter with Enlightenment: A Study of Japanese Ethics* (Albany, NY: State University of New York Press, 2001), 105–6 and Paul Reps and Nyogen Senzaki, *Zen Flesh, Zen Bones: A Collection of Zen and Pre-Zen Writings* (Boston, MA: Tuttle Pub., 1998), 128–9. Some versions of this story translate Nansen's comment to Jōshū as "If you had been there, I could have spared the cat," implying that Jōshū, as an enlightened monk, could have said something to stop Nansen. See Yamada Kōun, *The Gateless Gate: The Classic Book of Zen Koans* (Boston, MA: Wisdom Publications, 2004), 70–3.

5 Carter, *Encounter with Enlightenment*, 80.

6 Ibid., 86–7.

7 Ibid., 86–7.

8 Hall and Ames state, "Persons are radically situated as persons-in-context, inhering as they do in a world defined by specific social, cultural, and natural conditions. Persons shape and are shaped by the field of things and events in which they reside." See David L. Hall and Roger T. Ames, *Thinking From the Han: Self, Truth, and Transcendence in Chinese and Western Culture* (Albany, NY: State University of New York Press, 1998), 264.

9 Carter, *Encounter with Enlightenment*, 88.

10 Ibid., 106.

11 Dōgen, *A Primer of Sōtō Zen*, 77.

12 See ibid., 7, 22, 50, 62 for some of the more important instances.

13 Dōgen, *The Heart of Dōgen's Shōbōgenzō* (trans. Norman Waddell and Masao Abe) (Albany, NY: State University of New York Press, 2002), 40–1.

14 Carter, *Encounter with Enlightenment*, 114–16.

15 Dōgen, *A Primer of Sōtō Zen*, 14.
16 This is Thomas Kasulis' translation of the *Shoakumakusa* passage: see *Zen Action, Zen Person* (Honolulu, HI: University of Hawaii Press, 1981), 94. Mikkelson also stresses the importance of this passage for Dōgen's ethics. See Douglas K. Mikkelson, "Who is Arguing About the Cat? Moral Action and Enlightenment according to Dōgen," *Philosophy East and West* 47, no. 3 (1997): 391.
17 Mikkelson interprets these categories as merely descriptive of the moral conduct of an enlightened person, but I believe Dōgen means them normatively as well. Within Buddhist ethics, harm (maleficence) can be understood as that which promotes suffering or ignorance. Good (beneficence) is that which minimizes suffering and promotes enlightenment. One must purify one's intentions to the point that one constantly wills the benefit of all beings. See Mikkelson, "Who is Arguing About the Cat?" 391.
18 Carter, *Encounter with Enlightenment*, 111.
19 Ibid., 101.
20 Ibid., 102–3. Damien Keown recounts the parable of the raft as another type of "transcendency thesis" in which normative precepts are left behind in favor of an ethic grounded in moral virtue. See Damien Keown, *The Nature of Buddhist Ethics* (New York: Palgrave, 2001), 92–6.
21 Kasulis, *Zen Action, Zen Person*, 89.
22 Kasulis, *Zen Action, Zen Person*, 29–30.
23 See Dōgen's *A Primer of Sōtō Zen*, 50, 55, 56, 72, for some of the more pertinent passages.
24 Dōgen, *A Primer of Sōtō Zen*, 56.
25 Ibid., 15, 43–4, 49, 84.
26 Ibid., 65–6.
27 Ibid., 37.
28 Ibid., 56.
29 Ibid., 72.
30 Ibid., 71.
31 Ibid., 14.
32 Carter, 107.
33 Ibid., 107.
34 Søren Kierkegaard, *Fear and Trembling (with Repetition)* (trans. and ed. Howard V. Hong and Edna H. Hong) (Princeton, NJ: Princeton University Press, 1983), 54–5.
35 Lori Gruen, "The Moral Status of Animals," in *The Stanford Encyclopedia of Philosophy*, ed. Edward N. Zalta (Stanford, CA: Stanford University Press, 2010). Hugh LaFollette also makes this point in "Animal Rights and Human Wrongs," in *Ethics and the Environment*, ed. N. Dower (London: Gower Press, 1989), 79–90.
36 See Mary Anne Warren, "Difficulties with the Strong Animal Rights Position," in *Contemporary Moral Problems*, 8th ed., ed. James E. White (Belmont, CA: Thomson Wadsworth, 2006), 396–403. Her criteria for personhood are articulated in her discussion of the personhood of a human fetus: Mary Anne Warren, "On the Moral and Legal Status of Abortion," in *Contemporary Moral Problems*, 8th ed., ed. James E. White (Belmont, CA: Thomson Wadsworth, 2006), 114–25. Her perspective on animal rights was articulated in 1987 and her views on abortion appeared a decade later, but we can infer from both of these articles how her "moral community" criteria would apply to animals. Warren mentions that these criteria apply to "moral rights of women and of nonhuman animals." Warren, "On the Moral and Legal Status of Abortion." Her views will be discussed in greater detail later in this chapter.
37 Carter, *Encounter with Enlightenment*, 110.
38 Of course, I mean "self" here in the nominal sense: it is a spatio-temporal aggregate rather than an absolute entity.
39 Dōgen, *Moon in a Dewdrop: Writings of Zen Master Dōgen* (ed. Kasuaki Tanahashi) (San Francisco, CA: San Francisco Zen Center, 1985), 146.

40 Ibid., 79. This is a double entendre: rat and tiger refer to both animals and hours of the day (each two-hour interval was named after a creature from the Chinese zodiac).
41 Ibid., 41. Answering "*mu*" to the *kōan* indicates that the question is empty because all thing exist only nominally.
42 Ibid., 65.
43 Damien Keown, *Buddhist Ethics: A Very Short Introduction* (Oxford: Oxford University Press, 2005), 39–42, 49. Also see Dōgen, *Moon in a Dewdrop*, 339.
44 Dōgen, *Moon in a Dewdrop*, 46.
45 Ibid., 106–7.
46 Ibid., 328.
47 Ibid., 90.
48 Ibid., 105.
49 Ibid., 35.
50 Deane Curtin, "Dōgen, Deep Ecology, and the Ecological Self," *Environmental Ethics* 16 (1994): 195–213.
51 Masao Abe, *A Study of Dōgen: His Philosophy and Religion* (trans. and ed. Steven Heine) (Albany, NY: State University of New York Press, 1992), 54–5.
52 Dōgen, *Moon in a Dewdrop*, 58.
53 Dōgen, *A Primer of Sōtō Zen*, 72.
54 Keown, *Buddhist Ethics*, 46.
55 Ibid.
56 Ibid., 42, 45–7.
57 Abe, 37–8.
58 Abe, 38–9.
59 Ibid., 110, 146.
60 Tom Regan, *The Case for Animal Rights* (Berkeley, CA: University of California Press, 1985).
61 Warren, "Difficulties with the Strong Animal Rights Position," 403.
62 The third section of the chapter deals with these relevant exceptions in detail.
63 Dōgen, *A Primer of Sōtō Zen*, 72.
64 As we shall see in the next section, Dōgen believes these extenuating circumstances must be extreme to justify a violation of the precepts.
65 Keown, *Buddhist Ethics*, 48–9.
66 Dōgen, *The Heart of Dōgen's Shobogenzo*, 3. Also see Kasulis, *Zen Action, Zen Person*, 70.
67 Dōgen, *A Primer of Sōtō Zen*, 43.
68 Ibid., 21.
69 Ibid., 7.
70 See Carl Cohen, "Do Animals Have Rights?" *Ethics and Behavior* 7, no. 2 (1997), 91–102.
71 Keown, *Buddhist Ethics*, 49–50.
72 Carter, *Encounter with Enlightenment*, 106.
73 Mikkelson, "Who is Arguing About the Cat?" 386–91. *Hishiryō* is the state of mind associated with enlightenment. Unlike *shiryō* (thinking via discursive reasoning) or *fushiryō* (not thinking at all), *hishiryō* is a state in which the individual experiences the world as it truly is without thinking of any one thing in particular.
74 Hee-Jin Kim, *Dōgen on Meditation and Thinking: A Reflection on His View of Zen* (Albany, NY: State University of New York Press, 2007), 30–2.
75 Taigen Dan Leighton, *Visions of Awakening Space and Time: Dōgen and the Lotus Sutra* (New York: Oxford University Press, 2007), 14–15.
76 Ibid., 15.
77 LaFollette makes a similar point: suffering is unnecessary if the being that suffers does not stand to benefit from it in any way. LaFollette, "Animal Rights and Human Wrongs," 80, 83.

78 Kim, *Dōgen on Meditation and Thinking*, 30–2.
79 Keown, *The Nature of Buddhist Ethics*, 146–63.
80 Carter, *Encounter with Enlightenment*, 105–7.
81 Ibid., 171.
82 John Schroeder, *Skillful Means: The Heart of Buddhist Compassion* (Delhi: Motilal Banarsidass Publishers, 2004), 139. Also see Dōgen, *Moon in a Dewdrop*, 175–83.
83 Dōgen, *A Primer of Sōtō Zen*, 9, emphasis added.
84 Mikkelson addresses this idea at length, interpreting "cutting the cat in one" as the non-dualistic thinking associated with *hishiryō*. Upon hearing the pivot word, a student can "realize/actualize without-thinking and see the cat as it really is." Mikkelson, "Who is Arguing About the Cat?" 387.
85 Takuan Sōhō, *The Unfettered Mind* (trans. William Scott Wilson) (Tokyo: Kodansha, 1986), 81–2. Also see Yagyū Munenori, *The Life-Giving Sword* (trans. William Scott Wilson) (New York: Kodansha International, 2003).
86 Dōgen, *A Primer of Sōtō Zen*, 9.
87 Ibid.
88 Alison McIntyre, "Doctrine of Double Effect," in *The Stanford Encyclopedia of Philosophy* (ed. Edward N. Zalta) (Stanford, CA: Publishing House, 2010). Also see Albert R. Jonsen, Mark Siegler, and William J. Winslade, *Clinical Ethics*, 7th ed. (New York: McGraw-Hill, 2010), 145.
89 MacIntyre, "Doctrine of Double Effect."
90 Dōgen, *A Primer of Sōtō Zen*, 9.
91 Simon P. James, *Zen Buddhism and Environmental Ethics* (Burlington, VT: Ashgate, 2004), 56.
92 Ibid., 57.
93 The author would like to thank Clifford Chalmers Cain and Richard Geenen for their kind assistance in preparing this essay for publication. Mahalo nui loa.

Bibliography

Abe, Masao. *A Study of Dōgen: His Philosophy and Religion.* Translated and edited by Steven Heine. Albany, NY: State University of New York Press, 1992.

Carter, Robert. *Encounter with Enlightenment: A Study of Japanese Ethics*. Albany, NY: State University of New York Press, 2001.

Cohen, Carl. "Do Animals Have Rights?" *Ethics and Behavior* 7, no. 2 (1997): 91–102.

Curtin, Deane. "Dōgen, Deep Ecology, and the Ecological Self." *Environmental Ethics* 16 (1994): 195–213.

Dōgen. *A Primer of Sōtō Zen: A Translation of Dōgen's Shōbōgenzō Zuimonki*. Translated by Reihō Masunaga. Honolulu, HI: University of Hawaii Press, 1971.

Dōgen. *Moon in a Dewdrop: Writings of Zen Master Dōgen.* Translated and edited by Kasuaki Tanahashi. San Francisco, CA: San Francisco Zen Center, 1985.

Dōgen. *The Heart of Dōgen's Shōbōgenzō*. Translated by Norman Waddell and Masao Abe. Albany, NY: State University of New York Press, 2002.

Gruen, Lori. "The Moral Status of Animals." In *The Stanford Encyclopedia of Philosophy.* Edited by Edward N. Zalta. Stanford, CA: Stanford University Center for the Study of Language and Information, 2010 (accessed May 26, 2012) http://plato.stanford.edu/archives/fall2010/entries/moral-animal/.

Hall, David L. and Ames, Roger T. *Thinking from the Han: Self, Truth, and Transcendence in Chinese and Western Culture.* Albany, NY: State University of New York Press, 1998.

James, Simon P. *Zen Buddhism and Environmental Ethics.* Burlington, VT: Ashgate, 2004.

Jonsen, Albert R., Siegler, Mark, and Winslade, William J. *Clinical Ethics*, 7th ed. New York: McGraw-Hill, 2010.

Kasulis, Thomas. *Zen Action, Zen Person*. Honolulu, HI: University of Hawaii Press, 1981.

Keown, Damien. *Buddhist Ethics: A Very Short Introduction*. Oxford: Oxford University Press, 2005.

Keown, Damien. *The Nature of Buddhist Ethics*. New York: Palgrave, 2001.

Kierkegaard, Søren. *Fear and Trembling (with Repetition)*. Translated and edited by Howard V. Hong and Edna H. Hong. Princeton, NJ: Princeton University Press, 1983.

Kim, Hee-Jin. *Dōgen on Meditation and Thinking: A Reflection on His View of Zen*. Albany, NY: State University of New York Press, 2007.

Kōun, Yamada. *The Gateless Gate: The Classic Book of Zen Koans*. Boston, MA: Wisdom Publications, 2004.

LaFollette, Hugh. "Animal Rights and Human Wrongs." In *Ethics and the Environment*. Edited by Nigel Dower, 80–90. London: Gower Press, 1989 (accessed May 26, 2012) www.hughlafollette.com/papers/animal.rights.and.human.wrongs.pdf.

Leighton, Taigen Dan. *Visions of Awakening Space and Time: Dōgen and the Lotus Sutra*. New York: Oxford University Press, 2007.

McIntyre, Alison. "Doctrine of Double Effect." In *The Stanford Encyclopedia of Philosophy*. Edited by Edward N. Zalta. Stanford, CA: Stanford University Center for the Study of Language and Information, 2010 (accessed May 26, 2012) http://plato.stanford.edu/archives/fall2011/entries/double-effect/.

Mikkelson, Douglas K. "Who is Arguing About the Cat? Moral Action and Enlightenment according to Dōgen." *Philosophy East and West* 47, no. 3 (1997): 383–97.

Munenori, Yagyū. *The Life-Giving Sword*. Translated by William Scott Wilson. New York: Kodansha International, 2003.

Regan, Tom. *The Case for Animal Rights*. Berkeley, CA: University of California Press, 1985.

Reps, Paul and Senzaki, Nyogen. *Zen Flesh, Zen Bones: A Collection of Zen and Pre-Zen Writings*. Boston, MA: Tuttle Pub., 1998.

Schroeder, John. *Skillful Means: The Heart of Buddhist Compassion*. Delhi: Motilal Banarsidass Publishers, 2004.

Sōhō, Takuan. *The Unfettered Mind*. Translated by William Scott Wilson. Tokyo: Kodansha, 1986.

Warren, Mary Anne. "Difficulties with the Strong Animal Rights Position." In *Contemporary Moral Problems*, 8th ed. Edited by James E. White, 396–403. Belmont, CA: Thomson Wadsworth, 2006.

Warren, Mary Anne. "On the Moral and Legal Status of Abortion." In *Contemporary Moral Problems*, 8th ed. Edited by James E. White, 114–25. Belmont, CA: Thomson Wadsworth, 2006.

7 Nonhuman animals and the question of rights from an Asian perspective

Christopher Key Chapple

Worldview and cosmology set up the conditions for ethics and decision-making. From the time of Descartes' pronouncements on the machine-like nature of animals, compounded with the rise of industrialized, technology-enhanced food production, there has been a growing distance between human and nonhuman animals, underscored by the general ignorance of the public in regard to the realities of factory farming, product testing, and other infelicitous uses of animals.

From an Asian perspective, where until recently slaughter has been largely small scale and in full view, meat remains, for the most part, a delicacy and makes up a significantly smaller portion of the average person's diet than in other parts of the world. Of course, this is changing due to the inevitable globalization of the American lifestyle and the rise of fast food restaurants in Asia. Nonetheless, the underlying belief systems of India (Hindu, Jaina, Sikh), East Asia (Buddhism, Confucianism, Taoism), and Southeast Asia (Buddhism, Christianity, Islam) generally, perhaps with the exception of Confucianism, contain strong messages that animals must be protected.

Hindus, Jainas, Buddhists, and Sikhs all believe in the idea of reincarnation or rebirth (*saṃsāra*). Hence, each person has endured and perhaps enjoyed past lives within the realm of animals and can feel empathy for their reality. Taoism, like Yoga, developed complex sequences of movement in imitation of animals, harnessing shamanic forms of connection.

This chapter begins with an examination of the United Nations Declaration of Human Rights, the Earth Charter, a document that disseminates key points about environmental ethics, and the core ideas of the Great Ape Project, which advocates personhood rights for higher nonhuman primates. Each of these documents probes the language of rights as it pertains, respectively, to human beings, the living systems of the earth community, and high functioning primates. This "rights" approach will be juxtaposed with Asian views of personhood and the continuities between nonhuman and human animals. I will argue that the Asian view of life, which claims that humans have been animals and that animals might become humans in future lives, suggests the need to reconsider earlier definitions of rights. Even beyond the Great Ape project championed by Peter Singer, humans might need to expand their categories to include a broader view of what constitutes a "person" to include nonhuman animals.

Uniting nations, the Earth, and nonhuman primates

We will start with an investigation of the United Nations Declaration of Human Rights. Its acceptance is so widespread that it endures as a global document of conscience. The United Nations Declaration of Human Rights set an idealistic, optimistic tone for the rebuilding of the world order following World War II. It crafted a language for assessing the human person that emphasized rights and responsibilities that accord to men and women based on their innate dignity. With close investigation of the history of the development of human rights language used in the document, it can be discerned that the drafters of the United Nations Declaration were quite thorough in their attempt to be inclusive of the world's philosophical perspectives. Additionally, gender played an important role in the drafting of the document, both in terms of the ideas contained in the document and the leadership of the commission. Eleanor Roosevelt (1886–1962) served as the Chair of the Human Rights Commission of the United Nations from its inception in 1947 until 1951. Hansa Mehta, an independence activist and legislator from newly created free India served on the drafting committee and played a significant role, as we will see, in ensuring a special place for women in the document. The Declaration created a benchmark for public policy in the latter half of the twentieth century and, it can be argued, helped prevent greater strife through the difficult period of the Cold War. It also provided a model for the drafters of the Earth Charter and similar platforms for public discussions on rights and responsibilities.

Work on the UN Declaration of Human Rights began within months of the end of the Second World War. Groundwork for the document was laid in San Francisco in 1945, with the signing of the United Nations Charter. The actual Declaration appeared in six preliminary drafts starting in June 1947 before the ratification of the Universal Declaration of Human Rights on December 10, 1948. A series of meetings leading up to the final document was held in London, Lake Success (a suburb of New York), and Geneva, before ratification in Paris.

The first version was based on a broad outline drafted by a Canadian member of the committee, John Humphrey. It was recast the same month by René Cassin of France. However, despite the early role of these decidedly Western diplomats, from the very beginning multiple voices were included in the draft and their influence can be seen in the final document. Two philosophers on the committee were of particular note: P.C. Chang and Charles Malik. Chang insisted on including the Chinese Confucian *Ren*, which he translated as "two-man mindedness." The sense of this delicate concept was eventually rendered as the word "dignity,"[1] though from the nuanced language of the document, a sense of the original intent can be gleaned.

Charles Malik, of Lebanese origin, had studied with Heidegger at Freiburg University and completed his doctoral dissertation at Harvard on "The Metaphysics of Time in the Philosophies of Whitehead and Heidegger."[2] Though at first resistant to the realm of politics, Malik eventually took over the chairmanship of the Human Rights Commission in 1951. He consistently resisted what he considered to be the hegemony of collectivism, emphasizing consistently that "the human being is more important than any national or cultural group to which he may belong" and that "a person's mind and conscience are his most sacred and inviolable possessions."[3] However, under the influence of others on the team, he yielded to the more community and family oriented rhetoric that pervades the document.

Teilhard de Chardin sent in a recommendation to focus on "man in society" rather than isolated individuals,[4] highlighting the balance that the drafters sought to achieve between the role of the government and freedom of conscience. Though he had passed away, Franklin Roosevelt cast a long shadow on the proceedings, particularly as his wife reminded the group from time to time of his advocacy of "four freedoms": freedom of speech and belief, and freedom from fear and from want.[5] These latter two freedoms hold implications beyond the exclusively human domain.

As noted, two women served on the original drafting committee: Eleanor Roosevelt and Hansa Mehta. Mehta, from India, was particularly effective in broadening the language of the document so as to steer away from male universals. At her insistence, and over the objections of Eleanor Roosevelt, the preamble reads "inherent dignity … of all members of the human family" rather than "mankind" and the first article states: "All human beings are born free and equal in dignity and rights."[6] As Mary Ann Glendon has noted, Mehta "made sure the Declaration spoke with power and clarity about equal rights for women well before they were recognized in most legal systems."[7] Mehta had been imprisoned by the British during the anti-colonial struggle and was "battling back home against purdah, child marriage, polygamy, unequal inheritance law, and bans against marriages among different castes."[8] She warned that the language "all men" would explicitly ban women, while Roosevelt insisted that the term would include women as well. Eventually, Roosevelt yielded.

The influence of the document extended beyond the political to the religious. We have already noted that the Jesuit Teilhard de Chardin offered suggestions to the drafting committee. Eleanor Roosevelt, a prolific columnist who held great sway on public opinion, wrote in 1951, after attending a world religions conference, "I think I believe that the Lord looks upon His children with compassion and allows them to approach Him in many ways."[9] Pope John Paul XXIII, who convened the Second Vatican Council, praised the Universal Declaration of Human Rights in his encyclical *Peace on Earth*[10] and used its dignatarian language of rights in the document *Pacem in Terris* (217).[11] *Nostra Aetate*, the official Vatican II document that pronounces the presence of truth in all the world's religious traditions, might be seen as parallel to Eleanor Roosevelt's above statement. Martin Luther King, Jr., also embraced the Declaration and referred to it in his sermons and speeches.

The Declaration, in a sense, created a world context for women's leadership, particularly in Asia. Hansa Mehta, sensitive to the suffering caused by misogyny in the world, emphatically insisted that gender be put upon the world table as an issue to be recognized, confronted, and negotiated. South Asia saw the rise of the world's first female prime ministers, in India, Sri Lanka, Pakistan, and Bangladesh. The political success of women might have benefited from the deep cultural sense of woman as mother-leader and source of strength (*śakti*). However, the rise of women's leadership has been noteworthy, particularly given the entrenched role of male leadership in Hindu, Buddhist, and Islamic traditions.

The first statement of the preamble to the Declaration of Human Rights emphasizes the importance of dignity: "Whereas recognition of the inherent dignity and of the equal and inalienable rights of all members of the human family is the foundation of freedom, justice and peace in the world." The first five proclamations assert rights that can easily be reconsidered and perhaps extended to nonhuman animals. The Declaration begins as follows:

> **Article 1**. All human beings are born free and equal in dignity and rights. They are endowed with reason and conscience and should act towards one another in a spirit of brotherhood.
>
> **Article 2**. Everyone is entitled to all the rights and freedoms set forth in this Declaration, without distinction of any kind, such as race, colour, sex, language, religion, political or other opinion, national or social origin, property, birth or other status. Furthermore, no distinction shall be made on the basis of the political, jurisdictional or international status of the country or territory to which a person belongs, whether it be independent, trust, non-self-governing or under any other limitation of sovereignty.
>
> **Article 3**. Everyone has the right to life, liberty and security of person.
>
> **Article 4**. No one shall be held in slavery or servitude; slavery and the slave trade shall be prohibited in all their forms.
>
> **Article 5**. No one shall be subjected to torture or to cruel, inhuman or degrading treatment or punishment.[12]

The last 25 articles of the Declaration focus on explicitly human concerns: courts, education, marriage, nationality, and so forth, categories which could not presumably be extended to nonhuman animals. However, the first five articles highlight values that in a limited way could be re-interpreted to include nonhuman animals. Philosophers and biologists such as Peter Singer, Tom Regan, Colin Allen, and Marc Bekoff have argued that nonhuman animals are worthy of dignity, freedom, right-to-life, security, and freedom from slavery and cruelty.[13] Nonhuman animals can be said to possess dignity, the right to live, the right to be free, and not to be subjected to cruelty. Although nonhuman animals are not mentioned in the Declaration, research about animal cognition has revealed that, in their own fashion, nonhuman animals deserve to be treated with dignity and without cruelty.

Implications for animals

The Declaration of Human Rights is clearly anthropocentric. It seeks to guarantee autonomy of thought and action on the part of human beings. The world was recovering from the terrible trauma of World War II and the real possibility of human self-destruction. In the ensuing decades, other issues have surfaced. Women's issues such as marriage rights (article 16)[14] and property ownership rights (article 17)[15] are addressed in the Declaration and have continued to be significant. The well-being of the planet is now considered to be imperiled by the threat of climate change. A new discourse of rights has emerged, including the landmark case made for animal rights by Peter Singer in his 1975 book *Animal Liberation* and the drafting of the Earth Charter (1994–2000).

Rosemary Radford Ruether, Carol Adams, and other feminist scholars have proclaimed a relationship between the subjugation of animals and that of slaves and women.[16] At the Parliament of World Religions in Cape Town, South Africa, 1999, Dada Vasvani of the Radhoaswami movement, stated that the eighteenth century brought the liberation of men, the nineteenth century brought the liberation of slaves, and that the twentieth century brought the liberation of women. He went on to proclaim that the twenty-first century must and will bring the liberation of animals.[17]

As we examine the United Nations Declaration of Human Rights, we can see how these moments of liberation can be tied to the core concept of dignity, mentioned earlier. Dignity, a translation of the Chinese Confucian term *Ren*, internalizes the sense of worthiness. Why do persons merit protection by the law? By ascribing dignity to persons, we find an implicit expectation that their behavior will be virtuous. True to Eleanor Roosevelt's inherent optimism and her vision for a harmonious world, all protections flow in the articulation of human rights. Beyond its obvious concern for human well-being, this document, in its preamble and the first five articles, holds implications that may extend beyond the human, and, as we will see, set the stage for the Earth Charter fifty years later as well as the premises of the Great Ape Project.

The Earth Charter

The Earth Charter has been described as "a declaration of fundamental principles for building a just, sustainable and peaceful global society in the 21st century … for the well-being of the whole human family, the greater community of life, and future generations."[18] The result of a decade-long process begun in 1995, this document has been endorsed by more than 4,500 organizations, including governments and non-profit, non-governmental groups. The Earth Charter Commission, with representatives from the Americas, Africa, Australia, Asia, and Europe, is chaired by Steven L. Rockefeller, former religion professor and dean at Middlebury College. The document was formally launched in 2000 with the support of Queen Beatrix of the Netherlands at the Peace Palace at The Hague.

In comparison to the United Nations Universal Declaration of Human Rights, the Earth Charter takes a broader view, more inclusive of life systems rather than merely focusing on human concerns:

> **Preamble**
> We stand at a critical moment in Earth's history, a time when humanity must choose its future. As the world becomes increasingly interdependent and fragile, the future at once holds great peril and great promise. To move forward we must recognize that in the midst of a magnificent diversity of cultures and life forms we are one human family and one Earth community with a common destiny. We must join together to bring forth a sustainable global society founded on respect for nature, universal human rights, economic justice, and a culture of peace. Towards this end, it is imperative that we, the peoples of Earth, declare our responsibility to one another, to the greater community of life, and to future generations.
>
> **Earth, Our Home**
> Humanity is part of a vast evolving universe. Earth, our home, is alive with a unique community of life. The forces of nature make existence a demanding and uncertain adventure, but Earth has provided the conditions essential to life's evolution. The resilience of the community of life and the well-being of humanity depend upon preserving a healthy biosphere with all its ecological systems, a rich variety of plants and animals, fertile soils, pure waters, and clean air. The global environment with its finite resources is a common concern of all peoples. The protection of Earth's vitality, diversity, and beauty is a sacred trust.

Of the sixteen sections of the Earth Charter, one, the second to the last, takes up the issue of animals:

> **15. Treat all living beings with respect and consideration.**
>
> a. Prevent cruelty to animals kept in human societies and protect them from suffering.
> b. Protect wild animals from methods of hunting, trapping, and fishing that cause extreme, prolonged, or avoidable suffering.
> c. Avoid or eliminate to the full extent possible the taking or destruction of non-targeted species.[19]

The Earth Charter advances the cause of animals in several ways. First, it begins with a concern for life forms beyond the human, recognizing that all human flourishing requires the resources and abundance of a healthy planet. The Charter identifies the importance of science and evolution and in its Preamble lauds Earth's "rich variety of plants and animals" as quoted above. It also expresses deep concern for the suffering of animals. This document has been widely disseminated through the internet and has been used extensively in classrooms, church study groups, and community salons. It represents a great advance in the expansion of the idea of rights to not only nonhuman animals but to the very systems that comprise Earth.

The Great Ape Project

The Great Ape Project describes itself as "an international movement that aims to defend the rights of the nonhuman great primates: chimpanzees, gorillas, orangutans, and bonobos."[20] Established in 1994 and now based in Brazil, the Project operates four chimpanzee sanctuaries. It has issued the world Declaration on Great Primates that asserts the need to protect the right to life, freedom to live in the wild, and freedom from torture for these animals.

The Great Ape Project makes the case that certain primates, including chimpanzees, orangutans, and gorillas, carry sufficient similarity to human primates that they too should be exempt from slavery and other forms of abuse. Using the language of rights as universalized in the UN Declaration of Human Rights, Peter Singer, Paola Cavalieri, and others suggest that the Great Apes could be repatriated to United Nations Trust Territories where they could be released and rehabilitated to "nonhuman independent territories."[21] Cavalieri and Singer posit their project as follows:

> What we envision is thus an international movement that can play, for the liberation of the other great apes, the role that in the past was played for humans in the Anti-Slavery Society. Its immediate goal will be to ensure that, both morally and legally, chimpanzees, gorillas, and orangutans are removed from the category of property, and included in the category of "another" i.e., in the class of beings who are credited with personhood.... Its international impact and resonance make it reasonable to hope that it could, over the next few years, gain enough political support to relegate the assumption that we are entitled to enslave and exploit our closest kin to the junkyard of discredited ideas.[22]

Interestingly, their argument on behalf of primate species rests upon their genetic similarity to humans. The Great Ape Project does not take as its core concern the well-being of all nonhuman animals, only those who resemble humans. The argument is not about animal protection as a whole, but about protecting animals that are the closest of human kin. Humans remain the measure of worth. To provide an alternate viewpoint, we turn now to worldviews from Asia that propose a different approach, based less on the human as the standard and more on a recognition of the innate dignity not only of humans and their close biological kin, but of all living, breathing beings.

Asian perspectives on personhood

> Heaven is my father and earth is my mother, and even such a small creature as I find an intimate place in their midst. Therefore that which extends

> throughout the universe I regard as my body and that which directs the universe I consider as my nature. All people are my brothers and sisters, and all things are my companions.[23]

According to most schools of Asian thought, the force that energizes the universe and all aspects of creation cannot be separated from the force that drives the human. Animals are seen as kin. Many Asian traditions and cultures ascribe dignity to animals. Hinduism, Jainism, and Buddhism have helped shape cultural norms and practices throughout the region, exerting influence beyond the subcontinent to Southeast Asia, Indonesia, and, in the case of Buddhism, all parts of northern and eastern Asia. Attitudes toward animals in these Asian traditions have supported and continue to support advocacy for the well-being of all living beings. Through their stories and even in their complex cosmologies, Hindu, Jaina, and Buddhist traditions accord high status to animals as friends and relatives from past lives.

Animals in yoga

Yoga postures, often of animals, emerged as a distinct expression of religious devotional practice over a course of many hundreds of years. Early images from the Indus Valley Civilization of Mohenjodaro and Harappa (*ca.* 3000 BCE) depict humans surrounded by animals, both fierce and domestic, in an idyllic tableau. Terracotta sculptures show humans imitating the countenance of animals, most notably the tiger.[24] Historian of religion, Mircea Eliade, in his classic work on shamanism, noted that imitation of animals can be found among shamans worldwide. He wrote that "forgetting the limitations and false measurements of humanity [in imitating animals, one] ... found a new dimension in life: spontaneity, freedom, sympathy with all the cosmic rhythms and hence bliss and immortality."[25] The earliest image of what might be deemed a proto-Yogi shows a cross-legged figure sitting upon an animal skin, adorned with a headdress that includes horns from a buffalo or antelope. This combination is not unlike the Native American tradition of donning the skins and horns of a totem animal, indicating that one has harnessed the special power associated with that particular animal.

In the medieval period, detailed Yoga manuals were composed to provide instruction on how to mimic the stance and mood of specific animals. Many postures (*āsana*) carry the names of animals. The *Haṭha Yoga Pradīpikā* (*HYP*), written by Svātmārāma in the fifteenth century, lists several poses named after animals. Some examples are the Cow Head's Pose (*Gomukhāsana*) [*HYP* 20], the Tortoise Pose (*Kūrmāsana*) [*HYP* 24], the Rooster Pose (*Kukkuṭāsana*) [*HYP* 25], the Peacock Pose (*Mayūrāsana*) [*HYP* 32], and the Lion's Pose (*Siṃhāsana*) [*HYP* 52–4].[26] Additionally, later Yoga manuals, such as the *Gheraṇḍa Saṃhitā*, include several additional poses named for animals, including the Serpent Pose (*Nāgāsana*), the Rabbit Pose, the Cobra Pose (*Bhujaṅgāsana*), the Locust Pose (*Śalabhāsana*), the Crow Pose (*Kākāsana*), the Eagle Pose (*Garuḍāsana*), the

Frog Pose (*Maṇḍūkāsana*), and the Scorpion Pose (*Vṛśchikāsana*), to name a few.[27] By imitating animals through the practice of Yoga, one takes on the qualities associated with each, from the regal bearing of a lion to the great balance and insight of an eagle. Rather than drawing upon abstract notions regarding moral standing and rights in terms of the relationship between animals and humans as found in the Earth Charter and the Great Ape Project, the approach of Yoga to nonhuman animals is much more visceral, suggesting an emotional continuity or porous fluidity between animal and human realities. Through the practice of Yoga, one potentially gains intimacy with the outlook of animals; from this intimacy might arise care and concern.

Animals in Hinduism

The Vedas, which date from before 1500 BCE and serve as the foundation for various forms of Hinduism, extol the cow in dozens of hymns, likening the beneficence of the cow to the dawn, to speech, to the rain clouds, and creation itself.[28] The Upaniṣads introduce the idea of reincarnation, with the *Kauṣītaki Upanisad* stating: "[One] is born again here according to [one's] deeds (*karma*) as worm, or as a moth, or as a fish, or as a bird, or as a lion, or as a wild boar, or as a snake, or as a tiger, or as a person."[29] In the later Purāṇic period, an abundance of gods and goddesses arise in both literature and in the arts. Animals themselves became elevated to deity status in Hinduism, such as the Eagle Garuḍa, the Monkey Hanuman, and the Elephant-headed Gaṇeśa. Each anthropomorphic deity has a well-known companion animal, including Gaṇeśa's rat, Durgā's lion, Sarasvatī's peacock, Lakṣmī's elephant, and Śiva's bull.

The *Yogavāsiṣṭha*, a Hindu Kashmiri text from the eleventh century, includes a story in its section known as the *Upaśama Prakaraṇa* that tells about two brothers who grapple with the death of their parents. In a playful cascade of poetic description, this story describes the process of reincarnation. It suggests that because all humans have once been animals, insects, and even trees, that we can feel empathy for each of these life forms. Through reflecting on these other existences, we can lessen our attachment to this particular precious human birth.

Puṇya, the older brother, has attained the state of liberation (*jīvanmukti*). Their father, a holy man named Dīrghatapā, dies. His wife and the mother of the boys, using yogic techniques, follows him in death. Pāvana, the younger brother, is inconsolable in his grief. Puṇya instructs him regarding the fleeting nature of the body and eventually frees his brother from his affliction, bringing him to liberation through tales of birth and rebirth. His teachings admonish Pāvana to remember his past births as myriad beings. By reflecting on the joys and pains of various past births, Puṇya prompts his brother to gain a new perspective on his current circumstance. Ultimately, this insight liberates Pāvana. The dialogue includes the following:

> You are a spiritual substance (*liṅga śarīra*)
> and have undergone many births.

You have had many friends and properties in your past lives.
Why not think of them also?
You had many friends in the flowery plains
where you had your pasture in your former form as a stag.
Why not think of those deer,
who were once your dear companions?
Why do you not lament for your lost companions of swans,
in the pleasant pools of lotuses, where you dove
and swam in the form of a gander?
Why not lament for your fellow trees in the woodlands,
where you once stood as a stately tree among them?
You had comrades of lions on the rugged crags of mountains.
Why not lament for them also?
You had many friends among the fishes
in clean lakes adorned with lotuses.
Why not lament your separation from them?
You have been a monkey in the green woods of Daśārṇa.
You have been a prince in the land of frost.
You have been a raven in the woods of Puṇḍra.
You have been an elephant in the land of Haihayas,
a donkey in Trigarta, a dog in the country of Śalva,
a bird in the wood of sāl trees.
You have been a peepal tree on the Vindhya Mountains,
a wood insect in a large oak,
a rooster on the Mandara Mountain,
and then you were born as a Brahmin in one of its caverns.
You were a Brahmin in Kosala, a partridge in Bengal,
a horse in the land of snows,
and a beast at the sacred grounds of Puṣkara.
You have been an insect in the trunk of a palm tree,
a gnat in a big tree, and a crane in the Vindhya woods.
Now you are my younger brother.
You had been an ant for six months,
laying within the thin bark of a bhugpetera tree
in a glen of the Himalayan foothills.
You are now born as my younger brother.
You were a millipede in a dung-hill at a distant village,
where you dwelt for a year and a half.
Now you are my younger brother.
You were once the baby of a hill tribe woman
and dwelt at her breast like a honey-sucking bee…
You are now my younger brother.
In this manner, you were born in many other shapes
and had to wander all about this continent for years.
You are now my younger brother.[30]

Under the tutelage of his older brother, Pāvana achieves liberation through reflecting on the many past lives that he has experienced. By seeing his connections with past embodiments, Pāvana gains the dispassion needed to heal his grief and engage the world through a state of equanimity. According to Vasiṣṭha, the two brothers lived for many years in the forest, perfect in their spiritual knowledge (*jñānavijñānāparāgau*). Though moving himself away from self-concern, Pāvana becomes free to act again within the world without depression or fear, important lessons for the young Rāma.

The view of animals in this narrative is fraught with affect. Rather than an animal standing for or representing some human emotion or conveying some moral message as in *Aesop's Fables*, the animals here are portrayed for themselves as animals. They serve as reminders of the continuity of life. Puṇya describes deer, swans, lions, fishes, monkeys, ravens, elephants, donkeys, dogs, partridges, horses, ants, millipedes, and more. By pointing out the variety of life forms and noting the environments in which they dwell, Puṇya exhibits a knowledge of and interest in life forms other than human. By asking his brother to consider his link with this menagerie, he effectively rousts him from his perch of sadness. Though connecting with his own biological history, Pāvana regains equilibrium and momentum.

Animals in Jainism

The Jaina faith arose more than 2,500 years ago on India's northern Gangetic plain. Its founding figures, Pārśvanātha (*ca.* 850 BCE) and Mahāvīra (*ca.* 500 BCE) are regarded to be the twenty-third and twenty-fourth of a long line of spiritual teachers (Tīrthaṅkaras). They taught and lived a way of life that emphasizes the practice of nonviolence (*ahiṃsā*). This commitment to nonviolence, which includes vegetarianism and rejection of occupations that involve the harm of animals, is designed to release the fettering *karmas* that occlude the luminous nature of the soul (*jīva*). Because of violence committed in this life and in past lives, dimly colored *karmas* have cloaked one's innate pure consciousness with ignorance and desire. By the careful application of the Jaina vows of nonviolence, truthfulness, not stealing, sexual restraint, and non-possession, one expels these afflicted *karmas*, advancing toward a state of liberation, known as *kevala*.

The Jina, one of the early teachers of Jainism, also known as Mahāvīra (*ca.* 500 BCE) was described as containing animal-like qualities:

> His senses were well protected like those of a tortoise;
> He was single and alone like the horn of a rhinoceros;
> He was free like a bird;
> He was always waking like the fabulous bird Bharunda;
> Valorous like an elephant, strong like a bull;
> Difficult to attack like a lion…
> Like the earth he patiently bore everything;
> Like a well-kindled fire he shone in his splendor[31]

In the iconography of the Jaina tradition, each great teacher, or Tīrthaṅkara, seems nearly identical, seated in meditation. To distinguish between the 24 different individuals, one needs to consult the insignia at the base of each sculpture. Ṛṣabha's companion is the bull; Ajita is marked by an elephant; Saṃbhava, a horse; Abhinanda, an ape; Sumati, a partridge. The two historical Tīrthaṅkaras, Pārśvanātha (*ca.* 800 BCE) and Mahāvīra (*ca.* 500 BCE), are signified by a snake and lion, respectively.[32]

According to Jainism, each human person has endured countless lives as a nonhuman animal. The Jaina teaching of reincarnation (*punarjanma*) specifies that un-purged *karma* in this life will carry over to shape one's future life. Hence, all people have a history that intertwines animal narratives with one's current human narrative. The second reason why animals are important relates to ethics. Ethical behavior, particularly as listed in the vows above, determines the course of present and future life. One way to improve one's ethical and future ontological status is to treat animals with benevolence. Acts of kindness toward animals can help release the binding *karmas* that otherwise would cause an inauspicious rebirth. From a Jaina perspective, all humans have been nonhuman animals and good treatment of animals can help improve one's lot both in this life and in the next.

In Jainism, all animals possess consciousness. Jainas identify ascending gradations of consciousness, beginning with a consciousness that arises with the sense of touch and culminating in the human form, possessing the gift of self-awareness and the capacity to refine moral action. Jainas attribute consciousness even to entities that in Aristotelian thought are inanimate. For instance, rocks are said to possess the sense of touch and hence hold their own consciousness. The same is true for water, whether in droplets or oceans, fire, and gusts of wind, as well as the innumerable micro-organisms that pervade each and every environment and every plant, large and small. Most cultures would not consider rocks or lumps of ice or palm trees to be "animals." For Jainas, they merit recognition for their ability to touch and, presumably, their ability to convey certain moods.

The lowliest of animal forms, according to the Jainas, can be found in the realm of worms. Dwelling within the earth and within various decaying or diseased bodies, worms gnaw and tunnel. According to the Jaina worldview, these worms possess both the sense of touch and the sense of taste. They are considered to be higher level beings, and must be spared from harm. Whereas it is permissible to walk upon the earth and to breathe air and to make food from plants, it would not be acceptable to cause harm to worms, as such harm would further deepen the *karma* that shrouds the soul. Higher than worms, insects such as crawling bugs and ants are said to possess the sense of smell. They also merit protection. The next station in Jaina taxonomy names butterflies, bees, flies, and moths as adding the sense of sight to the foundations of touch and taste and smell. Water snakes add the sense of hearing. All mammals, reptiles, and birds fall under the highest category, those beings that possess all six senses, including the ability to think.

This worldview is reinforced in the daily life of Jainas and also can be seen as somewhat reflected in the overall attitude toward animals in India where animals are part of daily life, with cows, goats, elephants, and camels spilling into the streets and sidewalks. The Jainas assiduously, for more than 2,500 years, have advocated against animal sacrifice and for vegetarianism. They influenced the practices of Buddhism and Hinduism, and successfully appealed to the Mughal rulers for increased regard for animals. Jainas have opened and maintained thousands of shelters throughout the subcontinent for the protection of animals. In the recent Jaina diaspora, they have lent support to animal shelters and to various causes that work for the protection of animals worldwide.

The stories of animals include a famous tale about King Yaśodhara who, due to anger and jealousy and maltreatment of a rooster made of flour, is reborn in turn as a peacock, a mongoose, a fish, a goat, and a chicken, enduring difficult lives and gruesome deaths, before regaining human form and taking up the religious life. Sixteen of the twenty-four great teachers or Tīrthaṅkaras can be identified by their companion animal. Pārśvanātha is always seen with snake, Mahāvīra with a lion. Jaina animal shelters, known as *pinjrapoles*, provide food and water to hundreds of thousands of ill or unwanted animals each year throughout all parts of India. Animals are said to possess an ethical compass, and animals who perform evil deeds can earn a birth in hell. The *Tattvārtha Sūtra* (*ca.* 400 CE) states that "birds can be born no lower than the third hell, quadrupeds not below the fourth, and snakes not below the fifth; only fish and human males are able to be born in the seventh hell."[33] This indicts the violence-generating ability of humans of the male gender to commit incredible acts of cruelty and the murderous capacity of predatory fish such as sharks.

The oldest text of Jainism, the *Ācārāṅga Sūtra* (*ca.* 300 BCE), gives Mahāvīra's foundational teaching on animals and the need for their protection:

> Some slay animals for sacrificial purposes, some slay animals for the sake of their skin, some kill them for the sake of their blood; others for the sake of their heart, their bile, the feathers of their tail, their tail, their big or small horns, their teeth, their tusks, their nails, their sinews, their bones; with a purpose and without a purpose. Some kill animals because they have been wounded by them or are wounded or will be wounded. He who injures these animals does not comprehend and renounce these sinful acts; he who does not injure these, comprehends and renounces these sinful acts. Knowing them, a wise man should not act sinfully towards animals, or cause others to act so, nor allow others to act so.[34]

According to Jainisim, by refraining from cruelty to animals, the human being can elevate himself or herself, recognizing that when we hurt other beings, human or nonhuman, we ultimately only hurt ourselves.

In some stories animals themselves perform great acts of merit, prompting Padmanabh S. Jaini to write:

> Like humans, animals are able to assume the religious vows.... This similarity with humans may partly explain the penchant of Indians—and

particularly Jainas—to consider all life as inviolable. While this is not the same as exalting animals as holy beings, as some Hindus have done, it has prompted many Indians to renounce all violence toward living beings, and recognize the sacredness of all forms of life.[35]

Animals in Buddhism

The Buddha told many stories of his past births in the collection of narratives known as the Jātaka Tales. These stories include references to more than seventy different types of animals. The Buddha himself took many animal forms, including as different monkeys, elephants, jackals, lions, crows, deer, birds, and fish.[36] The Buddha, when he lived as a wealthy prince, had a close relationship with many animals, most notably his white stallion Kanthaka.[37]

The Jātaka tales suggest that animals hold moral agency, learn from their mistakes, and suffer or benefit from the consequences. In one particularly robust tale, the Buddha dwelt deep in the forest as a tree spirit. A ferocious lion and tiger lived in this forest, who were so effective and rapacious in their killing that they left behind copious offal to fester and decay. Out of fear, no humans dared enter the forest, even to fell a tree. One of the future Buddha's fellow tree spirits was deeply offended by the stench oozing from the predators' victims. One day, the tree spirit assumed a dreadful form and scared off the tiger and the lion. The people of a nearby village noticed that the feared predators were no longer leaving tracks into the forest, and began harvesting trees. Soon, the entire forest was gone, the land was brought under cultivation, and all the tree spirits lost their homes, moving on to new births.[38] This fable, like many of the rebirth stories, speaks of human greed, and the inevitability (and sorrow) of change.

Animals with dignity

Humans maintain a remarkable intimacy with animals on the Indian subcontinent. No place in the world can claim a more pervasive and diverse vegetarian cuisine. Cows, water buffalo, goats, camels, and elephants ply the same roadways with humans, providing labor that, in the developed world, is supplied by machinery. To honor such working animals, celebrations are held each year, such as Poṅgal, when animals are given a special day of rest and decorated with brightly colored dots and patterns.

But animals are not always treated kindly in India. People within India fear roving bands of marauding elephants and predatory tigers. Monkeys have become a major nuisance within urban areas, requiring special "monkey whisperers" to manage and remove them. Sometimes animals are perceived to present a threat that elicits harsh treatment.

Animal sacrifice, which was practiced extensively during the Vedic period, still persists in small pockets, particularly in Nepal and eastern India. Sanctified, particularly in the ritual known as the horse sacrifice, such rituals make magical correlations between the parts of the animals, the human body, and the cosmos.

The *Bṛhadāraṇyaka Upaniṣad* proclaims of the sacrificed horse that "the sun is his eye; the wind, his breath; universal fire, his open mouth; the sky, his back; the atmosphere, his belly;... days and nights, his feet; rivers, his entrails; plants and trees, his hair."[39] The text goes on to state that the forces of the universe dwell within the human frame, and that by gaining intimacy with the senses and with the body, one can grow to deeply understand and empathize with all things. Years ago, horse sacrifice was replaced with the sacrifice of smaller animals, particularly goats, and in most places today, such sacrifices are strictly forbidden in India. However, the popular press of India provides descriptions of ritual killing by the Nepalese royal family, as well as by movie stars, who give thanks through such rituals.[40] Buddhists, from the onset, have decried and condemned the practice of animal sacrifice, and along with the Jainas, helped convince many Hindu rulers to abandon this practice. In fact, many Buddhists in China, Korea, and Japan, participate in an alternative ceremony of releasing animals. However, like the stranded bunnies and newly hatched chicks who are abandoned after Easter, many "released" animals do not escape abuse and are often re-captured to be sold yet again, to another client with pious intentions.[41]

Nonetheless, India maintains an extensive network of organizations that advocate animal welfare. The most famous of these is the Goshala, the shelters that exist across India for unwell and elderly cattle.[42] Though perhaps less well known, the Jaina Pinjrapoles, which number in the thousands, give shelter, food, and medical care to countless birds and animals. While visiting one of their bird shelters, I witnessed the care and attention given to each individual wounded or sick pigeon and sparrow.[43] Their work is not limited to India. The Jain Society of Greater Detroit has developed a service project that benefits both humans and birds. Youth from the Jain Center in Farmington Hills, Michigan, build, install, and maintain bird feeders outside the windows of convalescent and nursing homes, providing tender bonds between young and old, human and nonhuman.[44]

Bishnoi animal activism: protecting personhood

Perhaps the most famous animal activism movement in India can be found in the work and life of the Bishnoi. The founder, Jambheśvara, also known as Jambhoji, was born in Pipasar, a rural region of Rajasthan, in 1451, and died in 1536. According to some accounts, his father was a Rajput prince and his mother was a Muslim. Both Hindu and Muslim communities lay claim to his story. Though they self-identify as Hindu, the Bishnoi maintained practices associated with Islam; they bury their dead and keep no images of deities in their temples. Before partition of India from Pakistan at the time of independence in 1947, the shrine table devoted to his memory was covered with a green cloth, indicating a connection with Islam. Since partition, the color of the cloth has been saffron.[45] Having served as a cowherd for more than twenty years before receiving a religious vision, Jambheśvara established the Bishnoi community in 1485 for the protection of humans, animals, and plants. He composed twenty-nine rules to be followed by all members of this community, which include the following:

18. Be compassionate towards all living beings;
22. Provide common shelter for goats and sheep to avoid them being slaughtered in abattoirs;
23. Do not castrate bulls;
28. Do not eat meat or non-vegetarian dishes.[46]

Another of his works, the *Jambha Sāra*, lays out six rules to avoid violence:

> First is the *Jhampari Pāl* that prohibits the animal sacrifice. Second is the *jeevani vidhi* to filter water and milk. Third is putting the water-creatures back into the water. Fourth is to make sure that the firewood and the cowdung for fuel do not have any creatures or insects that might be accidentally burnt. Fifth is the *badhiyā*, to avoid harming the bullocks, to not sell them to the butchers, or to send them to animal shelter centers. Sixth is the protection of deer in forests like cows, goats and other non-violent beasts.[47]

According to traditional lore, the Bishnoi commitment to the protection of plants and animals has cost hundreds of them their lives since the fifteenth century, including a group of 363 Bishnoi who, under the leadership of Amrita Devi, a woman, resisted deforestation in 1730. Because of this tragedy, the ruler of Jodhpur, Maharaj Abhay Singh, apologized and issued the following decrees that would prevent such slaughter in the future:

(A) All cutting of green trees and hunting of animals within the revenue boundaries of Bishnoi villages was strictly prohibited.
(B) If by mistake any individual violated this order, he would be prosecuted by the state and severely penalized.
(C) Even the members of ruling families were not permitted to shoot animals in or near the Bishnoi Villages.[48]

Amrita Devi inspired the Chipko tree protection movement in the 1970s. To this day, the animals within the Bishnoi area, which includes most of Rajasthan and parts of Gujarat and Haryana, are afforded extraordinary protection. In 2000, the Amrita Devi Award was given to the family of Gangaram Bishnoi, who lost his life while protecting a Chinkara deer. In 2004, the same award was bestowed on the family of Chhailuram Singh Rajput, a Bishnoi who lost his life saving a Blackbuck. In 1998, Hindi film actor Salman Khan was sentenced to five years in prison for killing a Blackbuck in Bishnoi territory. In modern times, Bishnoi have established the Community for Wildlife and Rural Development Society, and the All India Jeev Raksha Bishnoi Sabha, a wildlife protection organization. The Bishnoi maintain an active website, which includes the posting of an award winning film about their movement, *Willing to Sacrifice*.[49]

Conclusion

This chapter began with an assessment of the United Nations Declaration of Human Rights, the Earth Charter, and the Great Ape Project. Providing careful arguments, these documents urge the protection of rights for men and women, for the integrity of the ecosystems, and for primates of high mental capacity. Each of these documents appeals to human reason more than emotion. We then consulted Asian resources, primarily from the Hindu, Buddhist, Jaina, and Yoga traditions on the topic of animals. From earliest recorded history, through the Buddhist and the Jaina condemnation of animal sacrifice and the Bishnoi animal protection movement, animal advocacy has been an integral part of Indian culture. Animals have been accorded respect and are said to carry an innate dignity. It is believed that each human person has endured and experienced countless lives as an animal, and most humans can expect a future animal birth.

The core philosophies of India hold animals in great regard, not only for their gifts, but also for their very being. From India, the world can learn a great deal about building an ethic of animal advocacy. Lively stories of past animal births, philosophies that emphasize the inter-connectedness of life, and a long history of women and men willing to make sacrifices to protect trees and animals constitute a substantial reservoir of inspiration. These narratives tend to appeal to sentiment more than reason. Personhood in these traditions dwells not only in the human form and not only with the higher primates. According to the Asian view, all beings can be seen as companions. By developing this view, one can recover a sense of connectedness, leading to empathy and ultimately to animal protection. The view that animals and humans exist symbiotically and that all humans have experienced an animal birth, places the human in a place of humility and great responsibility.

Notes

1 Mary Ann Glendon. *A World Made New: Eleanor Roosevelt and the Universal Declaration of Human Rights* (New York: Random House, 2001), 100.
2 Ibid.,126.
3 Ibid., 39.
4 Ibid., 76.
5 Ibid., xviii.
6 Accessed October 15, 2010 www.un.org/endocuments/udhr/.
7 Glendon, *A World Made New*, xx.
8 Ibid., 90.
9 Eleanor Roosevelt, *My Day: The Post-War Years, 1945–1952*, ed. David Emblidge (New York: Pharos, 1990), 247, as quoted in Glendon, *A World Made New*, 231.
10 Glendon, *A World Made New*, 132.
11 Ibid., 217.
12 *Universal Declaration of Human Rights* (December 10, 1948), articles 1–5, accessed October 15, 2010 www.un.org/en/documents/udhr/index.shtml.
13 See Peter Singer, *Animal Liberation* (New York: Random House, 1975); Tom Regan, *The Case for Animal Rights* (Berkeley, CA: University of California Press, 2004); and

Colin Allen and Marc Bekoff, *Species of Mind: The Philosophy and Biology of Comparative Ethology* (Cambridge, MA: MIT Press, 1997).

14 UN, *Universal Declaration*, article 16.

15 Ibid., article 17.

16 See Rosemary Radford Ruether, *Gaia and God: An Ecofeminist Theology of Earth Healing* (San Francisco, CA: HarperSanFrancisco, 1992); Carol Adams, *The Sexual Politics of Meat: A Feminist-Vegetarian Critical Theory* (New York: Continuum, 1990); Carol Adams, "Why feminist-vegan now?" *Feminism and Psychology* 20, no. 3 (2010): 302–17; Carol Adams and Josephine Donovan, eds. *Animals and Women: Feminist Theoretical Explorations* (Durham, NC: Duke University Press, 1995); Carol Adams and Josephine Donovan, eds. *Beyond Animal Rights: A Feminist Caring Ethic for the Treatment of Animals* (New York: Continuum International Publishing Group Inc., 1996); Karen J. Warren, "The Power and the Promise of Ecological Feminism," *Environmental Ethics* 12 (1990): 125–46.

17 Parliament of the World's Religions, Cape Town, South Africa, 1999.

18 The Earth Charter Initiative, accessed October 15, 2010 www.earthcharterinaction.org.

19 Ibid.

20 The Great Ape Project, accessed July 18, 2012 www.greatapreproject.org.

21 Paola Cavalieri and Peter Singer, "The Great Ape Project and Beyond," in *The Great Ape Project*, eds. Paola Cavalieri and Peter Singer (New York: St. Martin's Griffin, 1993), 304–12.

22 Peter Singer and Paola Cavalieri, "The Great Ape Project: Premises and Implications," in *Bioethics and the Use of Laboratory Animals: Ethics in Theory and Practice*, eds. A. Lanny Kraus and David Renquist (Dubuque, IA: Gregory C. Benoit Publishing, 2000), 168.

23 Zhang Zai (1021–77), "*Ximing* or the Western Inscription," in *Sources of Chinese Traditions*, ed. William T. deBary (New York: Columbia University Press, 1960), 25.

24 Jonathan Kenoyer, *Ancient Cities of the Indus Valley Civilization* (Karachi: Oxford University Press, 1998), 82, 167.

25 Mircea Eliade, *Shamanism: Archaic Techniques of Ecstasy* (Princeton, NJ: Princeton University Press, 1953), 460.

26 Svatmarama, *The Hatha Yoga Pradipika* (trans. Pancham Sinh) (New Delhi: Munshiram Manoharlal, 1997).

27 Gheranda, *The Gheranda Samhita* (trans. Rai Bahadur Srisa Chandra Vasu) (Delhi: Sri Satguru Publications, 1979).

28 For a sampling of verses, see Ralph T.H. Griffith, *The Hymns of the Rgveda* (Delhi: Motilal Banarsdiass, 1973), 684 [revised reprint].

29 Robert Ernest Hume, trans., *The Thirteen Principal Upanishads* (Oxford: Oxford University Press, 1921), 303.

30 Adapted from Vihari Lal Mitra, trans., *The Yoga Vasistha of Valmiki: Sanskrit Text and English Translation* (ed. Ravi Prakash Arya) (Delhi: Parimal Publications, 1998), Book V, Chapter 20, verses 8–22.

31 Hermann Jacobi, trans., *Jaina Sutras Translated from the Sanskrit. Part I. The Acaranga Sutra and the Kalpa Sutra* (Oxford: Clarendon Press, 1884), 261.

32 Christopher Key Chapple, "Inherent Value without Nostalgia: Animals and the Jaina Tradition," in *A Communion of Subjects: Animals in Religion, Science & Ethics*, eds. Paul Waldau and Kimberley C. Patton (New York: Columbia University Press, 2006), 245.

33 Padmanabh S. Jaini, *The Jaina Path of Purification* (Berkeley, CA: University of California Press, 1979), 174.

34 Jacobi, *Jaina Sutras*, 12.

35 Padmanabh S. Jaini, *Collected Papers on Jaina Studies* (Delhi: Motilal Banarsidass, 2000), 264.

36 See Christopher Key Chapple, "Animals and Environment in Buddhist Birth Stories," in *Buddhism and Ecology: The Interconnection of Dharma and Deeds*, eds. Mary Evelyn Tucker and Duncan Ryuken Williams (Cambridge, MA: Harvard University Center for the Study of World Religions, 1997), 134.

37 William Clarke Warren, *Buddhism in Translations* (Cambridge, MA: Harvard University Press, 1896), 62–7.

38 Edward B. Cowell, *The Jātaka Tales or Studies of the Buddha's Former Births*, six volumes (London: Pali Text Society, 1895), story 121, I:267–9.

39 Hume, *The Thirteen Principal Upanisads*, 73.

40 See Lance Nelson, "Cows, Elephants, Dogs, and Other Lesser Embodiments of Atman: Reflections on Hindu Attitudes Toward Nonhuman Animals," in *A Communion of Subjects: Animals in Religion, Science & Ethics*, eds. Paul Waldau and Kimberley C. Patton (New York: Columbia University Press, 2006), 180.

41 See Duncan Ryuken Williams, "Animal Liberation, Death, and the State: Rite to Release Animals in Medieval Japan," in *Buddhism and Ecology: The Interconnection of Dharma and Deeds*, eds. Mary Evelyn Tucker and Duncan Ryuken Williams (Cambridge, MA: Harvard University Center for the Study of World Religions, 1997), 149–62.

42 See Nelson, "Cows, Elephants, Dogs, and Other Lesser Embodiments of Atman" and Steven J. Rosen, *Holy Cow: The Hare Krishna Contribution to Vegetarianism and Animal Rights* (New York: Lantern Books, 2004).

43 For a full description of this tradition and instances of particular *pinjrapoles*, see Derkyck O. Lodrick, *Sacred Cows, Sacred Places: Origins and Survivals of Animal Homes in India* (Berkeley, CA: University of California Press, 1981).

44 Conversation with Manish Mehta, Director, Jain Society of Greater Detroit, October 19, 2007.

45 See Pankaj Jain, *Dharma and Ecology of Hindu Communities: Sustenance and Sustainability* (Aldershot, UK, and Burlington, VT: Ashgate, 2011), 55.

46 Ibid., 59. Also see www.bishnoi.org.

47 Pankaj Jain, "Dharma and Ecology of Hindu Communities," PhD dissertation, University of Iowa, 2008, 109.

48 Accessed September 15, 2010 www.bishnoi.org.

49 Accessed September 15, 2010 www.bishnoi.org.

Bibliography

Adams, Carol. *The Sexual Politics of Meat: A Feminist-Vegetarian Critical Theory*. New York: Continuum, 1990.

Adams, Carol. "Why feminist-vegan now?" *Feminism and Psychology* 20, no. 3 (2010): 302–17.

Adams, Carol and Donovan, Josephine, eds. *Animals and Women: Feminist Theoretical Explorations*. Durham, NC: Duke University Press, 1995.

Adams, Carol and Donovan, Josephine, eds. *Beyond Animal Rights: A Feminist Caring Ethic for the Treatment of Animals*. New York: Continuum International Publishing Group Inc., 1996.

Allen, Colin and Bekoff, Marc. *Species of Mind: The Philosophy and Biology of Comparative Ethology*. Cambridge, MA: MIT Press, 1997.

Cavalieri, Paola and Singer, Peter. *The Great Ape Project: Equality Beyond Humanity*. New York: St. Martin's Griffin, 1993.

Cavalieri, Paolo and Singer, Peter. "The Great Ape Project: Premises and Implications." In *Bioethics and the Use of Laboratory Animals: Ethics in Theory and Practice*. Edited by A. Lanny Kraus and David Renquist, 163–70. Dubuque, IA: Gregory C. Benoit Publishing, 2000.

Chapple, Christopher Key. "Animals and Environment in Buddhist Birth Stories." In *Buddhism and Ecology: The Interconnection of Dharma and Deeds*. Edited by Mary Evelyn Tucker and Duncan Ryuken Williams, 131–48. Cambridge, MA: Harvard University Center for the Study of World Religions, 1997.

Chapple, Christopher Key. "Inherent Value without Nostalgia: Animals and the Jaina Tradition." In *A Communion of Subjects: Animals in Religion, Science & Ethics*. Edited by Paul Waldau and Kimberley C. Patton, 241–9. New York: Columbia University Press, 2006.

Cowell, Edward B. *The Jātaka Tales or Studies of the Buddha's Former Births*, six volumes. London: Pali Text Society, 1895.

The Earth Charter Initiative, accessed July 18, 2012 www.earthcharterinaction.org.

Eliade, Mircea. *Shamanism: Archaic Techniques of Ecstasy*. Princeton, NJ: Princeton University Press, 1953.

Gheranda. *The Gheranda Samhita*. Translated by Rai Bahadur Srisa Chandra Vasu. Delhi: Sri Satguru Publications, 1979.

Glendon, Mary Ann. *A World Made New: Eleanor Roosevelt and the Universal Declaration of Human Rights*. New York: Random House, 2001.

The Great Ape Project, accessed July 18, 2012 www.greatapreproject.org.

Griffith, Ralph T.H. *The Hymns of the Rgveda*. Delhi: Motilal Banarsidass, 1973.

Hume, Robert Ernest, trans. *The Thirteen Principal Upanisads*. Oxford: Oxford University Press, 1921.

Jacobi, Hermann, trans. *Jaina Sutras Translated from the Sanskrit. Part I. The Acaranga Sutra and the Kalpa Sutra*. Oxford: Clarendon Press, 1884.

Jain, Pankaj. *Dharma and Ecology of Hindu Communities: Sustenance and Sustainability*. Ashgate, UK, and Burlington, VT: Ashgate, 2011.

Jain, Pankaj. "Dharma and Ecology of Hindu Communites," PhD dissertation, University of Iowa, 2008, 109.

Jaini, Padmanabh S. *The Jaina Path of Purification*. Berkeley, CA: University of California Press, 1979.

Jaini, Padmanabh S. "Indian Perspectives on the Spirituality of Animals." *Collected Papers on Jaina Studies*. Delhi: Motilal Banarsidass, 2000.

Kenoyer, Jonathan. *Ancient Cities of the Indus Valley Civilization*. Karachi: Oxford University Press, 1998.

Lodrick, Deryck O. *Sacred Cows, Sacred Places: The Origin and Survival of Animal Homes in India*. Berkeley, CA: University of California Press, 1981.

Mehta, Manish, Director, Jain Society of Greater Detroit, Personal conversation, October 19, 2007.

Mitra, Vihari Lal, trans. *The Yoga Vasistha of Valmiki: Sanskrit Text and English Translation*. Edited by Ravi Prakash Arya. Delhi: Parimal Publications, 1998.

Nelson, Lance. "Cows, Elephants, Dogs, and Other Lesser Embodiments of Atman: Reflections on Hindu Attitudes Toward Nonhuman Animals." In *A Communion of Subjects: Animals in Religion, Science & Ethics*. Edited by Paul Waldau and Kimberley C. Patton, 179–93. New York: Columbia University Press, 2006.

Regan, Tom. *The Case for Animal Rights*. Berkeley, CA: University of California Press, 2004.

Roosevelt, Eleanor. *My Day: The Post-War Years (1945–1952)*. Edited by David Emblidge. New York: Pharos, 1990.

Rosen, Stephen J. *Holy Cow: The Hare Krishna Contribution to Vegetarianism and Animal Rights*. New York: Lantern Books, 2004.

Ruether, Rosemary R. *Gaia and God: An Ecofeminist Theology of Earth Healing*. San Francisco, CA: HarperSanFrancisco, 1992.

Singer, Peter. *Animal Liberation.* New York: Random House, 1975.

Svatmarama. *The Hatha Yoga Pradipika.* Translated by Pancham Sinh. New Delhi: Munshiram Manoharlal, 1997.

UN General Assembly, *Universal Declaration of Human Rights*, December 10, 1948 (accessed September 15, 2010) www.un.org/en/documents/udhr/index.shtml.

Vasvani, Dada. Presentation at the Parliament of World Religions in Cape Town, South Africa, December 1–9, 1999.

Warren, Karen J. "The Power and the Promise of Ecological Feminism." *Environmental Ethics* 12 (1990): 125–46.

Warren, William Clarke. *Buddhism in Translations.* Cambridge, MA: Harvard University Press, 1896.

Wiley, Kristi. "Five Sensed Animals in Jainism." In *A Communion of Subjects: Animals in Religion, Science & Ethics*. Edited by Paul Waldau and Kimberley C. Patton, 250–5. New York: Columbia University Press, 2006.

Zai, Zhang. "*Ximing* or the Western Inscription." *Sources of Chinese Traditions.* Edited by William T. deBary. New York: Columbia University Press, 1960.

8 Bovine *dharma*

Nonhuman animals and the Swadhyaya Parivar

Pankaj Jain

Introduction

This chapter is about the perspectives towards nonhuman animals[1] that are exemplified by *Swadhyayis*—Swadhyaya practitioners—in the Indian state of Gujarat. The Swadhyaya movement arose in the mid-twentieth century in India as a new religious movement, led by its founder, late Pandurang Shastri Athavale (1920–2003). In my research, I have discovered that there is no category of "environmentalism" in the "way of life" of Swadhyayis. I argue, however, that the concept of *dharma* can be effectively applied as an overarching term for the sustainability of ecology, environmental ethics, and the religious lives of Swadhyayis.[2] *Dharma* synthesizes their way of life with environmental ethics, based on its multidimensional interpretations, as I show with respect to their perspectives towards cows and other nonhuman animals.[3]

Swadhyaya's dharmic ecology

Having heard about the Swadhyaya, I called their office in Mumbai to visit one such site during my trip to India in the summer of 2006. Soon, I found myself on my way to Valsad in Gujarat. I arrived at the home of a Swadhyaya volunteer, Maheshbhai,[4] who took me to a cattle-shelter site managed by local Swadhyayis. All of them expressed warmth and enthusiasm when welcoming me, explaining various activities and ideologies of the Swadhyaya movement. As they began explaining the way they perceive nature and the vision of their guru Athavale, I asked questions related to environmentalism. What I present below is based on several such interviews with Swadhyaya followers. I have also extracted relevant information from the vernacular literature of Swadhyaya, based on the video-recorded discourses of Athavale.

Swadhyaya is one of the least known new religious movements, arising in the mid-twentieth century in the Western states of India. This movement now has presence in several Western countries such as the United States, Canada, and the United Kingdom.[5] Athavale started giving discourses on the Vedas, the Upaniṣadas, and the Bhagavad Gita in 1942 in Mumbai and continued to preach until his death in 2003. In his discourses, Athavale repeatedly emphasizes that the main goal of Swadhyaya is to transform human society based on the Upanishadic concept of "Indwelling God," i.e., the Almighty resides in everybody and that one should develop a sense of *spiritual* self-respect for oneself irrespective of *materialistic* prestige or possessions. In addition to one's own dignity, the concept of "Indwelling God" also helps transcend the divisions of class, caste, and religion and Athavale exhorted his followers to develop the Swadhyaya community based on the brotherhood of humans under the fatherhood of God. Activities of Swadhyaya are woven around this main principle.

Before I begin introducing the ecological work of Swadhyaya, it is important to mention that their environmental significance is denied by the Swadhyayis themselves. In fact, one of the Swadhyayis was taken aback when I told him about my topic of research:

> You might misrepresent Swadhyaya if you choose to research it from [an] ecological perspective. Swadhyaya and its activities are only about our devotion to [the] Almighty; ecology is not our concern. Environmental problems are due to industrialization and the solution lies beyond Swadhyaya's activities. Swadhyayis are not environmentalists!

Based on my observations of Swadhyaya's activities, however, I tend to agree with him. Although environmentalism is neither the means nor the goal of Swadhyaya's activities, natural resources such as the earth, the water, the trees, and the cattle are revered and nurtured by Swadhyayis based on the understanding that the Almighty resides in every particle of the universe. Environmentalism does come out as an important by-product of Swadhyaya's multi-faceted activities and this was noted during a 1992 conference in Montreal where Swadhyaya was invited to present its ecological philosophy and work.[6] In what follows, I nevertheless argue that a multivalent term like *dharma* can comprehend and describe the Swadhyaya phenomenon and the way it relates to ecology. Swadhyaya followers do not regard environmentalism as their main duty, their *dharma*; however, one can regard their *dharma* and their cultural practices as ecologically sustainable, as I will demonstrate. I also want to note that my observations are based on their activities in rural parts of India, since the urban and the diaspora Swadhyayis do not yet have such ecological projects.

Pandurang Shastri Athavale and Swadhyaya's bovine ecology[7]

In several explanations from Indic texts,[8] Athavale develops a set of preaching that I call "bovine *dharma*," which is based on the qualities of cows that emerged as *gorasa* (literally, essence of cattle), a project to nurture the cows. Athavale cites a Sanskrit verse to show that seven forces sustain the earth, cows, Brahmins, Vedas, Satis (noble women), truthful people, charitable people, and people without lust and greed.[9] The cow gives all of her belongings to humans: milk and other dairy products strengthen us, bullocks are utilized in farming, cow dung is utilized as a fertilizer, and urine is used as an Ayurvedic medicine. After her death, the cow's bones are utilized in the sugar industry, her skin is used in the leather industry, and her horns are used to make combs. According to Athavale, humans should be eternally grateful to cows and Indians do not just exploit cows for materialistic benefits but instead regard them as mothers. Only humans drink the milk of other species such as cows. Regarding cows as mothers expresses our gratitude and respect for them. Like our biological mothers, they nourish us with their milk. According to Athavale, Indian villagers used to feed their cows before taking their own meals, as a sign of love and respect. Even today, many families observe the tradition of *go-grāsa*, the offering of symbolic food to cows before meals. Athavale mentions Kṛṣṇa's love for cows and says that Kṛṣṇa turned into Gopālakṛṣṇa (Kṛṣṇa, the cow caretaker) out of his love for cows. Kṛṣṇa used to attract cows with his sweet flute in Gokul. He cites a Sanskrit verse from the *Padma Purāṇa* to show the importance of cows in ancient India, "Let cows be ahead of me, behind me, inside my heart. I should reside in the midst of cows."[10] Similarly, the *Brahma Vaivarta Purāṇa* mentions that all the gods and pilgrimages reside in the cows.[11]

Athavale explains that the cow has a quality of chewing her food thoroughly before swallowing it. He interprets this chewing as a preaching that we should also chew every new thought before accepting it. Only after carefully analyzing it, should we accept it. Such carefully accepted thoughts will not only help our own intellectual development but will also benefit broader society. Extending the bovine dharmic discourse further, Athavale cites the famous Bhagavad Purana verse in which all the Upaniṣadas are called cows, Kṛṣṇa as the milkman supplying milk to Arjuna. We should always be nourished by the teachings of the Upaniṣads and the Bhagavad Gita.[12]

Athavale also cites another verse by Kālidāsa and extends the meaning of the Sanskrit word *go*. *Go* has several meanings such as cow, physical power, eyes, and speech. He preaches cow-worship in all its different meanings, i.e., that we should respect cows (animals), that the rulers should be powerful, that women should possess long-term vision, and that scholars should convey good thoughts to the masses. Any kind of ritual is incomplete without *Pancāmṛta*, consisting of the three dairy products, milk, yogurt, and ghee, in addition to honey and sugar, all of which serve as metaphors. First, milk signifies purity. Our life, character, reputation, actions, mind, and heart, all should be pure and untainted. Second, Athavale explains that just a small quantity of yogurt transforms a large quantity of milk. Noble people should also develop this quality. They may be small in number but they can transform huge sections of societies. Third, ghee has a unique lubricating quality. Our life should also be lubricated with love for everybody. As described above, Athavale very skillfully utilizes several metaphors, analogies, myths, and legends to inspire his followers.

Athavale developed a project for cows called *Gorasa*. He established dairies in villages where people could get the milk throughout the year at a nominal price and the profit earned from such collective efforts was distributed to needy local families or saved for future projects. This stopped the earlier practice of selling the milk to far-away cities. Since the intermediaries involved in selling were eliminated, the purity of milk was ensured, and the cost was minimized. This has also inspired farmers to domesticate more cows.

As has been seen, Athavale sought to develop what I have called a "bovine *dharma*," a dharmic environmental ethics for cows, which is inspired by the virtues of cows. Athavale describes the inherent qualities and virtues of the cows, i.e., *the* dharma *of the cows*. By observing and following the dharmic qualities of a cow, one can develop one's moral and ethical qualities, *the* dharma *of a human being*. Here again, we see several meanings of *dharma* interplaying with one other. The *dharma, inherent quality*, can inspire the *dharma, virtue*, and this can help develop the *dharma* to care for the animals and environment, *environmental ethics*.

In the following section, I will consider some other animals besides cows as they are discussed in Athavale's discourses. Athavale repeatedly highlights instances of God's divine presence in different species. Among animals, he is Kāmadhenu among cows, Vāsuki among snakes, Uccaiśravas among horses, Airāvata among elephants, lion among wild animals, eagle among birds, and crocodile among fishes. These are the references in the tenth chapter of the Bhagavad Gita.

Perspectives towards other nonhuman animals

Athavale derives several inspirations from various animals as mentioned in the Bhagavad Purana (11.7–9). This is evident in the dialogue between Yadu and Avadhūta in which the avadhūta describes his twenty-four gurus from different objects of nature including the earth, air, sky, water, fire, moon, sun, pigeon, python, the ocean, moth, honeybee, elephant, the deer, the fish, the prostitute Pingala, the eagle, the child, the young girl, arrow maker, serpent, spider, and the wasp.[13] In line with the theme of this volume, I am including below only nonhuman animals from this list of twenty-four gurus as preached by Athavale in his discourses. Each animal's qualities are very skillfully connected with human ethics as is evident below.

Pigeon. The avadhūta considers the pigeon his eighth guru. This bird teaches how excessive attraction for a thing can delude one's mind. The pigeon dies when a hunter caught his family. His attachment to his family causes his own death also. We have to learn from the pigeon not to forget the self and the God. One should spend all one's energy for one's development and for God.

Python. The avadhūta says that the python is his ninth guru who taught him how to live without self-insistence. A python does not have his own insistence about his food. He just sits with his mouth open and eats whatever comes into his mouth. One should live with all his personal insistence and desires surrendered to God and accept only what is sent by God. One should live with indifference towards materialistic pleasures and should not run after them. Whatever is to be sent by God will definitely come our way so there is no need to spend our energy pursuing it. We should rather utilize our energy for our development.

Bee. The bee collects the essence of flowers. He collects the juice of flowers from several flowers instead of from one. We should not limit ourselves to a single book but should rather learn from different scriptures. Even an ascetic should not settle at one place but should keep roaming to avoid attachment to a place or a person.

Honeybee. The honeybee teaches the art of accumulation; he collects the honey but someone else takes it away. We should also accumulate the wealth for the sake of others. Wealth has three states: consumption, donation, or destruction. If we do not consume for ourselves or donate for others, it will be destroyed eventually.

Elephant. The next animal mentioned is a male elephant that desires to touch a female elephant. Even a powerful animal like the elephant falls due to his lust for the opposite sex. Lust should be replaced by a sacred reverence for beauty. We should sublimate our desires rather than suppress them.

Deer. A hunter could catch a deer with the aid of pleasant music. An obscene art or obscene music is to be renounced. Art that obstructs one's development should not obsess a seeker.

Fish. Just as an angler catches a fish by bait, a person who is a slave to his senses remains a slave to materialistic pleasures. A seeker should rise beyond these pleasures.

Bird. A bird holding a piece of meat lures other birds for that meat. However, when the bird throws away that piece of meat, other birds no longer bother her. This teaches Avadhūta the quality of non-possessiveness.

Snake. The avadhūta tells that an ascetic should learn five things from a snake. First, he should live like a snake without building a permanent house. Second, he should avoid the crowd and live alone in secret like a snake. Third, an ascetic should not allow spare things to accumulate, just as a snake does not even have hands to accept things. Fourth, he should practice his penance secretly just as a snake lives in secret places. Fifth, he should remain silent like a snake. According to Athavale, snake worship is one of the most unique aspects of Indian culture.

In addition to the utilitarian value of snakes, as a deterrent against rats and other creatures harmful for agriculture, snakes also have several other qualities that humans should learn. A snake likes the fragrance of sandalwood and other fragrant flowers. Humans should also have the fragrance of noble qualities to attract everyone. A snake stores the poison and does not waste it away by biting harmless people; she only bites in self-protection. Humans should also store and control their strengths and use them only for self-protection and for the protection of others. Some snakes have jewels on their heads. Humans should also adorn their minds with divine qualities exemplified by great visionaries. In the famous Puranic tale of sea churning, the snake Vāsuki becomes an instrument for noble work. Similarly, Lord Vishnu and Lord Shiva have accepted snakes in their vicinity. These examples show that even snakes are dear to gods if they are instrumental in divine work or are attracted to divine qualities.

Insect. Later, the avadhūta observes an insect shutting off its dwelling from another insect. Later it thinks about the invading insect and eventually becomes like it. This teaches Avadhūta the importance of thinking. One should think about sacredness that can change one's life. An insect gets attracted by a candle and burns in her. Beauty attracts and instead of escaping from it, we should consider it divine.

Spider. A spider spins her web and after some time, she swallows her own web. God also designs the universe with a thought and then dissolves it at the end of a cosmic cycle. This is the teaching that the avadhūta learns from a spider.

Conclusion

Anil Agarwal had mentioned that Hindu beliefs, values, and practices, built on a "utilitarian conservationism," rather than "protectionist conservationism," could play an important role in restoring a balance between environmental conservation and economic growth.[14] The Swadhyaya perspectives that I have described above do not fall into either category. In fact, when I interviewed some of the Swadhyaya volunteers, they vehemently denied both utilitarian and protectionist motives behind their *prayogs* (experiments) and instead underscored the devotional motive.

The cow protection examples are Indian counterparts to what could be called "environmental activism." They are inspired by Indic religious traditions. When I asked Swadhyayis about the practical challenges or difficulties related to such work, they noted several challenges. One challenge is to be able to sustain the transformation based on the Swadhyaya's teachings. Without the dharmic perspective, the work can become "mechanical" or can take the form of another "religious ritual." If these activities fail to inspire people to develop an ethos, develop a bond with nature, or if Swadhyayis stop practicing these ethics in their daily life, then their work will take a "religious" shape, reducing dharmic work into another religious ritual without a deep foundation for environmental ethics. Another challenge is to take these activities and replicate them at a larger level. So far, these have remained smaller local models found at the district level rather than projects at the regional or national level. Some of the Swadhyaya volunteers also confessed that the number of volunteers available to work at different sites varies according to the intensity and depth of Swadhyaya's thoughts in the surrounding villages. Since the spread of Swadhyaya is not uniform across the different villages and towns of Gujarat and Maharashtra (and elsewhere in India and other countries), the number of volunteers working at such *prayogs* is also not uniform. Noted environmentalist Anupam Mishra aptly remarked:

> Even without involving the environmentalists, people are bringing out miracles at the grass-root level. Upon seeing them, we should humbly accept them. Even if they may not fit our measuring scale, our measuring scale itself may be inappropriate. A work that has already reached millions belongs to the people. Media reports only political parties but it cannot represent the people.[15]

Athavale had developed several more *prayogs* (experiments) to accomplish his mission for socio-spiritual transformation based on the dharmic philosophy of the "Indwelling God." I have described only some of them that relate to cattle (with the belief that the Almighty resides in cattle and in the rest of the universe). These *prayogs* do not label themselves as "environmental projects" and yet they have succeeded in sustaining natural resources in thousands of Indian villages. After the death of Athavale in 2003, the current leadership has not developed new ecological *prayogs*. The leadership instead seems focused on strengthening the existing *prayogs* by inspiring more villagers to join the movement. I agree with Ramachandra Guha's remark that there was no environmentalism before industrialization; there were only the elements of an environmental sensibility.[16]

The Swadhyaya followers also show similar sensibilities in their local activities in the villages. This sensibility in turn is inspired by a cosmology that is based on the texts, myths, and legends derived from the dharmic traditions. We do see a reflection of textual reverence for nature in the behavior of Swadhyayis. Whether this behavior will take a generic ecological ethos outside their familiar surroundings is yet to be seen. It is still a nascent movement fueled by the founder's charisma fresh in the memories of its followers. In this new century and in the absence of Athavale, will Swadhyayis become environmentalists? Swadhyaya is emerging as a movement around the globe. When Swadhyayis migrate to different parts of the world, will they connect their environmental sensibility to respond to the problems of climate change? Only time will tell the answers to these questions.

Notes

1 For the sake of simplicity throughout the chapter, I will use the term "animal" and "nonhuman animals" interchangeably.

2 For another argument along these lines, see Simon Weightman and S.M. Pandey, "The Semantic Fields of Dharma and Kartavy in Modern Hindi," in *The Concept of Duty in South Asia*, eds. Wendy Doniger and John Duncan Martin Derrett (Columbia, MO: South Asia Books for the School of Oriental and Africa Studies, 1978).

3 For an excellent overview of cow shelters in India, see Deryck O. Lodrick, *Sacred Cows, Sacred Places: Origins and Survivals of Animal Homes in India* (Berkeley, CA: University of California Press, 1981). Frank J. Korom, "Holy Cow! The Apotheosis of Zebu, or Why the Cow is Sacred in Hinduism," *Asian Folklore Studies* 59, no. 2 (2000): 181–203, and Doris Srinivasan, *Concept of Cow in the Rigveda* (Delhi: Motilal Banarsidass, 1979) likewise go in detail about Hindu perspectives towards cows in various texts.

4 In this chapter, I have used pseudonyms except for well-known personalities.

5 Between 1994 and 1996, some observers and scholars had visited the Swadhyaya villages. Their observations were compiled in an edited volume by Raj Krishan Srivastava, ed., *Vital Connections: Self, Society, and God: Perspectives on Swadhyaya* (New York: Weatherhill Publications, 1998). This is a helpful introduction of the movement. In addition, the following texts are useful: Dharampal-Frick, "Swadhyaya and the 'Stream' of Religious Revitalization," in *Charisma and Canon: Essays on the Religious History of the Indian Subcontinent*, ed. Vasudha Dalamia, Angelika Malinar, and Martin Christof (New Delhi, Oxford University Press, 2001); George A.

James, "Athavale" and "Swadhyaya," in *The Encyclopedia of Religion and Nature*, ed. Bron Taylor (New York: Thoemmes Continuum, 2005); John T. Little, "Video Vachana, Swadhyaya and Sacred Tapes," in *Media and the Transformation of Religion in South Asia*, eds. Laurence A. Babb and Susan S. Wadley (Philadelphia, PA: University of Pennsylvania Press, 1995); Makarand Paranjape, *Dharma and Development: The Future of Survival* (Delhi: Samvad India Foundation, 2005); Trichur S. Rukmani, "Turmoil, Hope, and the Swadhyaya," Paper presented at the CASA Conference, Montreal, Quebec, 1999; Arvind Sharma, "A Metaphysical Foundation for the Swadhyaya Movement (If It Needs One)," Unpublished paper, 1999; Betty Miller Unterberger and Rekha R. Sharma, "Shri Pandurang Vaijnath Athavale Shastri and the Swadhyaya Movement in India," *Journal of Third World Studies* 7, no. 1 (1990): 116–32. After completing this chapter, I also came to know that Ananta Giri has published a monograph on self-development and social transformation brought about by Swadhyaya: see Ananta Kumar Giri, *Self-Development and Social Transformations: The Vision and Practice of the Self-Study Mobilization of Swadhyaya* (Lanham, MD: Lexington Books, 2009).

6 This conference, "Living with the Earth: Cross-cultural Perspectives on Sustainable Development, Indigenous and Alternative Practices," took place April 30 to May 3, 1992. The Intercultural Institute of Montreal, Canada organized it. A three-page report titled "Presentation by Dīdī [the current leader of the movement] on the Swadhyaya Movement" was written by Robert Vachon in the proceedings of the conference. An interview with Dīdī was subsequently broadcast nationwide by the Canadian Broadcasting Corporation on a one-hour radio program called *Ideas*.

7 Information in this section is based on Swadhyaya's Hindi books such as *Saṃskṛti Pūjan* and *Eṣa Pantha Etad Karma Pūjan* (with my translations).

8 *Cow Hymn*, from the Atharva Veda 4.21 (my translation below).

1 The Cow is the mother of the Rudras, daughter of the Vasus, sister of the Aditisons, and treasure of the ghee-nectar. I have explained to every thoughtful person that they should never kill an innocent cow.
2 The cows have done favor for us here at our place. May they stay comfortably at our cow-shelter and fill the atmosphere with their music sounds. May these colorful cows produce different kinds of calves and give us ritual-milk before dawn.
3 May these cows neither be destroyed, nor stolen, nor be harmed by our enemies. May we receive the help of the cows, whose owner worships the gods and who is capable of donation. May the cows live with him forever.
4 May the cows be our chief wealth, may Indra provide us with this wealth, and may the milk with the soma be our blessed drink for our rituals. Whoever owns these cows, is virtually Indra himself. I want to worship Indra with my faithful heart and cow-products.
5 Cows! You strengthen a frail and enlighten a lackluster person. With your ennobling sounds, you make our homes noble. This is why, your glory is sung in the assemblies.
6 Cows! May you produce many calves, have enough food to graze upon, drink clean water in the ponds, be safe from thieves and violent animals, and may Rudra's weapon protect you from all evils.

Cow-Shelter Hymn, Atharva Veda 3.14.

1 Clean, prosperous, and beautiful cow-shelters should be built for the cows. Clean water should be fed to them and their skill to produce good calves should be maintained. They should be loved so much that the best materials should be given to them.
2 Aryamaa, Pushaa, Brihaspati, and Indra should nourish the cows and the milk from these cows should nourish me.

3 Healthy cows giving good fertilizer in the form of cowdung and good food in the form of milk should come and stay in our cow-shelter.
4 The cows should come to this cow-shelter. Nourished here, they should produce good calves, love their owner, and live happily here.
5 May this cow-shelter be beneficial to the cows, may they be nourished here, produce calves, and multiply in numbers. The owner himself should manage the cow-shelter.
6 The cows should live with their owner happily. This cow-shelter is nice and the cows should be well nourished here. Increasing their glory and health, the cows should grow here. We will obtain such cows and care for them.
7 By which cow, the three worlds (the heaven, the earth, and the space) are protected, we praise that milk-giving cow. One hundred persons are ready to milk it and one hundred caretakers are waiting for it. The gods that are nourished by it realize its importance.

9 *Gobhir vipraiśca vedaiścaḥ satibhiḥ satyavādibhiḥ. Alubhdhaiḥ dānśūraiśca saptabhirdhāryate mahīḥ* (my translation).
10 *Gāvo me agrath santu gāvo me santu pṛṣthath. Gāvo me hṛdaye santu gavām madhye vasāmyahaṃ*. (Padma Purāṇa, Sṛstī Khanḍa 57. 152, my translation).
11 *Sarve devā gavāmange tīrthāni tatpadeṣu* (Brahma Vaivarta Purāṇa, Śri Kṛṣṇa Janma Khanḍa 21.91, my translation).
12 *Sarvopaniṣado gāvo dogdhā gopālanandanaḥ. Pārtho vatsaḥa sudhīrabhokta dugdham bhagvadgitāmṛtaṃ mahat*. (Bhagavad Gita Mahātmyaṃ verse 6, my translation).

13 *Pṛthvi vāyur ākāśam, āpogniś candramā ravih, kapotojagarah sindhuh*
Patango madhukṛd gajah, madhu-hā harino mînah, pingalā kurarorbhakah
Kumāri śarakṛt sarpa, urnanābhih supeśakṛt, ete me guravo rājan
Caturviṃśatir āśritāh, śikśā vṛttibhir eteṣām, anvaśikṣam ihātmanah
(Bhagavad Purana, 11.7.33–5, my translation)

14 Christopher Key Chapple and Mary Evelyn Tucker, eds. *Hinduism and Ecology: The Intersection of Earth, Sky, and Water* (Cambridge, MA: Harvard University Press, 2000), 165–82.
15 Anupam Mishra, *Aaj Bhi Khare Hain Talab* (Delhi: Gandhi Peace Foundation, 1993).
16 Ramachandra Guha, *How Much Should a Person Consume? Environmentalism in India and the United States* (Berkeley, CA: University of California, 2006), 6.

Selected bibliography

Chapple, Christopher Key and Mary Evelyn Tucker, eds. *Hinduism and Ecology: The Intersection of Earth, Sky, and Water*. Cambridge, MA: Harvard University Press, 2000.

Dharampal-Frick, “Swadhyaya and the ‘Stream’ of Religious Revitalization,” in *Charisma and Canon: Essays on the Religious History of the Indian Subcontinent*, ed. Vasudha Dalamia, Angelika Malinar, and Martin Christof, 274–92. New Delhi: Oxford University Press, 2001.

Giri, Ananta Kumar. *Self-Development and Social Transformations? The Vision and Practice of the Self-Study Mobilization of Swadhyaya*. Lanham, MD: Lexington Books, 2009.

Guha, Ramachandra. *How Much Should a Person Consume? Environmentalism in India and the United States*. Berkeley, CA: University of California, 2006.

Korom, Frank J. “Holy Cow! The Apotheosis of Zebu, or Why the Cow is Sacred in Hinduism.” *Asian Folklore Studies* 59, no. 2 (2000): 181–203.

Little, John T. "Video Vachana, Swadhyaya and Sacred Tapes." In *Media and the Transformation of Religion in South Asia*. Edited by Laurence A. Babb and Susan S. Wadley, 254–81. Philadelphia, PA: University of Pennsylvania Press, 1995.

Lodrick, Deryck O. *Sacred Cows, Sacred Places: Origins and Survivals of Animal Homes in India.* Berkeley, CA: University of California Press, 1981.

Mishra, Anupam. *Aaj Bhi Khare Hain Talab*. Delhi: Gandhi Peace Foundation, 1993.

Paranjape, Makarand. *Dharma and Development: The Future of Survival.* Delhi: Samvad India Foundation, 2005.

Rukmani, Trichur S. "Turmoil, Hope, and the Swadhyaya." Paper presented at the CASA Conference, Montreal, 1999.

Sharma, Arvind. "A Metaphysical Foundation for the Swadhyaya Movement (If It Needs One)." Unpublished paper, 1999.

Srinivasan, Doris. *Concept of Cow in the Rigveda.* Delhi: Motilal Banarsidass, 1979.

Srivastava, Raj Krishan, ed. *Vital Connections: Self, Society, and God: Perspectives on Swadhyaya.* New York: Weatherhill Publications, 1998.

Unterberger, Betty Miller and Sharma, Rekha R. "Shri Pandurang Vaijnath Athavale Shastri and the Swadhyaya Movement in India." *Journal of Third World Studies* 7, no. 1 (1990): 116–32.

Weightman, Simon and Pandey, S. M. "The Semantic Fields of Dharma and Kartavy in Modern Hindi." In *The Concept of Duty in South Asia.* Edited by Wendy Doniger and John Duncan Martin Derrett, 216–27. Columbia, MO: South Asia Books for the School of Oriental and Africa Studies, 1978.

9 Snakes in the dark age

Human action, karmic retribution, and the possibilities for Hindu animal ethics

Amy L. Allocco

Introduction

Snake worship is both old and widespread on the Indian subcontinent, where Hindu traditions have long regarded snakes (*nāga*s) as divinities linked with water, fertility, and anthills. In textual sources and iconographic representations, snakes are associated with a range of Hindu deities: Vishnu reclines on the great serpent Adishesha, Krishna dances atop the hoods of the venomous Kaliya, *nāga* hoods curve over Mariyamman's (and other local goddesses') heads, snakes ornament Shiva and accompany Murugan, and Ganesha wears a *nāga* as his sacred thread. In South India, where *nāga*s are understood as female divinities, snake goddess (*nāgāttammaṉ*) worship is a common feature of everyday Hindu devotional life. Here ritual practices honoring divine snakes are overwhelmingly the domain of female devotees, who may perform them to secure protection, prosperity, good marriage prospects, and, especially, the blessing of children.[1]

At first glance, at least, the reverence accorded to divine snakes fits well with broader Hindu attitudes toward landscape and natural phenomena, where mountains, rivers, trees, and animals—even the earth itself—may be considered sacred and worshiped as deities. But as Lance Nelson has observed, "the attitudes toward nonhuman animals within Hinduism are immensely complex and often … strike the observer as antithetical."[2] Indeed, while a number of scholars have proposed that elements of Hindu traditions may be marshaled as positive resources for environmental conservation and stewardship, others have documented how and why such attitudes may not be consistently indexed to ecological consciousness and responsibility.[3] Using the *Ṛgveda* as an example, Laurie L. Patton shows how even a single authoritative and ancient Hindu text may cut both ways, offering models for balanced and harmonious relationships between humans and nature alongside explicit scenes of destruction.[4] Despite the presence of both textual prescriptions and vernacular practices testifying to the sanctity of trees, animals, natural features, and elements of the broader natural world, deforestation, water shortages, and pollution of all sorts rank among India's most pressing environmental realities. At the same time, on the basis of both religious and secular principles, issues like animal sacrifice and dam projects generate significant controversy and are vigorously contested. Such asymmetries have posed interpretive difficulties for scholars, environmentalists, and practitioners. For example, in her study of India's sacred trees Albertina Nugteren points to India's sacred geography as a powerful asset for responding to the environmental crisis,[5] but also notes that, "Delving into the cultural heritage with the objective of finding inspiration for the present may thus result in a wealth of beautiful imagery, but its merit can hardly be claimed to be congruent with historical facts and everyday reality."[6]

Whether because of their frightening visages, potentially fatal bites, or their dissimilarity to humans (factors which have combined to produce an array of unflattering characterizations highlighting their cold-blooded and supposedly deceitful natures), *nāga*s have neither attracted the commitment of animal rights activists nor become the focus of protective institutions that other animals, such as the sacred cow, have enjoyed in contemporary India.[7] Despite this relative neglect, snakes have, on the whole, not been threatened or targeted, although this is largely due to the fact that they are not generally regarded as useful to humans. That is, in India they are not sought after for meat, labor, or clothing in the ways that other animals have been. Still, in local understandings problems ensue between snakes and humans when *nāga*s, considered creatures of the unruly/undomesticated forest, venture into the settled life of the village/city (and, most perilously, the home) and when humans intrude on and domesticate snake habitats in the course of clearing land for habitation or cultivation. The wild forest and the settled realm of the village/city are conventionally understood as appropriately separate and distinct and, as such, any porosity between them is believed to engender confusion and entail danger. Indeed, as we shall see below, anxiety about such interpenetrations surfaced frequently in my fieldwork interviews, where informants advocated a respect for snakes and their territory, which they understood as best kept distinct from the spaces claimed by humans.

Accounts elicited from ritual specialists, Sanskrit scholars, astrologers, and both male and female worshipers in the South Indian state of Tamil Nadu highlight the esteem in which sacred snakes are held, the range of powers with which they are believed to be endowed, and the blessings as well as curses they may confer. While these narratives testify to the divine status of *nāga*s and to their standing as forms or embodiments of the snake goddess, they cast the reverence with which they must be treated squarely in terms of the disastrous consequences that may befall those who harm or kill them rather than in terms of snakes' intrinsic value and worth. For example, a woman from an agricultural family told me that if a farmer accidentally kills a cobra in his or her fields, milk offerings are made and a simplified version of the Hindu death rite is performed. She hastened to add that this ceremony is not done because the snake is considered inherently sacred but rather because the snake may pronounce a curse (*sarpa cāpam*) against its murderer if s/he does not atone for its death.[8] Such formulations cast doubt on the presence of a developed animal ethic in the oral texts concerning snake goddesses that I collected and raise questions about whether a broader indigenous environmental ethic might be retrieved from the vibrant snake worship traditions found in contemporary South India. Some constructive resources might be located, however, where narratives about divine snakes intersect with Hindu understandings of cosmic time, particularly the *yuga*s, the expansive world ages in Hindu cosmology. Many of the descriptions of the punishments that befall those who mistreat *nāga*s were embedded in larger discourses lamenting the panoply of changes associated with "modern times" and, especially, the current and final of the four *yuga*s, the Kali Yuga. Among the multiple influences that could contribute to a locally inflected ecological awareness, here I focus on the possibility that a fruitful model for ethical relations between humans, nonhuman animals, and the natural world may be discernible in narratives that highlight human interactions with snakes in the context of the disregard for the environment that characterizes the last of these four world epochs.

I first offer a condensed account of my research setting before moving to briefly contextualize *nāga* traditions and identify the forms that the snake goddess takes in contemporary Tamil Nadu. I then offer an overview of the practices associated with snake goddess worship in South India and summarize some of the reasons for its increasing popularity. While a number of factors are operative in this local context, one particular concept—*nāga dōṣam*—surfaced repeatedly in my interviews and conversations and thus merits our consideration here. A malignant astrological condition, *nāga dōṣam* (literally, "snake blemish") is widely believed to result from killing or harming a snake. After providing this background and introducing these concepts, I expand my scope and shift my focus to examine how classical Hindu ideas about the world ages, or *yuga*s, intersect with regional beliefs about relationships and interactions between humans and *nāga*s and local narratives about *nāga dōṣam*. In concluding, then, I suggest that a constructive environmental ethic—indeed, an alternative paradigm for human participation in the biological community—may be discernible in the oral traditions concerning *nāga*s in the Kali Yuga, the present and most degenerate of these four world ages.

Framing: context and background

A dissertation project focused on *nāga* traditions brought me to the South Indian state of Tamil Nadu for fourteen continuous months of research between 2006 and 2007. Two preliminary stints of ethnographic research, in the summers of 2004 and 2005, had convinced me of the vibrancy and expanding popularity of snake worship practices, its growing prominence across a broad spectrum of Hindu women, and the fact that it was consistently linked in local analyses to what are perceived as the "modern" problems of delayed marriage and infertility. Regular connections were drawn by my informants between *nāga dōṣam* and the Kali Yuga in the narratives I recorded during this extended time in the field, but it was not until I undertook follow-up research in the summers of 2008 and 2011 that I was able to develop a more sustained focus on the details of this association and to extend my inquiries about the Kali Yuga beyond the upper-caste informants who typically introduced it without my prompting.[9]

Although I took frequent trips to rural temples and villages for ritual events and religious celebrations during these periods, I have always made my Indian home in Chennai, Tamil Nadu's capital and one of India's largest cities. There I conduct my research at urban temples ranging from grand edifices with Brahmin priests, long histories, and wealthy patrons, to modest neighborhood temples with popular annual festivals and some regional reputation, to roadside shrines with devoted local followings but little broader recognition. My days are dictated by the rhythms of the Hindu ritual calendar, with its many festivals, pilgrimages, and astrologically determined periods of religious in/activity, and filled with stories and explanations provided by devotees, priests, scholars, astrologers, and other ritual experts. I also consulted an array of Tamil-language pamphlets and religious manuals concerned with snake worship and *nāga dōṣam*, and translated passages related to *nāga* traditions from various genres of Sanskrit texts.

Although *nāga* worship is ubiquitous in India today, it has received little sustained attention as a vernacular tradition in its own right, particularly from contemporary scholars.[10] Because *nāga* traditions fall within the realm of non-textual, vernacular religious practices, they have occupied a somewhat marginal position relative to Hindu traditions identified with the Sanskrit textual tradition, Brahminic ritual, well-defined sectarian traditions, and large temple complexes. *Nāga* traditions are characterized by a diverse array of ritual practices and thus have proved difficult to classify or categorize. Further, these traditions are inflected very differently in their varied regional contexts; in most parts of north and central India snakes are regarded as male deities, while across southern India and in parts of eastern India *nāga*s are imaged and worshiped as snake goddesses. Despite the lack of attention *nāga* traditions have received in the scholarly literature, in contemporary Tamil Nadu the worship of snake goddesses, or *nāgāttammaṉ*, is a dynamic, enormously popular, and rapidly expanding tradition. It is increasingly visible, appealing to a surprising cross-section of castes and sects, and host to an innovative and evolving ritual tradition. So that we can understand how *nāga* worship provides a space to reflect on potential models for human interaction with animals and the wider biological community, I first describe what exactly constitutes a snake goddess and outline the practices through which devotion to this deity may be expressed in contemporary South India.

Manifestations of the snake goddess in Tamil Nadu

In Tamil Nadu, in India's southeastern corner, the snake goddess takes a variety of physical forms and thereby offers her mostly female devotees several modes through which to approach her. The four most common are her manifestations as an anthropomorphic goddess, an anthill, a divine serpent, and a stone *nāga* image. When she is represented as an anthropomorphic goddess, the snake goddess's figure is typically sculpted from black stone or cast in a range of metals. Her face is benign and beautiful, and above the tall crown that indicates her divinity an arc of snake hoods shields her head. The snake goddess may be installed in the *sanctum sanctorum* of temples that are dedicated to her and where she is the main divinity, or her likenesses may occupy subsidiary shrines at temples (especially those dedicated to Shiva or to various local goddesses) where she is not the principal deity. The snake goddess sometimes appears in a full-body image, with legs and two or more arms, and at other times only her head is sculpted (see Figure 9.1). Temple priests daily bathe and anoint these anthropomorphic *nāgāttammaṉ*s, dress them in lustrous silks, and adorn them with jewelry, colored powders, and flowers. Devotees bring offerings to snake goddess temples similar to those they present at other shrines; these include coconuts, fruit, flower garlands and blossoms, milk, incense, and camphor.

Second, the snake goddess takes the form of an anthill (*puṟṟu*; sometimes referred to as a termite hill or white-ant hill), which is conceived of as a *svayambhū* (self-manifest) eruption of the goddess from the earth. The soil of the anthill is believed to have curative powers and is ingested by those who seek healing from disease, illnesses, and malevolent possession. At temples where anthill mud is distributed as *prasādam* (literally, "favor"; a substance infused with the deity's grace), devotees may also consume a pinch of it. These conical earthen mounds feature tunnel-like passages where snakes are believed to enter and exit; it is at these openings where devotees will typically place their offerings. The emergence of these anthills, natural signifiers of the snake goddess, is often the initial indication that she has chosen to reveal herself in a particular place. Many oral narratives and written temple histories (*sthala purāṇam*) concerning the origins of individual snake goddess temples note that the anthill appeared first, worship followed, and a shrine with an anthropomorphic image was constructed much later. One non-Brahmin man who administers a small, private snake goddess temple in Chennai described how an anthill formed and began to grow against the outer wall of his house and he realized that it heralded the goddess's presence:

> The anthill is a sign of her grace. It is her body, slowly growing from the dirt of the earth. It is only because of the anthill's appearance that we built this temple. The snake goddess is in the anthill and she is the anthill. We worship the anthill and the snake; both the snake and the anthill are deities [*cāmi*].[11]

Anthills are also understood as the dwelling places of actual serpents, and these snakes are recognized as a third form that the snake goddess takes. In one of our conversations a female healer contextualized the goddess's reptilian manifestation this way: "The goddess came and sat in an anthill. We see her there as a snake. Both the anthill and the snake are the goddess. Sometimes she is a snake, sometimes she is an anthill. Always she is power [*śakti*]."[12] Although Tamils acknowledge that anthills are built by ants or termites and not by the snakes themselves, many believe that snakes take up residence in anthills and thus sanctify them by virtue of their divine presence, rendering them worthy of

Figure 9.1 Installed in a roadside Hindu temple in Chennai, India, this snake goddess's anthropomorphic image has been dressed and adorned as part of a daily worship ceremony (*pūjā*) (source: photo credit, Amy L. Allocco (2007)).

worship.[13] For the snake goddess in her serpentine form, then, the anthill is understood to serve as either a house where she takes shelter, or a temple wherein her presence dwells. One female devotee, who embodies her chosen deity in possession, put it this way:

> The snake goddess lives inside the anthill, which is her temple. Much as we live in a house to protect ourselves from the sun and the rain, so she lives in her temple. She will not reveal herself to many people, because they will fear her form. But she has appeared to me and to others like me who have overwhelming devotion [*bhakti*].[14]

While serpents are widely understood as manifestations of the snake goddess and are considered divine, in contemporary Tamil Nadu there is little propitiation of live snakes. That is to say that *nāga*s are not captured or otherwise brought to temples for ritual purposes in South India, although I was told that such practices do occur in regions of northern India, particularly in connection with the annual Naga Panchami festival that honors and entreats snakes for protection.[15] I encountered the deliberate inclusion of actual snakes in worship only once in my research, while doing fieldwork on traditions associated with the snake goddess Manasa in the northeastern states of Assam and West Bengal. By contrast, Tamil devotees are generally content to visit places where they believe snakes are present, albeit concealed (such as in anthills), and to leave offerings there for *nāga*s to partake of when they emerge. As will be described below, families may also establish shrines on their property to make offerings to snakes who periodically visit their homes or to regularly propitiate protective snakes who are understood to be permanently attached to a family's lands and residence.

Finally, the snake goddess also takes the form of snake stones (*nāgakkal or nāga cilai*), which may be stone slabs featuring carved snake likenesses or three-dimensional sculptures of coiled serpents (see Figure 9.2). Typically installed under sacred trees at temples, these *nāga* images exhibit a variety of representations: they may show one polycephalous snake, two intertwined snakes, or a single coiled snake with an extended hood. Snake stones are established and enlivened in *pratiṣṭhā* rites which kindle breath and life (*uyir*) in these stone forms, and devotees and priests identify these images as *nāgāttammaṉ* only after this ritual has been completed. Like any permanently installed temple image, these stone *nāga*s require daily worship after this enlivening ceremony is performed. *Nāga* stones are not only exceptionally common in contemporary Tamil Nadu, they also function as the snake goddess's most accessible forms, since devotees are able to bathe, anoint, and decorate them with their own hands in embodied displays of devotion that are typically impossible with her anthill and anthropomorphic manifestations, which are administered by priestly intermediaries.[16] It is important to note that the snake goddess's multiple forms are by no means mutually exclusive; they share space at many temples, offering devotees multiple modes of approach and multiple possibilities for participation in ritual

Figure 9.2 Set beneath a sacred tree in a Hindu temple's courtyard, these stone snake images (*nāgakkal* or *nāga cilai*) have been anointed with turmeric powder, offered pieces of turmeric root, and decorated with a flower garland by devotees (source: photo credit, Amy L. Allocco (2004)).

relationships with her. These physical forms of the snake goddess are often joined by others among her signifiers, such as sacred trees and tridents (see Figure 9.3). Further, while this repertoire of embodiments covers the forms of the south Indian snake goddess it hardly exhausts all *nāga* forms.

Worshiping the snake goddess and the curse of *nāga dōṣam*

Now that we have been introduced to the forms that the snake goddess may take in Tamil Nadu, we may turn our attention to how and why she is venerated. This discussion is especially important given our focus on animal and environmental ethics here, because without further contextualization the presence of a snake deity and a host of popular ritual practices dedicated to this goddess might invite a too-facile appraisal or excessively positive interpretation of attitudes toward nonhuman animals. I noted above that worship of the snake goddess is overwhelmingly the practice of women; in addition to the ritual practices I already outlined, it is almost exclusively women who embody the snake goddess in possession and speak her prophecy (*aruḷ vākku*). These devotees undertake a wide range of vows to honor and propitiate her: they may fast, conduct cycles of ritual

Figure 9.3 At this urban temple, the snake goddess receives worship in multiple forms: here her anthill (*puṟṟu*) and snake stone (*nāgakkal* or *nāga cilai*) manifestations are joined by another of her marks, the trident (*cūlam*) (source: photo credit, Amy L. Allocco (2007)).

worship (*pūjā*), and promise her pleasing gifts of saris, jewelry, and other items if their wishes are fulfilled. During the goddess's festival season in the sultry Tamil month of *Āṭi* (July to August), when the goddess is believed to heat up and expand, these vows also intensify and may include firewalking (*tīmiti*), ritual piercings (*alaku*), carrying milk pots in procession (*pāl kuṭam*), cooking for and ritually feeding the goddess her favorite foods (such as *kuḻ* and *poṅkal*), and dancing her presence in possession events. Although *nāgāttammaṉ*s are certainly worshiped for generalized prosperity, protection, and well-being, they are primarily entreated for fertility, and it is concern about conception that has catalyzed new ritual interest in the snake goddess in Tamil Nadu in recent years.

Specifically, *nāga* worship is increasingly visible and popular in connection with *nāga dōṣam* (snake blemish), the malignant condition mentioned in this chapter's introduction. An astrological flaw in an individual's horoscope that is believed to result from having harmed or killed a snake, *nāga dōṣam* is primarily faulted for delayed marriage and infertility and disproportionately affects women. When individuals experience difficulty arranging their marriages or with conception they typically consult with an astrologer, who examines their horoscopes to determine whether a *nāga dōṣam* diagnosis is warranted and then prescribes one or more ritual therapies to mitigate or remove this horoscopic "blemish." The repertoire of ritual treatments employed to counteract *dōṣam* includes relatively simple and inexpensive practices, such as worshiping one of the snake goddess's multiforms, as well as more elaborate and costly rites, such as retaining a priest to install a new snake stone and instill divine life in it, offering sterling silver (or gold) snake images to Brahmins as ritual gifts, and/or making a pilgrimage to one or more of the regionally important temples associated with *nāga dōṣam.*

While rituals to relieve this horoscopic defect can be scheduled on an individual basis with priests at any number of Hindu temples, special *dōṣam*-removal *pūjā*s are conducted throughout the day at the Shri Kalahasti Temple in the nearby state of Andhra Pradesh, and temple officials there told me that they sell in excess of 2,000 tickets for these rites each day (see Figure 9.4).[17] One of Kalahasti's priests linked the burgeoning interest in these ceremonies to the increasing prevalence of sin (*pāvam*) in the modern world and to people's desire to avail themselves of painless solutions for the suffering induced by their karmic flaws.

> When we started these *pūjā*s the number of people who came was smaller. It developed gradually and today many people are coming.... People are sinning more and more. For remedies [*parikāram*] they come here. This sin increases in every *yuga* and in the Kali Yuga people want "quick service."[18] They want an immediate remedy for their suffering and Kalahasti has provided this "service."[19]

Like others with whom I spoke, this priest framed his discussion of escalating sinful behavior in terms of the Kali Yuga, which functions as one indigenous

Figure 9.4 The courtyard at the Shri Kalahasti Temple is filled with rows of stone snake images (*nāgakkal* or *nāga cilai*) installed during rituals performed to counteract *nāga dōṣam* and other, related horoscopic flaws (source: photo credit, Amy L. Allocco (2011)).

category for classifying changes perceived as negative or threatening, and the precarious nature of modern social life.

Although space constraints prevent me from carefully detailing the reasons why there is such widespread concern about later marriage ages and fertility in Tamil Nadu today, and thus why *nāga* traditions are expanding and being self-consciously framed in innovative ways, I can briefly outline some of the relevant issues here. Factors as disparate as later marriage ages, shifting gender expectations and social values, changes in diet, higher incidence of obesity and diabetes, and even the introduction of close-fitting, Western-style men's briefs have combined to produce what has been called "an emergent 'crisis of infertility'" in Tamil Nadu.[20] Data collected between 2005 and 2006 and released by the International Institute for Population Sciences in the third National Family Health Survey (NFHS-3) in 2008 reveals that this state is tied with two others for the nation's lowest total fertility rate (TFR) at 1.8 children per woman, which is far beneath India's average of 2.7 children per woman as well as below the replacement level of fertility.[21] Indigenously, however, late marriage, difficulty conceiving, and infertility are often perceived as "modern" afflictions attributable to sins committed against snakes that then manifest in inauspicious planetary alignments in an individual's horoscope, producing *nāga dōṣam* and ultimately blocking marriage and conception. Delayed marriage and infertility disrupt the traditional social order, gender roles, and expectations about the individual life cycle, and—because of the quite old association between *nāga*s and fertility—these are understood as problems that the snake goddess is particularly well poised to rectify. *Nāga* traditions, then, have been revised and revitalized to address this contemporary need and now function as an indigenously meaningful framework through which to understand and respond to these disconcerting conditions, as, interestingly, do classical Hindu formulations about cosmic cycles of time, or the *yuga*s.

Harming snakes in the Kali Yuga

Among the complex cosmic cycles propounded by Hindu traditions, Luis González-Reimann suggests that the *yuga*s, which "provide a mythological and historical framework," have emerged as particularly relevant "with respect to social circumstances and everyday life."[22] The *yuga*s devolve from the Kṛta Yuga, the first and perfect age, to the Kali Yuga, the final, most degraded, and present epoch, which is often called "the dark age" or "the age of discord." In a co-authored essay Randy Kloetzli and Alf Hiltebeitel assert that the *yuga*s connect lived time with divine time and that its descriptions in ancient Hindu texts provide "a self-evident tale of decline and imminent toppling."[23] The inevitable deterioration associated with the *yuga* cycle was underscored by a range of individuals I encountered during my fieldwork, many of whom evidenced disapproving attitudes toward and disgust about the gradual debasement of religion and the degradation of the environment. The Kali Yuga was also explicitly invoked as a rationalization for *nāga dōṣam*; speaking in English, one Brahmin father of two daughters put it succinctly, "Nowadays, *nāga dōṣam* has become excessive. The main reason is the Kali Yuga."[24]

Much like my informants in South India, González-Reimann regards the Kali Yuga, whose "negative characteristics explain the difficult world we live in," as the focal point of the system.[25] The Sanskrit *Purāṇa*s portray this most degenerate age as a time when human behavior strays quite treacherously from the codes of *dharma*, ritual practice is degraded, religious knowledge is lost, and the gods fail to receive appropriate worship.[26] The *Kūrma Purāṇa* states that as the *yuga*s progress virtue will wane among the earth's greedy and selfish inhabitants until, by the Kali Yuga, it is "lost altogether."[27] Significantly, environmental destruction and alienation from the natural world feature prominently in *purāṇic* descriptions of the Kali Yuga: these narrations foretell a housing shortage, a shrinking number of trees, and a diminished food supply and conjure an earth that will be whipped by harsh winds, scorched by intense heat, frozen by extreme cold, lashed by torrential rain, and parched from lack of water. The *Kūrma Purāṇa*, for example, asserts that "in the Kali there is fatal disease, continuous hunger and fear, awful dread of drought and revolution in the lands,"[28] while the *Viṣṇu Purāṇa* promises that "the destruction of the world will occur" and "humankind will be utterly destroyed."[29] In these textual sources such ominous developments and harsh conditions are squarely attributed to human avarice and decadence, underscoring the correlation between moral decay and environmental devastation.

A number of informants attributed the rise in *nāga dōṣam* to the fact that as encroaching human settlements displace snakes from their natural habitats, these creatures may be prevented from mating, have their nests destroyed, or be killed, thus exposing the perpetrators of such sinful acts to this astrological malady. Others discussed their concerns about urbanization, deforestation, and the move away from traditional agricultural practices and leave ancestral homes and lands, all of which they saw as indicative of the moral degeneracy of this present age and linked to the prevalence of *nāga dōṣam*. Informants also disapproved of a host of social and religious changes; they cited trends including the non-performance of annual death ceremonies for family members, the failure to meet other ritual obligations (including worshiping *nāga*s), disrespect shown to elders, the neglect of menstrual codes, shifts in gender expectations, and the breakup of joint families. Several narratives revealed the tensions engendered by the blurring of the undomesticated territory of the forest and the settled realm of the village/city that were introduced earlier in this chapter. One priest's emphatic comments are representative:

> In the olden days when farmers worked in the fields, many snakes would be seen in villages and in fields. Those areas were inhabited by many snakes. *We* were farming in *their* place. *We* were farming where *they* lived. So, many farmers happened to kill snakes, fearing that the snakes may kill them.[30]

In the eyes of my interlocutors these disturbances and intrusions form part of a larger complex of human selfishness, non-performance of rituals, the breakdown of the joint family, and other changes that are understood as uniquely indexed to the Kali Yuga and, by extension, to the recent rise in cases of *nāga dōṣam*.

Ann Grodzins Gold reports strikingly similar perspectives from the opposite corner of the subcontinent, where Rajasthani villagers linked deforestation and decreasing rainfall with a decline in *dharma* and morality.[31] Many of them associated the Kali Yuga with alterations in human character, relationships, and interactions with the natural environment and viewed agricultural advancements not as improvements or an indication of "progress," but rather as something of a loss. Gold notes that in both textual depictions of the Kali Yuga from the Sanskrit *purāṇa*s and the narratives she elicited "ecological breakdown and moral laxness have a thoroughly interpenetrating logic";[32] in the "moral ecology" articulated by her informants in which changes in the environment, religious conduct, caste relations, sexual morality, agricultural practices, and human character were intimately related.[33] Vasudha Narayanan also explores connections between the decline of *dharma* in the Dark Age and the ravaging of the earth; in her exploration of issues including overpopulation, consumption, and gender hierarchies she discusses characterizations of the *yuga*s drawn from the *purāṇa*s as well as examples of contemporary Indian ecological initiatives.[34] In the context of a discussion about serpents and fertility in her recent book A. Whitney

Sanford writes that the causal connection between *dharma* and agricultural prosperity is an "enduring idiom" in India, and Kelly D. Alley points out places where Banarsi priests, activists, and devotees leaned on understandings of the Kali Yuga to explain the polluted state of the Ganges River and the degeneracy of the present day.[35]

I noted above that as a specific karmic outcome, *nāga dōṣam* accrues to an individual who beat or killed a snake and is then "cursed" by the offended *nāga*; this condition is also believed to affect individuals who committed such sinful acts in a previous life as well as those whose ancestors may have done so. Local analyses of this etiology emphasize that whether harming or killing the snake was intentional or accidental has no bearing on whether this malefic condition will afflict a person, or how severe its negative effects might be. The motif of human action interfering with a snake's breeding (and thus denying it the continuation of its lineage) surfaced frequently in narratives and provides important clues toward explaining why the offended *nāga* seeks its retribution by obstructing human fertility. Speaking in English, an astrologer described a consultation with an old friend who thoughtlessly tortured and killed a baby snake during his childhood:

> He told me that harming that snake has resulted in a defect in his life. I asked him, "What is the defect?" He said that his babies do not live. At least three or four of his children have died. This is the result of killing that small kid, that snake.

Correspondences such as the one proposed by this astrologer suggest a quite literal karmic calculus in which the perpetrator suffers precisely the same fertility problems he or she has visited upon her reptilian counterpart. These karmic consequences can travel over an individual's multiple rebirths and may affect up to seven generations of the person's family.

Such conceptions—both that particular sinful deeds may result in very specific karmic outcomes, and that *dōṣam* may endure beyond temporal and cyclic boundaries—fit with larger understandings of *karma* in Hindu traditions and have been noted by other scholars. In an essay examining aspects of animal slaughter in Sanskrit textual sources and the development of a vegetarian ethic, Edwin Bryant details the colorful karmic retributions outlined in the epics and *purāṇa*s for those who kill or torture animals.[36] He recounts a narrative from the *Mahābhārata* in which a sage who once pricked an insect with a blade of grass is later impaled by thieves on a pike;[37] this relatively literal karmic consequence serves as a fulfillment of the epic's promise that one will suffer "similar torment" in future births to that one inflicts on other creatures in this life.[38] The sense that negatively impacting a snake's reproduction at any point—from conception to newly hatched babies—invites precisely the same kinds of problems for the offending individual through the curse of *nāga dōṣam* is also evident in the vernacular texts focusing on this malignant condition, as well as in Sanskrit manuals concerned with *nāga dōṣam*'s ritual remedies.

Related to the theme of dislodging snakes from their rightful territory were the stories about what I might call patron snakes. These narratives fell into two broad categories: the first concerns *nāga*s who belong to and protect individual plots of uninhabited or forested land. In cases where humans wish to clear and take up residence on this property but fail to propitiate these snakes in advance of constructing a dwelling, these snakes may be displaced from their inherited lands and curse the humans involved.[39] One ritual specialist made this observation about a client he had diagnosed with *nāga dōṣam*:

> In the previous birth he would have killed or harmed a snake. While building his house he might have killed some snakes that came out from the "ground" [i.e., plot of land]. These kinds of sins will return to him as *nāga dōṣam*.[40]

Anxiety about evicting snakes was expressed by informants with much less religious training and ritual knowledge, as well. A laborer, who had been hired by a would-be homeowner to drain water from a vacant lot and rid it of snakes so that construction could begin, told me that he refused to interfere with the snakes and ultimately quit this job.

> I told him [the boss] many times that this is not proper work for me. I can run the pump, drain the water, and level the ground, but only a priest can make offerings and ask the snakes to depart without offending them. If I force them [the snakes] from their home so that he [the boss] can build one, will he come and save me if those snakes curse me or bite me?[41]

The second class of stories involves house snakes (*maṉai pāmpu*) who are charged with protecting the inhabitants of specific dwellings. These *nāga*s, most of whom were originally attached to a plot of land and then successfully propitiated during a home's construction such that they became protective house snakes, may over time have harms inflicted on or neglect shown to them by the occupants. Narratives about indigenous snakes with relationships to particular residences also highlight the changes wrought by modern times and contrast the current ill treatment of these patron *nāga*s with the reverence with which they were treated in previous *yuga*s. One non-Brahmin man told me that as the relationships that extended families or castes have traditionally shared with native villages and ancestral lands weaken in modern times, especially when family homes that once housed joint families are closed up and people migrate to cities for employment and educational opportunities, house snakes are often forgotten or abandoned.[42] In addition, this gentleman also reflected on what he viewed as the gendered responsibility to provide for one's patron snake. He described how a new daughter-in-law might ignore her affinal family's house snake, and suggested that as women increasingly take on jobs outside the home, they may not have the time or inclination to leave offerings for these guardian snakes. At least one South Indian shrine, the Mannarasala Shri Nagaraja Temple in Kerala, has in recent years made its expansive, forested grounds available to meet these new ritual exigencies. Identified in some narratives as the site of the Khandava Forest from the *Mahābhārata* and in others as associated with an episode featuring Parashurama, an incarnation of Vishnu, the temple has become the final resting place for hundreds of stone *nāga* images that have been placed there by families who find that they can no longer tend their ancestral snake shrines. Significant numbers of additional snake stones are likewise offered there annually by childless couples, who may also seek the individual counsel and blessings of the temple's hereditary priestess.[43]

The dark age and possibilities for animal and environmental ethics

Cornelia Dimmitt and J.A.B. van Buitenen observe:

> the most important function of the notion of these four Ages seems to lie in the negative moral judgment leveled on present society, for we are always living in the Kali Age, in the time just before the coming of dissolution of the universe, when men are both weak and evil.[44]

In the context of my fieldwork, at least, this tendency to critique current social and environmental conditions in terms of the *yuga* paradigm was certainly evident, although the link between denunciation and action was not always apparent. While scholars like Nelson evidence a measured optimism in concluding that, "there is material in the Hindu tradition that may well lend itself to the emergence of a new vision of human–animal relations"[45] others, such as Nugteren, caution that associating environmentalism with religious traditions may be "dangerous."[46] Calling religion both an "incentive" and "obstruction" to environmental consciousness,[47] Nugteren counts the Kali Yuga concept in the latter category because it may simply be blamed for current degraded environmental conditions.[48] Narayanan notes that the ominous *purāṇic* accounts of the degradations associated with each successive eon signal that they are predestined and thus inevitable, and wonders "if human beings are powerless against such cosmic configurations."[49] The perspective of a Sanskrit scholar I interviewed seem to validate these assessments; in response to my question about India's environmental challenges he referenced the Khandava Forest episode from the *Mahābhārata*—a story in which the fire god Agni, who wishes to devour the forest, presses Krishna and Arjuna to assist him with this incendiary project[50]—in order to point out that what he called "habitat destruction" is a cyclical process that follows the rhythm of the *yugas*. He seemed dismissive of the possibility that humans could (or should) strive to address contemporary ecological concerns in these Kali Yuga days, and instead framed his attitude toward these issues in light of the classical narrative of inexorable decline.

This traditional scholar was not representative of most of my informants, however. The vast majority of them advocated the need to work even harder in this degraded epoch to behave in a morally responsible manner, to uphold religious values, and to resist the trajectory of environmental decline that they perceived to be all around them. The oral narratives that I recorded were, on the whole, not pessimistic about the possibility of at least stemming the tide of deterioration; instead, many of my informants urged a renewed commitment to religious sincerity, moral accountability, and responsible environmental stewardship. They encouraged a less self-centered and greedy attitude toward the natural world and predicted that we would see a downturn in *nāga dōṣam* (and thus delayed marriage and infertility) if humans would stop harming snakes, let them live in peace, and resume worshiping them. These views corroborate Gold's contention that, while degradation may not be reversible, the understandings her informants expressed regarding how sin and selfishness impact the environment "appear to be important sources of practical and ideological strength infusing India's environmental movements."[51]

Despite acknowledging that doomsday predictions about the Kali Yuga could lead to human passivity about social and environmental conditions, other scholars, too, noted some fruitful resources. Narayanan, for example, draws hope from the textual tradition. She observes that there is "no Hindu text focusing on *dharma* or this-worldly righteousness that advises us to be passive and accept the end-of-the-world scenario with a life-negating philosophy." Instead, she argues, many texts advise us to be committed to and proactive in enhancing our quality of life.[52] Nugteren points out that the Kali Yuga designation has become "a metaphor, a manner of speech, a common denominator for bad times" that it is regarded as the encompassing cause of all types of degradation, and labels this a "defeatist attitude" in terms of environmental matters.[53] Still, she holds open the possibility that the Kali Yuga could inspire positive attitudes and environment activism rather more than a merely "fatalist indifference" and "license for inconsiderate behavior."[54]

It is obvious that the field of relationships between snakes and humans in India is qualitatively different from the more consumptive mode of relating to animals that humans categorize as desirable to eat or whose bodies—or body parts—they might have other uses for. For the most part, *nāga*s are either harmed or killed accidentally or, if deliberately, by persons who fear if they do not kill that snake it may otherwise kill them. While Indians may understand themselves in relationships of karmic continuity with snakes and other beings (who might have been human in a previous birth or might be passing through this animal incarnation en route to a human one), explicit hierarchies persist whereby the animal form is marked as a "lower" birth that will necessitate a human rebirth before that being can hope to escape the cycle of *samsara*. Beliefs about the ways in which harming snakes will ripen into decidedly unpleasant karmic fruits, whether for oneself or one's descendants, in this or a future birth, are widespread; in addition to causing the dreaded late marriage and infertility, a snake's curse is associated with diseases like skin conditions and leprosy, failed crops, and untimely death.

If we follow out the indigenous logic, it is clear that the anxiety about harming snakes is intensely self-interested. This is not, on the whole, a discourse focused on sentience or consciousness, species preservation, or biodiversity, nor is it a conversation pertaining to the inherent value of snake life. Rather, it is an articulated "cause-and-effect" or "you reap what you sow" narrative that spells sorrow and suffering for the human who perpetrates harm on a snake. And although *nāga*s are considered divine and stand at the center of a quite robust and currently expanding ritual tradition, their status does not generate an environmentally centered ethic. We find similar disjunctions between traditional religious categories and a contemporary environmental logic in Vijaya Rettakudi Nagarajan's concept of "intermittent sacrality" with respect to Bhu Devi, the earth goddess, and in Alley's work on the Ganges River, where Hindus' identification of elements of the natural world as goddesses does not prevent them from throwing trash on or in or otherwise polluting the earth and the river, which are seen as these goddesses' bodies.[55] Thus, the divine status of Indian *nāga*s is not what insulates or protects them from harm; instead, it is their well-known power to curse those who afflict them and the threat of them delivering either instant or delayed karmic consequences. The prevailing human orientation toward snakes we see, therefore, is an anthropocentric one, fundamentally predicated on the desire to avert the potentially disastrous repercussions for harming them.

However clear the self-serving, instrumental logic is here, from absence I'd like to at least raise the possibility of theorizing an indigenous ethics of non-harm that could potentially be applied more broadly and be extended to include other nonhuman animals. As is often the case, I'd like to take my cue from the indigenous categories and emphases. For the most part my consultants did not invoke the degraded Kali Yuga fatalistically, or with the intent of opening up a hundreds-of-thousands-of-years-long loophole and absolving themselves of moral responsibility. Rather, they engaged this cyclical framework and pushed back against its dire pronouncements, consistently urging me to take seriously the ethical imperatives they saw in the textual tradition, broadly conceived, and heed their critiques of present-day conduct. Maybe the best way to highlight this strand of thinking and to raise the question about the potential implications of such a way of reasoning about the Kali Yuga and human responsibility is to end with the words of one priest, who understands the lack of respect for sacred knowledge as part and parcel with environmental degradation. He spoke to me as he sat underneath his temple's sacred tree, carefully bathing the grouping of snake stones installed there:

> From the simplest life form to more advanced creatures, including plants and trees, every being has feelings. Simply because a tree cannot talk you cannot just cut it down—you will get the curse. If you kill or commit some other sin, in some way that curse will fall on you. But if we say this in the Kali Yuga no one listens. Our holy texts [*śāstras*] have been saying this for so many years, but now [in the Kali Yuga] is not the time for *dharma* to be followed. Why would anyone cut a tree?

It is worth asking what it would mean if others join him in articulating a vision whereby human behavior does not fatalistically submit to the discouraging characterizations of the Kali Yuga set out in the textual tradition and, instead, intentionally and deliberately develops a positive sense of connection to and moral responsibility for nonhuman animals and the natural world.

Notes

1 See my "Snake Goddess Traditions in Tamilnadu," in *Contemporary Hinduism*, ed. P. Pratap Kumar (Durham, UK: Acumen, 2013), 191–203.

2 Lance Nelson, "Cows, Elephants, Dogs, and Other Lesser Embodiments of *Ātman*: Reflections on Hindu Attitudes Toward Nonhuman Animals," in *A Communion of Subjects: Animals in Religion, Science & Ethics*, eds. Paul Waldau and Kimberley C. Patton (New York: Columbia University Press, 2006) 180–1.

3 Among the many available perspectives see, for example, the contributions in Lance E. Nelson, ed., *Purifying the Earthly Body of God: Religion and Ecology in Hindu India* (Albany, NY: State University of New York Press, 1988) and Christopher Key Chapple and Mary Evelyn Tucker, eds., *Hinduism and Ecology: The Intersection of Earth, Sky, and Water* (Cambridge, MA: Center for the Study of World Religions, Harvard Divinity School, 2000), as well as David L. Haberman, *River of Love in an Age of Pollution: The Yamuna River of Northern India* (Berkeley, CA: University of California Press, 2006) and Vasudha Narayanan, "Water, Wood, and Wisdom: Ecological Perspectives from the Hindu Traditions," *Daedalus* 130, no. 4 (Fall 2001). A. Whitney Sanford summarizes some of this literature with special attention to Vaishnava traditions; see her *Growing Stories from India: Religion and the Fate of Agriculture* (Lexington, KY: University Press of Kentucky, 2012).

4 Laurie L. Patton, "Nature Romanticism and Sacrifice in Ṛgvedic Interpretation" in *Hinduism and Ecology: The Intersection of Earth, Sky, and Water*, eds. Christopher Key Chapple and Mary Evelyn Tucker (Cambridge, MA: Center for the Study of World Religions, Harvard Divinity School, 2000), 40–1.

5 Albertina Nugteren, *Belief, Bounty, and Beauty: Rituals around Sacred Trees in India* (Leiden: Brill, 2005), 384.

6 Ibid., 364.

7 But see Nikhil Ghorpade, "For God's Snake!" PuneMirror.in, July 24, 2012 (accessed August 3, 2012) www.punemirror.in/article/2/20120724201207240903024 53e2662628/For-God%E2%80%99s-snake.html.

8 Interview, July 9, 2011, Chennai, India.

9 The ethnographic fieldwork and textual study on which this chapter relies was generously supported by an American Institute of Indian Studies Junior Fellowship; research grants from Emory University's Graduate School of Arts and Sciences and Fund for International Graduate Research; and a Hultquist Stipend as well as other faculty development and research funds awarded by Elon University. I am very grateful to all of these institutions. Thanks are also due to Neil Dalal and Chloë Taylor for the invitation to participate in the workshop that led to this publication and, as always, to Brian K. Pennington.

10 For a review of the relevant scholarly literature on *nāga*s and snake worship, see Amy L. Allocco, "Snakes, Goddesses, and Anthills: Modern Challenges and Women's Ritual Responses in Contemporary South India," PhD dissertation, Emory University, 2009, especially 49–64.

11 Interview, August 20, 2005, Chennai, India.

12 Interview, August 1, 2007, Chennai, India.

13 The belief that snakes take over dwellings established by ants is captured in a Tamil proverb that says, "Ants serve as the snake's carpenters."

14 Interview, July 26, 2005, Chennai. India.

15 For a discussion of this festival in Tamil Nadu see my "Fear, Reverence, and Ambivalence: Divine Snakes in Contemporary South India," in *Charming Beauties and Frightful Beasts: Non-Human Animals in South Asian Myth, Ritual and Folklore*, eds. Fabrizio M. Ferrari and Thomas Dähnhardt (Sheffield, UK: Equinox Publishing, 2013), 217–35.
16 Laurie Cozad argues that Indian snake worship traditions have endured across centuries precisely because the figure of what she calls the "supernatural snake" as well as snake rituals have historically been directly accessible to ordinary people, as opposed to being limited to kings or Brahmins, and that this accessibility accounts for why women are particularly active in this ritual tradition. Laurie Cozad, *Sacred Snakes: Orthodox Images of Indian Snake Worship* (Aurora, CO: The Davis Group, 2004) 3, 148–9.
17 Interview, July 27, 2011, Kalahasti, India.
18 Words or phrases in quotation marks indicate that they were spoken in English in the context of an interview otherwise conducted in Tamil.
19 Interview, November 1, 2006, Kalahasti, India.
20 Gillian Marie Goslinga, "The Ethnography of a South Indian God: Virgin Birth, Spirit Possession, and the Prose of the Modern World," PhD dissertation, University of California at Santa Cruz, 2006, 115.
21 *National Family Health Survey (NFHS-3), India, 2005–06: Tamil Nadu* (Mumbai: International Institute for Population Sciences (IIPS) and Macro International, 2008), 4.
22 Luis González-Reimann, "Cosmic Cycles, Cosmology, and Cosmography," in *Brill's Encyclopedia of Hinduism*, Vol. 1, ed.-in-chief Knut A. Jacobsen (Leiden: Brill, 2009), 421.
23 Randy Kloetzli and Alf Hiltebeitel, "Kāla," in *The Hindu World*, eds. Sushil Mittal and Gene Thursby (New York and London: Routledge, 2004), 568.
24 Interview, August 15, 2006, Chennai, India.
25 González-Reimann, "Cosmic Cycles," 421.
26 For translations of passages concerning the *yuga*s from particular *purāṇa*s see Cornelia Dimmitt and J.A.B. van Buitenen, eds. and trans., *Classical Hindu Mythology: A Reader in the Sanskrit Purāṇa*s (Philadephia, PA: Temple University Press, 1978) 36–44 and Wendy Doniger O'Flaherty, ed. and trans., *Textual Sources for the Study of Hinduism* (Chicago, IL: University of Chicago Press, 1988) 65–73.
27 Dimmitt and van Buitenen, *Classical Hindu Mythology*, 40.
28 Ibid.
29 Ibid., 41.
30 Interview, October 11, 2006, Chennai, India.
31 Ann Grodzins Gold, "Sin and Rain: Moral Ecology in Rural North India," in *Purifying the Earthly Body of God*, ed. Lance E. Nelson (Albany, NY: State University of New York Press, 1988) 165.
32 Ibid., 168.
33 Ibid., 182.
34 Vasudha Narayanan, "'One Tree is Equal to Ten Sons': Hindu Responses to the Problems of Ecology, Population, and Consumption," *Journal of the American Academy of Religion* 65 no. 2 (1997): 291–332.
35 Sanford, *Growing Stories from* India, 66; Kelly D. Alley, "Idioms of Degeneracy: Assessing Gaṅgā's Purity and Pollution," in *Purifying the Earthly Body of God*, ed. Lance E. Nelson (Albany, NY: State University of New York Press, 1988), 297–330.
36 Edwin Bryant, "Strategies of Vedic Subversion: The Emergence of Vegetarianism in Post-Vedic India," in *A Communion of Subjects: Animals in Religion, Science & Ethics*, eds. Paul Waldau and Kimberley C. Patton (New York: Columbia University Press, 2006) 194–203.
37 Ibid., 198.
38 Ibid., 199.

39 It is worth pointing out here that Sanskrit texts associated with the Indian *vāstu* tradition, the science of architecture, describe initial rites to propitiate the snakes belonging to a plot of land before that land is consecrated in preparation for building a dwelling; for more on such beliefs and ceremonies as well as a summary of the relevant academic literature on these topics see Allocco, "Snakes, Goddesses, and Anthills," 142–6.
40 Interview, August 1, 2005, Chennai, India.
41 Interview, July 2008, Chennai, India.
42 Interview, July 19, 2011, Chennai, India.
43 For other discussions of the Mannarasala Shri Nagaraja Temple see Christopher Key Chapple, "Hinduism and Deep Ecology," in *Deep Ecology and World Religions: New Essays on Sacred Grounds*, eds. David Landis Barnhill and Roger S. Gottlieb (Albany, NY: State University of New York Press, 2001) 64–6; L.K. Bala Ratnam, "Serpent Worship in Kerala," in *Through the Vistas of Life and Lore: Folkloric Reflections on Traditional India*, ed. R.M. Sarkar (Calcutta: Punthi Pustak, [1946] 2000) 621–42; and T.K. Gopal Pannikar, *Malabar and Its Folk* (New Delhi: Asian Educational Services, [1900] 1995).
44 Dimmitt and van Buitenen, *Classical Hindu Mythology*, 21.
45 Nelson, "Cows, Elephants, Dogs," 190.
46 Nugteren, *Belief, Bounty, and Beauty*, 435.
47 Ibid., 437.
48 Ibid., 435.
49 Narayanan, "One Tree is Equal to Ten Sons," 292.
50 See Christopher Framarin, this volume; for another perspective on the environmental implications of this story see Philip Lutgendorf, "City, Forest, and Cosmos: Ecological Perspectives from the Sanskrit Epics," in *Hinduism and Ecology: The Intersection of Earth, Sky, and Water*, eds. Christopher Key Chapple and Mary Evelyn Tucker, 275–6 (Cambridge, MA: Center for the Study of World Religions, Harvard Divinity School, 2000).
51 Gold, "Sin and Rain," 188.
52 Narayanan, "One Tree is Equal to Ten Sons," 292.
53 Nugteren, *Belief, Bounty, and Beauty*, 379.
54 Ibid., 381.
55 Vijaya Rettakudi Nagarajan, "The Earth as Goddess Bhū Devī: Toward a Theory of 'Embedded Ecologies' in Folk Hinduism," in *Purifying the Earthly Body of God*, ed. Lance E. Nelson (Albany, NY: State University of New York Press, 1988) 270, 277–9 and Alley, "Idioms of Degeneracy," 297–330.

Bibliography

Alley, Kelly D. "Idioms of Degeneracy: Assessing Gaṅgā's Purity and Pollution." In *Purifying the Earthly Body of God*. Edited by Lance E. Nelson, 297–330. Albany, NY: State University of New York Press, 1988.

Allocco, Amy L. "Fear, Reverence, and Ambivalence: Divine Snakes in Contemporary South India." In *Charming Beauties and Frightful Beasts: Non-Human Animals in South Asian Myth, Ritual and Folklore*. Edited by Fabrizio M. Ferrari and Thomas Dähnhardt, 217–35. Sheffield, UK: Equinox Publishing, 2013.

Allocco, Amy L. "Snake Goddess Traditions in Tamilnadu." In *Contemporary Hinduism*. Edited by P. Pratap Kumar, 191–203. Durham, UK: Acumen, 2013.

Allocco, Amy L. "Snakes, Goddesses, and Anthills: Modern Challenges and Women's Ritual Responses in Contemporary South India." PhD dissertation, Emory University, 2009.

Bala Ratnam, L.K. "Serpent Worship in Kerala." In *Through the Vistas of Life and Lore: Folkloric Reflections on Traditional India*. Edited by R.M. Sarkar, 621–42. Calcutta: Punthi Pustak, [1946] 2000.

Bryant, Edwin. "Strategies of Vedic Subversion: The Emergence of Vegetarianism in Post-Vedic India." In *A Communion of Subjects: Animals in Religion, Science & Ethics*. Edited by Paul Waldau and Kimberley C. Patton, 194–203. New York: Columbia University Press, 2006.

Chapple, Christopher Key. "Hinduism and Deep Ecology." In *Deep Ecology and World Religions: New Essays on Sacred Grounds*. Edited by David Landis Barnhill and Roger S. Gottlieb, 59–76. Albany, NY: State University of New York Press, 2001.

Chapple, Christopher Key and Tucker, Mary Evelyn, eds. *Hinduism and Ecology: The Intersection of Earth, Sky, and Water*. Cambridge, MA: Center for the Study of World Religions, Harvard Divinity School, 2000.

Cozad, Laurie. *Sacred Snakes: Orthodox Images of Indian Snake Worship*. Aurora, CO: The Davis Group, 2004.

Dimmitt, Cornelia and van Buitenen, J.A.B., eds. and trans. *Classical Hindu Mythology: A Reader in the Sanskrit Purāṇa*s. Philadephia, PA: Temple University Press, 1978.

Gold, Ann Grodzins. "Sin and Rain: Moral Ecology in Rural North India." In *Purifying the Earthly Body of God*. Edited by Lance E. Nelson, 165–95. Albany, NY: State University of New York Press, 1988.

González-Reimann, Luis. "Cosmic Cycles, Cosmology, and Cosmography." In *Brill's Encyclopedia of Hinduism*, Volume 1. Editor-in-chief Knut A. Jacobsen, 411–28. Leiden: Brill, 2009.

Goslinga, Gillian Marie. "The Ethnography of a South Indian God: Virgin Birth, Spirit Possession, and the Prose of the Modern World." PhD dissertation, University of California at Santa Cruz, 2006.

Haberman, David L. *River of Love in an Age of Pollution: The Yamuna River of Northern India*. Berkeley, CA: University of California Press, 2006.

Kloetzli, Randy and Hiltebeitel, Alf. "Kāla." In *The Hindu World*. Edited by Sushil Mittal and Gene Thursby, 553–86. New York and London: Routledge, 2004.

Lutgendorf, Philip. "City, Forest, and Cosmos: Ecological Perspectives from the Sanskrit Epics." In *Hinduism and Ecology: The Intersection of Earth, Sky, and Water*. Edited by Christopher Key Chapple and Mary Evelyn Tucker, 269–89. Cambridge, MA: Center for the Study of World Religions, Harvard Divinity School, 2000.

Nagarajan, Vijaya Rettakudi. "The Earth as Goddess Bhū Devī: Toward a Theory of 'Embedded Ecologies' in Folk Hinduism." In *Purifying the Earthly Body of God*. Edited by Lance E. Nelson, 269–95. Albany, NY: State University of New York Press, 1988.

Narayanan, Vasudha. "'One Tree is Equal to Ten Sons': Hindu Responses to the Problems of Ecology, Population, and Consumption." *Journal of the American Academy of Religion* 65, no. 2 (1997): 291–332.

Narayanan, Vasudha. "Water, Wood, and Wisdom: Ecological Perspectives from the Hindu Traditions." *Daedalus* 130, no. 4 (Fall 2001): 179–206.

National Family Health Survey (NFHS-3), India, 2005–06: Tamil Nadu. Mumbai: International Institute for Population Sciences (IIPS) and Macro International, 2008.

Nelson, Lance. "Cows, Elephants, Dogs, and Other Lesser Embodiments of *Ātman*: Reflections on Hindu Attitudes Toward Nonhuman Animals." In *A Communion of Subjects: Animals in Religion, Science & Ethics*. Edited by Paul Waldau and Kimberley C. Patton, 179–93. New York: Columbia University Press, 2006.

Nelson, Lance E., ed. *Purifying the Earthly Body of God: Religion and Ecology in Hindu India*. Albany, NY: State University of New York Press, 1988.

Nugteren, Albertina. *Belief, Bounty, and Beauty: Rituals around Sacred Trees in India*. Leiden: Brill, 2005.

O'Flaherty, Wendy Doniger, ed. and trans. *Textual Sources for the Study of Hinduism*. Chicago, IL: University of Chicago Press, 1988.

Pannikar, T.K. Gopal. *Malabar and Its Folk*. New Delhi: Asian Educational Services, [1900] 1995.

Patton, Laurie L. "Nature Romanticism and Sacrifice in Ṛgvedic Interpretation." In *Hinduism and Ecology: The Intersection of Earth, Sky, and Water*. Edited by Christopher Key Chapple and Mary Evelyn Tucker, 39–58. Cambridge, MA: Center for the Study of World Religions, Harvard Divinity School, 2000.

Sanford, A. Whitney. *Growing Stories from India: Religion and the Fate of Agriculture*. Lexington, KY: University Press of Kentucky, 2012.

Index